Department of Economic and Social Affairs

World Economic and Social Survey 2013

Sustainable Development Challenges

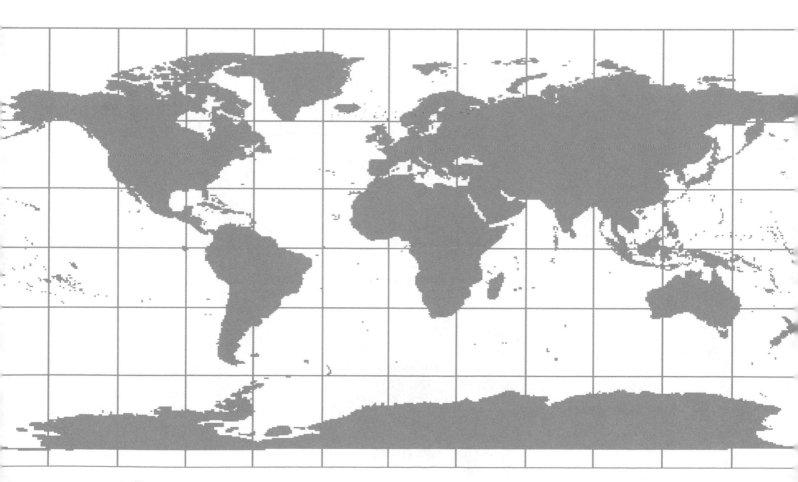

United Nations
New York, 2013

RIDER UNIVERSITY LIBRARY

DESA

The Department of Economic and Social Affairs of the United Nations Secretariat is a vital interface between global policies in the economic, social and environmental spheres and national action. The Department works in three main interlinked areas: (i) it compiles, generates and analyses a wide range of economic, social and environmental data and information on which States Members of the United Nations draw to review common problems and to take stock of policy options; (ii) it facilitates the negotiations of Member States in many intergovernmental bodies on joint courses of action to address ongoing or emerging global challenges; and (iii) it advises interested Governments on the ways and means of translating policy frameworks developed in United Nations conferences and summits into programmes at the country level and, through technical assistance, helps build national capacities.

Note

Symbols of United Nations documents are composed of capital letters combined with figures.

E/2013/50/Rev. 1
ST/ESA/344
ISBN 978-92-1-109167-0
eISBN 978-92-1-056082-5

United Nations publication
Sales No. E.13.II.C.1
Copyright @ United Nations, 2013
All rights reserved

RIDER UNIVERSITY LIBRARY

Preface

The present edition of the *World Economic and Social Survey* rightly focuses on the major issue of our time: sustainable development. As we work to reach the Millennium Development Goals by 2015 and shape a global vision for the period beyond, we must evaluate progress and look ahead to emerging challenges.

The global goal of halving poverty was achieved in 2010. We have seen remarkable gains in access to improved sources of water, the fight against malaria and tuberculosis, improved conditions for slum dwellers in cities, enrolment in primary education and the advancement of women.

At the same time, we must acknowledge that progress has been uneven and insufficient. Environmental sustainability is under threat, with accelerating growth in global greenhouse gas emissions and biodiversity loss. More than a billion people still live in extreme poverty. Nearly all of them suffer from hunger. Eradicating poverty must remain central to the international development agenda.

The United Nations Conference on Sustainable Development (Rio+20) reaffirmed commitment to sustainable development and adopted a framework for action and comprehensive follow-up. The *World Economic and Social Survey 2013* serves as a valuable resource as we look towards translating the outcome of Rio+20 into concrete actions. In particular, it offers in-depth analyses of some of the cross-sectoral issues identified at the Conference, notably urban sustainability, food and nutrition security and access to modern energy services for all.

Eradicating extreme poverty, promoting sustainable consumption and production, and managing the planet's natural resource base for the benefit of all are the overarching challenges of sustainable development. I commend the *World Economic and Social Survey 2013* and emphasize its value to all those seeking a solid understanding of these major issues which will underpin our progress towards the future we want.

BAN KI-MOON
Secretary-General

Acknowledgements

The *World Economic and Social Survey* is the annual flagship publication on major development issues prepared by the Department of Economic and Social Affairs of the United Nations Secretariat (UN/DESA).

The *Survey* was prepared under the general supervision and direction of Rob Vos, former Director of the Development Policy and Analysis Division (DPAD) of UN/DESA, and Willem van der Geest, Chief of the Development Strategy and Policy Unit of DPAD. The core team at DPAD included Diana Alarcón, Nicole Hunt, S. Nazrul Islam, Alex Julca, Marco V. Sánchez, Oliver Schwank, Sergio Vieira and Eduardo Zepeda. Administrative support was provided by Lydia Gatan. Michael Brodsky of the Department of General Assembly Affairs and Conference Management copy-edited the original manuscript. Israel Machado of DPAD and Ramona Kohrs and Jose Tatad of the Department of Public Information provided bibliographic support.

Substantive contributions were also made by Chantal Line Carpentier and Richard Alex Roehrl of the Division for Sustainable Development (DSD) of UN/DESA and by Shari Spiegel of the Financing for Development (FfD) Office of UN/DESA.

We gratefully acknowledge the background research contributions of Martín Cicowiez, Stephany Griffith-Jones, Mark Howells, Helena Molin Valdes, José Antonio Ocampo, Matteo Pedercini, Vladimir Popov, John Toye, Tom van der Voorn and David Woodward. Substantive feedback was also received from Rodolfo Lacy, Jorge Nunez, Paulo Saad, David Satterthwaite and Claudia Sheinbaum. Further thanks are due to the participants of several workshops, organized to facilitate the preparation of this *Survey*, for the insights they provided. They include, apart from the contributors mentioned above, Jorge Bravo, Barney Cohen, Sarah Cook, Barry Herman, Pingfan Hong, Bela Hovy, Ronald Lee, Eduardo Lopez Moreno, Deepak Nayyar, David O'Connor, Elina Palm, Jonas Rabinovitch, Hamid Rashid, Nikhil Seth, John Shilling, Maximo Torero and John Winkel.

Critical overall guidance was provided by Shamshad Akhtar, Assistant Secretary-General for Economic Development at UN/DESA.

Overview

Summary

- The world is faced with challenges in all three dimensions of sustainable development—economic, social and environmental. More than 1 billion people are still living in extreme poverty, and income inequality within and among many countries has been rising; at the same time, unsustainable consumption and production patterns have resulted in huge economic and social costs and may endanger life on the planet. Achieving sustainable development will require global actions to deliver on the legitimate aspiration towards further economic and social progress, requiring growth and employment, and at the same time strengthening environmental protection.

- Sustainable development will need to be inclusive and take special care of the needs of the poorest and most vulnerable. Strategies need to be ambitious, action-oriented and collaborative, and to adapt to different levels of development. They will need to systemically change consumption and production patterns, and might entail, inter alia, significant price corrections; encourage the preservation of natural endowments; reduce inequality; and strengthen economic governance.

- The *World Economic and Social Survey 2013* aims towards contributing to the deliberations on sustainable development with a focus on three important cross-sectoral issues: sustainable cities, food security and energy transformation. While the entire range of thematic areas identified for action and follow-up in section V of the outcome document of the 2012 United Nations Conference on Sustainable Development, entitled "The future we want" (General Assembly resolution 66/288, annex), cannot be covered comprehensively in this *Survey*, highlighting three of the cross-sectoral issues may hopefully contribute to the addressing of sustainable development challenges in the follow-up to the Conference.

Global sustainable development challenges post-2015

In September 2000, world leaders adopted the United Nations Millennium Declaration[1] which provided the basis for the pursuit of the Millennium Development Goals. A global consensus was successfully forged around the importance of poverty reduction and human development. Since then, the global community has managed to uplift a large segment of

---

[1] See General Assembly resolution 55/2.

the poor and vulnerable. The world reached the poverty target five years ahead of the 2015 deadline. In developing regions, the proportion of people living on less than $1.25 a day fell from 47 per cent in 1990 to 22 per cent in 2010. About 700 million fewer people lived in conditions of extreme poverty in 2010 compared with 1990. Still, results fall short of international expectations and of the global targets set to be reached by the 2015 deadline. It remains imperative that the international community takes bold and collaborative actions to accelerate progress in achieving the Millennium Development Goals.

Continuation of current development strategies will not suffice to achieve sustainable development beyond 2015. Moreover, relying on "business as usual" scenarios presents clear risks, because evidence is mounting that:

(a)   The impact of climate change threatens to escalate in the absence of adequate safeguards and there is a need to promote the integrated and sustainable management of natural resources and ecosystems and take mitigation and adaptation action in keeping with the principle of common but differentiated responsibilities;

(b)   Hunger and malnourishment, while decreasing in many developing countries, remain persistent in other countries, and food and nutrition security continues to be an elusive goal for too many;

(c)   Income inequality within and among many countries has been rising and has reached an extremely high level, invoking the spectre of heightened tension and social conflict;

(d)   Rapid urbanization, especially in developing countries, calls for major changes in the way in which urban development is designed and managed, as well as substantial increases of public and private investments in urban infrastructure and services;

(e)   Energy needs are likely to remain unmet for hundreds of millions of households, unless significant progress in ensuring access to modern energy services is achieved;

(f)   Recurrence of financial crises needs to be prevented and the financial system has to be redirected towards promoting access to long-term financing for investments required to achieve sustainable development.

Over the past years, the global challenges to sustainable development have been driven by a broad set of "megatrends", such as changing demographic profiles, changing economic and social dynamics, advancements in technology and trends towards environmental deterioration. A better understanding of the linkages among these trends and the associated changes in economic, social and environmental conditions is needed. The United Nations Conference on Sustainable Development, held in Rio de Janeiro, Brazil, from 20 to 22 June 2012, highlighted a range of interlinked challenges which call for priority attention, including decent jobs, energy, sustainable cities, food security and sustainable agriculture, water, oceans and disaster readiness.[2] The present *Survey* focuses on three of these cross-sectoral issues with immediate implications for realizing sustainable development, namely: (a) sustainable cities, (b) food and nutrition security and (c) energy transformation. The other challenges are important, but a comprehensive discussion of them is beyond the scope of this *Survey*.

---

2   See http://www.uncsd2012.org/about.html.

Partial convergence and persistence of inequalities

The progress that has been achieved in recent decades—and its unevenness—are tied intrinsically to changes in the global economy. Fast growth in some large emerging economies has led to a partial convergence in living standards, which exists side by side with abject poverty and a persistence of inequalities. Inequality undermines prospects for inclusive growth, equal access to social protection, and broader sustainable development by negatively affecting aggregate demand, investments in health care and education, and sociopolitical and economic stability.

In the decades ahead, diverse population dynamics have the potential to further exacerbate inequalities, both in developing and in developed countries, and at the global level. Increased urbanization, and rapid population growth, as well as population ageing, while reflecting rising prosperity in many countries, will put major stress on national and local infrastructures and public finance, as well as caregiving, health and education systems.

To address these challenges and to position for global sustainable development after 2015, a strengthened global development agenda will have to facilitate transformation in the way goods and services are produced, in the way jobs are created, in global consumption patterns, in the management of natural resources, and in the mechanisms of governance.

Strategies for pursuing sustainable development

Agenda 21 (United Nations, 1993) emphasized the interconnectedness among the three dimensions of sustainable development. Its actual implementation, however, arguably did not occur in the integrated manner envisaged. While the Millennium Development Goals focused attention on selected social and human development priorities, the world today witnesses emerging new challenges, aggravated by multiple financial, economic, food and energy crises, which have threatened the ability of all countries to achieve sustainable development. The United Nations Conference on Sustainable Development reaffirmed the political commitments of the international community to pursue sustainable development, under the principles of Agenda 21, including the principle of common but differentiated responsibilities.

Implementation process of Agenda 21 and the United Nations Conference on Sustainable Development

It is now clear that economic, social and environmental implementation efforts need to be reintegrated, and the tracks of discussion currently unfolding under the rubrics of the Millennium Development Goals and future sustainable development goals need to be thought of as dimensions of the sustainable development paradigm.

An important sustainable development challenge arises from unsustainable consumption and production patterns that have evolved in developed countries, a pattern that is increasingly being followed by developing countries. For example, per capita greenhouse gas emissions levels in developed countries are 20-40 times greater than needed for stabilization of the atmospheric greenhouse gas concentration. The per capita ecological footprints in developed countries are 4-9 times greater than their bio-capacity. The high degree of inequality that accompanies and promotes these patterns makes them socially unsustainable and constrains achievement of the human development goals. Without an effective global agenda, high-income households, in developed as well as developing countries, are likely to continue to adopt unsustainable consumption practices.

Need for inclusive strategies and technology innovation

The outcome document of the United Nations Conference on Sustainable Development[3] provides guidance for achieving the transition to sustainable development as a means of increasing the well-being of current and future generations in all countries. Sustainable development strategies need to be inclusive and take special care of the needs of the poorest and most vulnerable. Strategies need to be ambitious, action-oriented and collaborative, taking into account different national circumstances.

They will need to systemically change consumption and production patterns, and might entail, inter alia, significant price corrections; encourage the preservation of natural endowments; reduce inequality; and strengthen economic governance. Such a process will need to minimize the types of consumption and production that have negative externalities, while simultaneously seeking to maximize the types of consumption and production that create positive externalities. Examples of minimizing negative externalities include reduction of environmental pollution, while examples of positive externalities include, for example, technology adaptation, reduction of food waste and enhanced energy efficiency.

Technology will certainly play a major role in this transformation. Changes in consumption patterns can drive the creation of new technologies necessary for sustainability and their adoption and diffusion at the desired pace. Success in bringing about these changes will require substantial reorganization of the economy and society and changes in lifestyles. Economic and financial incentives for the creation and adoption of new technologies will be needed which may include innovative policy reforms.

Poverty eradication, changing unsustainable and promoting sustainable patterns of consumption and production, and protecting and managing the natural resource base of economic and social development are the overarching objectives of and essential requirements for sustainable development. In this large context, protection of climate and environment will need to be pursued as a universally shared goal. The global relocation of manufacturing and services sectors will also mean that appropriate technical regulation and social standards need to be adopted by developing and developed countries, with technical and financial support for developing countries.

The global sustainable development transformation entails, inter alia, significant price corrections, a strong commitment to preserving natural endowments, a reduction of inequalities, introduction of environmental accounting, strengthening of public spheres of life, redirection of the financial sector to the real economy and sharing of profit and employment. Transformation along these lines may be expected to increase the well-being of people, especially the poorest.

Sustainable development strategies of developing countries will continue to give priority to human development, with the eradication of poverty as its central goal. Human development requires more attention to be directed towards quality issues as well as coherence at the national level. Human development success depends to a large extent on using the opportunities created by globalization and on minimizing its negative

---

3   General Assembly resolution 66/288, annex.

effects. In this context, better management of capital flows and macroeconomic regulations may be necessary and coherence between national development strategies and global decision-making is important. Global institutions have to accommodate the special needs of developing countries, especially those of the least developed countries, the small island developing States, the landlocked developing countries and the countries in post-conflict situations. The global agenda will also need to attach greater importance to human rights, conflict prevention, good governance and reduction of inequality.

Developing countries have in fact put forward initiatives that are more advanced than those implemented by developed countries so far. For example, Ecuador and the Plurinational State of Bolivia enshrined the "rights of nature" in their recent constitutions. Many developing countries are developing their own sustainable lifestyle and consumption patterns, and offer aspirational models. Drawing on their traditional knowledge, they can in many areas leapfrog to more sustainable means of production, including greening of agriculture, industry and services. Developed countries can facilitate this process by offering appropriate cooperation in means of implementation, for example, through technology adaptation and transfer. Thus, both developed and developing countries can enter into a virtuous cycle of cooperation and engagement so as to ensure global sustainable development.

Towards sustainable cities

Urbanization provides new jobs and new opportunities for millions of people in the world, and has contributed to poverty eradication efforts worldwide. At the same time, rapid urbanization adds pressure to the resource base, and increases demand for energy, water, and sanitation, as well as for public services, education and health care.

Since 2007, more than half of the world's population has lived in urban centres and it is estimated that the proportion will have exceeded 70 per cent by 2050. Eighty per cent of the world's urban population will live in developing regions, especially in cities of Africa and Asia.

During 1950-2010, a net 1.3 billion people was added in small cities, more than double the number of people added in medium cities (632 million) or large cities (570 million). The policy implications of the rising significance of middle and large settlements in the next 15-20 years are worth noting. In the future, these cities will be primarily located in low- and middle-income countries. In many developing countries, rapid urbanization calls for additional resources, and capacity development of local governments has become a pressing issue. It should also be noted that urban areas are constantly evolving as a result of people's mobility, natural population growth, socioeconomic development, environmental changes, and local and national policies.

The number of people living in slums might triple by 2050 if no policy framework is established to address this issue

In many cities of low- and middle-income countries, access to public services (e.g., water, sanitation, electricity and health care) remains inadequate. Challenges to the institutional capacities for improving access to sound infrastructure, decent employment, and reducing vulnerability to pollution, natural disasters and other risks, loom large. Upper middle-

and high-income countries with urban centres that already have access to basic public services face the challenge of becoming more efficient in the use of energy and water, reducing the generation of waste and improving their recycling systems. Large and wealthier cities, in particular, may have well-managed resource systems but they also have larger ecological footprints.

Climate change impacts increase cities' vulnerabilities and put further stress on the adaptive capacities of the poor. Similarly, the ongoing economic crisis has increased underemployment of the educated youth in cities of poor and rich nations. Inequalities between rural and urban areas and within urban areas have been persistent features in many developing countries. About 1 billion people still live in slums lacking access to basic infrastructure and services such as water, sanitation, electricity, health care and education. There might be 3 billion slum dwellers by 2050 unless decisive actions are taken.

Effective urban management is a condition for cities' sustainability

The policy framework for the sustainable development of urban areas requires multilevel cooperation among local, national and global communities and partnerships to mobilize public and private resources. Democratic legitimacy and stakeholder consultation are important.

Sustainable development of urban areas requires integration and coordination, including regarding land-use issues, food security, employment creation, transportation infrastructure development, biodiversity conservation, water conservation, renewable energy sourcing, waste and recycling management, and the provision of education, health care and housing.

Synergies can be identified, e.g., between waste and recycling management (environmental management) and access to water and sanitation (social development), between air quality conservation and green public transportation, and between production and distribution of renewable energy sources and green energy access, as well as between the goal of reducing inequities (effective urban governance) and access to education and health care (social development).

The *Survey* proposes an integrated set of investments in infrastructure, public services and capacity development for different groups of countries. An integrated approach to rural and urban development is critical. Investment in economic and social infrastructure in rural areas might improve productivity, reduce poverty and inequity and create additional opportunities for sustainable livelihoods.

Sustainable development of cities in poor countries entails investment in infrastructure such as roads, water, sewers, electricity and services such as schools, public transportation and health care. Leapfrogging investment in a green industrial transformation can generate youth employment. In cities of middle- and high-income countries, investment in infrastructure, renewable energy, buildings, and improved electricity and water efficiencies is important. Investment in the reduction of waste production and improvement of waste collection and recycling systems is needed in most cities across the world. Providing access to modern energy services is a real challenge to urban authorities in developing countries which often do not have enough capacity to respond, nor the ability to raise the needed long-term financial resources for investment.

A "one size fits all" approach towards sustainable development in cities is precluded, since cities' priorities, objectives and paths are highly diverse. Policy frameworks need to promote a common integrated approach, while differentiating among the responsibilities of upper-, middle- and low-income countries. Consequently, measures of sustainable development progress also need to be tailored to the particular challenges and opportunities identified and prioritized by the cities' main stakeholders.

Ensuring food and nutrition security

It is essential to ensure that everyone in the world has access to enough nutritious food. The *Survey* highlights the challenges in this regard and the changes to the food system that are needed to ensure food and nutrition security by 2050.

The target of halving the proportion of people suffering from hunger in sub-Saharan Africa will not be met

Basic food insecurity still affects 1 billion people, as many as in 1970. However, the proportion of people who are undernourished declined from about 20 per cent in 1990-1992 to 15 per cent in 2008-2010. Progress has been uneven across regions and the 2007-2008 food and financial crisis posed additional challenges. Under current conditions, the target of halving the proportion of people suffering from hunger by 2015 will not be met in sub-Saharan Africa and South Asia.

Because of low quality and low diversity of available food, the challenge of malnutrition is broader than the issue of hunger or undernourishment. Individuals may take in enough calories for daily subsistence, but still suffer from "hidden hunger" with low levels of micronutrients owing to the lack of diversification of diets. This is a problem in both developing and developed countries, affecting 30 per cent of the world's population. The excess of calories is another rising major global public-health concern, as overweight and obesity result in more than 2.8 million deaths among adults every year.

Estimates indicate that food production will have to increase 70 per cent globally to feed an additional 2.3 billion people by 2050. Food demand is anticipated to continue to shift towards more resource-intensive agricultural products, such as livestock and dairy products, thereby exerting additional pressure on land, water and biodiversity resources.

On the supply side, meeting an increasing food demand is a major concern, given the rise of resource constraints. Current agricultural practices are a leading source of greenhouse gas emissions, while also leading to other problems, such as loss of soil fertility and water pollution from run-off. Increased temperatures and more volatile weather patterns caused by climate change may already be affecting crop yields, affecting incomes and agricultural production.

Increased land use for biofuels will increase constraints on the supply side and may lead to higher food prices, further affecting the most economically disadvantaged. Similarly, current urbanization trends accelerate the diversion of land use from agricultural production.

The food, water, energy, environment and climate nexus

An integrated approach to food security and the environment should take into consideration the food, water, energy, environment and climate nexus, while reorienting food production, distribution and consumption. Food security, while minimizing environmental impacts and increasing natural resource efficiency, will require increasing agricultural productivity, in particular in developing countries where agriculture accounts for a large share of gross domestic product (GDP) and where large productivity gaps still exist. Rapid increases in yields are deemed feasible, in particular where productivity gaps are high. At the same time, the protection of soil quality and crop and grazing land management, including restoration of degraded lands, have been identified as having the greatest agricultural potential to mitigate climate change, in addition to being cost-effective. Additional public investments in agriculture-related research and development will be crucial to increasing productivity.

The private sector will need to play a major role in expanding research, particularly in biotechnology, with a focus on food security. Special efforts are also needed to close the productivity gap of smallholder farms, which offer great potential for engagement in sustainable agricultural practices. Faster productivity gains among a large number of small-scale producers in very different agroecological regions will require improved dissemination and adaptation of technology to meet their specific needs.

A broad-based rural development strategy has to include infrastructural investments to better connect producers to output markets, including in rural-urban linkages and the improvement of distribution systems and storage facilities. The prospect of new economic opportunities, including institutional changes that facilitate access to input markets, as well as credit and insurance markets, will also encourage smallholders, especially women farmers, in developing countries to increase their productivity.

Social protection mechanisms, including social safety nets, must also be part of a broader rural development strategy to facilitate access of low-income households to food. This will not only protect the most vulnerable against short-term economic shocks, but also contribute to long-term resilience by facilitating their access to food and by strengthening the ability of smallholders to manage risks and adopt new technologies with higher productivity.

Reducing food wastage may contribute to the sustainability of the food system

To reorient food consumption towards diets that are less-resource intensive and more nutritious will also be crucial for food sustainability. In particular, reducing food wastage may contribute significantly to the sustainability of the food system. Currently, it is estimated that 32 per cent of the total food produced globally is wasted. In order to substantially reduce the quantity of food lost and wasted, changes have to take place at different levels of the food chain: production, storage, transportation and consumption. In developed countries, efforts are most needed at the retail and consumer end, owing in part to management practices and consumption habits. In developing countries, interventions are needed at the producer end, before food reaches the market, to address inadequate harvesting techniques and storage conditions. Speculation in land and water has to be addressed at both the national and the international level. More investment funds will be needed to help implement these strategies and to support other countries in developing their own strategies for reinforcing the resilience of food production systems.

The international community can help developing countries in their efforts to design and implement policies that increase resilience to food price volatility and to climate variability. Priority actions should include reviewing trade policies to ensure that they support food and nutrition security, while establishing a transparent food market information system with timely information on regional and international stocks. The reliability and timeliness of early warning systems need to be improved at both the national and regional levels, with a focus on countries that are particularly vulnerable to price shocks and food emergencies. The current global trading system also needs to be reformed so that the poorest can be provided with just and fair access to markets.

Changing the production and consumption patterns of wealthier countries and consumers, including dietary habits, could make a remarkable contribution to ensuring food and nutrition security. The livestock sector, which has grown rapidly to meet the increasing demand for meat, is a prime contributor to water scarcity, pollution, land degradation and greenhouse gas emissions. This trend will need to be reversed in the context of more sustainable diets, but as long as market prices do not reflect such scarcities, there will be insufficient incentives for behavioural changes. Publicity, advocacy, education and legislation will need to be used to bring about such cultural changes so as to reduce high levels of retail and domestic food waste in high- and upper middle income countries; furthermore, better policy instruments for promoting sustainable diets are still needed.

The energy transformation challenge

The transformation of the energy system needs to be a core element of the sustainable development agenda, in order to improve the living standards of people with equity and environmental sustainability. Under the Secretary-General's Sustainable Energy for All Initiative and in other contexts, explicit energy goals (or targets) have been suggested to end the dependence on traditional biomass as a source of thermal energy; to improve access to reliable, adequate and high-quality electricity; to facilitate convergence to best practices in the provision of energy services; and to ensure that unreliable or low-quality energy sources do not compromise the opportunities of the working poor who are self-employed or run household enterprises.

Transformation of the energy system needs to be a core element of the sustainable development agenda

The latest estimates confirm that emissions trends will likely lead to temperature increases with potentially catastrophic consequences. Even if all currently planned mitigation policies were fully implemented—including expanded use of renewable energy sources and improvements in energy efficiency—a stabilization of greenhouse gas emissions at 450 parts per million (ppm) will not have been achieved by 2050.

If one focuses on the rise in renewable energy, the advances in reducing pollution in some cities, the implementation of policies to improve sustainable development, and the adoption of international sustainability agreements, the world is undoubtedly greener today than it would have been if no actions had been taken. However, even after taking into account all of these factors, the likely outlook is that the desired emissions reduction targets will not be met.

According to some projections, emissions concentrations might reach between 650 and 700 ppm of carbon dioxide equivalent (CO_2e) by 2050 and between 800 and 1,300 ppm of CO_2e by 2100 (Organization for Economic Cooperation and Development, 2012c). These increases would be associated with increases in global average temperature of 2°C-3°C by 2050 and of 3.7°C-5.6°C by 2100.

Multiple pathways towards sustainable energy have been identified. There are many existing energy technology options for mitigating emissions and increasing welfare. Hundreds of scenarios have shown that the world can follow a large number of energy paths towards sustainable development which require, however, ambitious policies, improved international cooperation, including in means of implementation, behavioural changes and unprecedented levels of investment.

Sustainable development pathways share common features

Despite their variety, sustainable development pathways share common features. First, the sooner the implementation of policies starts, the greater the technological flexibility and the less costly the actions required. Second, policies increasing efficiency in the delivery of energy services can go a long way. Perhaps the most important insight provided by scenario analyses is that the world can go a long way towards controlling emissions, if it invests decisively in energy efficiency. Scenarios emphasizing improvements in end-use efficiency tend to meet sustainable development goals, such as ensuring (almost) universal access to electricity, maintaining air quality, and limiting global average temperature increases. However, if efficiency gains turn out to be small, the world will become highly dependent on rapidly improving innovation and increasing the supply of "clean" energy. Another insight is that sustainable development pathways have been devised that exclude nuclear power, and carbon capture and storage (and its bioengineering variants), technologies that face great sociopolitical and technical challenges. However, their exclusion would make the attainment of sustainable development much more challenging and require special measures to improve energy efficiencies and reduce demand.

Scenario results indicate that, in the absence of additional targeted pro-poor energy policies, by 2030, some 2.4 billion people will still rely on solid fuels for cooking, or 300 million more than the 2.1 billion so reliant in 2005. The implementation of a highly ambitious package of policies directly addressing the energy-poverty nexus has the potential to ensure access to modern energy of an additional 1.9 billion of people. The policy package would have to combine financing (including microfinancing), to cover the upfront costs of enabling access to modern energy and the purchase of appliances, with a 50 per cent fuel subsidy in relation to market prices. Even such an ambitious set of policies, however, would still leave 500 million people without access to modern energy, most of them in rural Africa and in remote areas. Additional specific targeted programmes implemented through international development cooperation would be needed for modern energy services.

Energy transformation can be compatible with economic and social inclusion

The sustainable energy transformation can be compatible with economic and social inclusion. In particular, near universal access to clean cooking fuels and electricity can be achieved in harmony with measures devised to contain the increase of emissions and, pertinently, at a comparatively modest investment cost.

The *Survey* does not view technology as the main limiting factor for energy transformation, but is less sanguine about the economic, social and cultural hurdles associated with the implementation of national policies and achievement of a commensurate level of international cooperation.

The complex challenges that a sustainable energy transformation faces range from issues of growth, macroeconomic balances, and technology innovation and its diffusion, to human development concerns. They confer great importance on policy coherence. Moreover, industrial policies, technological innovation, transfer and adaptation, and energy plans based on integrated energy assessments require decisive, ingenious and coherent national policymaking and international cooperation.

Low-carbon, inclusive growth requires that the set of conditions needed to create the "enabling environment" for change be in place: policy space and coherence; international financing; international cooperation; and enabling international institutions, establishing rules and norms. It requires an enabling environment for the industrial policies needed to accelerate economic growth and foster green sectors, as well as for large public and private investment projects. Adequate international financing needs to be available, especially to developing countries and the least developed countries. Domestic sources should be tapped to the extent possible, but the size of required investments will make international finance necessary. Designing national sustainable development strategies demands the integration of complex processes across the macroeconomy, the energy sector, and the deployment of technology, policies for social and economic inclusion, and the environment. Building national capacities and international cooperation in these areas will be important. The world needs a big push—one that is public investment-led, based on international development cooperation, and capable of catalysing private sector investment and innovation so as to sustainably transform the energy system.

Financing sustainable development

Responding to the above-mentioned challenges requires large-scale investments. It is recognized that the fulfilment of official development assistance (ODA) commitments is crucial. Innovative financing mechanisms can also make contributions to developing countries in respect of mobilization of additional resources for financing for development. Sustainable financing needs to be ensured across sectors, including agriculture, forestry, energy, health and education, as well as across economic segments, such as small and medium-sized enterprises, infrastructure and innovation, in both developed and developing countries. Special attention needs to be directed towards financing the global commons (e.g., the atmosphere, oceans, biodiversity and forests) and global health. This *Survey* shows that delivering on present commitments to achieve the Millennium Development Goals already requires substantial additional public expenditure. It also identifies financing challenges related to the *Survey*'s three focus areas: sustainable cities, food security and energy transformation.

Achieving the Millennium Development Goals requires stepping up public spending

Evidence drawn from country-level economy-wide modelling analyses for 27 developing countries suggests that achieving the Millennium Development Goals by 2015 requires significantly stepping up upfront public spending in developing countries.[4] First, a business-as-usual scenario assessed progress towards meeting the Millennium Development Goals under expected economic growth, existing public spending priorities and budget financing policies. This baseline scenario assessed whether the countries would be "on track" or "off track" to achieve the targets, taking into account non-linearities in the effectiveness of social spending in achieving those targets. All 27 country-level studies found that, while substantial human development progress would be made with the current public expenditure scenario, only two countries (Chile and Cuba) would fully meet, by 2015, a set of targets for primary school completion, reduction of child and maternal mortality rates, and expanded coverage of drinking water and basic sanitation.

For the cases in which business as usual was found not to be sufficient to achieve the goals, the analyses examined a number of policy scenarios under which public spending was stepped up as much as needed to achieve those goals from 2010 to 2015.

Meeting the human development targets was found to be affordable for only a minority of countries: 18 countries would need to raise their public spending by an extra 2 percentage points or more of GDP relative to the baseline with current policies. The public spending needed to meet the targets in the countries studied was estimated at about 7 per cent of GDP and, in some cases, the estimate was even higher.

An update of these analyses for six of the countries of Latin America and the Caribbean took into consideration the global financial crisis, by comparing social indicators under two scenarios, with and without the growth slowdown. It was found that the additional public spending requirements would have to rise by 1.6-3.4 per cent of GDP per year between 2010 and 2015 as a result of the economic growth slowdown—on top of the spending requirements that had been estimated for these six countries.

As indicated in the *Survey*, mitigation policies designed to curb carbon emissions through the adoption of renewable sources of energy will require substantial additional investments. Given the existing financing constraints, accelerated investments for sustainable development could overstretch countries' public finances.

Sustainable development requires coherence of fiscal policy and public investment allocations

Coherent policies for greenhouse gas mitigation, economic growth and human development need to be devised. The *Survey* presents evidence that taxing of greenhouse gas emissions in developed and developing countries can be useful. Not only could fiscal policy

---

4　These analyses were conducted by national researchers and government experts, with technical support from the Department of Economic and Social Affairs of the United Nations Secretariat and the World Bank. While Latin America has been comprehensively covered, only nine case studies for countries in Africa and Asia have been completed to date.

contribute to GHG mitigation, but—combined with a set of coherent policies—it could also change unsustainable consumption patterns, promote human development, and offset some of its potential economic costs. Three policy scenarios were simulated to illustrate that this may be the case, using the examples of three oil-importing developing countries. These scenarios are compared with a baseline which represents a continuation of currently expected economic growth and public spending interventions up to 2030.

The results show that, keeping all other things equal, unilateral taxes on the domestic price of fuel oil would depress intermediate and especially final consumption of fuel oil in the three countries. It is likely that carbon emissions would consequently be reduced and industries that supply oil-intensive goods for the domestic market and exports would be penalized. In fact, GDP growth is likely to be negatively affected.

If, alternatively, the new tax revenues were allocated to investing in public infrastructure, or expanding service delivery in education, instead of being used to reduce the budget deficit, the output loss would be offset partially or in some cases fully, mainly because such investments could spur productivity growth. Increased availability of public infrastructure or better-educated workers would tend to raise productivity growth above the baseline.

Increased public infrastructure or service delivery in education could also have a positive impact on human development. Without coherent policy interventions, taxing fuel oil consumption alone could reduce promotion rates in primary education, as households' demand for education decreases with decreasing economic activity.

Financing the sustainability of cities will require multilevel cooperation

A close partnership between local and national authorities is needed to finance the sustainable development of cities. While cities need to raise financial resources from capital markets directly, financial oversight mechanisms must be in place to manage risks so that municipal borrowing does not result in an excess of non-performing loans in the banking system or the incurring of huge financial liabilities by the central government.

Poorer cities need international cooperation and additional resources to support green technology adaptation, and capacity development, and to provide access to public transportation, housing of sound construction, water and sanitation, electricity, health care and education. It is indeed a daunting task to finance investment in public infrastructure, including adaptation to and mitigation of climate change, which often demands large sums of upfront finance whose returns would be reaped mainly in the medium and long terms.

Richer cities need policies to encourage renewable energy and to reduce inefficiency and wasteful consumption. Regulatory measures are important for determining pricing structures, taxes and subsidies for households and industry—for the development, for example, of compact neighbourhoods and the retrofitting of buildings. Various types of taxes can be used to finance the gap between the financial outlay and the actual cost of services, for example, lower fares for public transportation.

Thus, for poor and rich cities alike, part of the financing would have to be directed towards addressing global environmental challenges and the livelihoods of present and future generations.

City financing may entail the use of a wide variety of instruments

Financing strategies for sustainable development in cities can draw upon a wide range of instruments. Bond banks and resource pooling can be useful instruments for reducing risk. Cities in developing countries have successfully issued bonds (without a guarantee from the national Government) to finance water supply and sewerage projects. Public-private partnerships can also help raise funds for infrastructure projects, particularly in developing countries with limited access to long-term credit. Public-private partnerships have been used to finance the production of renewable sources of energy and waste management. Cities may also leverage the value of land to finance infrastructure, either through the outright sale of land by auction or by issuing leaseholds to leverage the land's value. These instruments can generate the initial capital needed to cover start-up costs of infrastructure investments. However, land-based financing instruments require relatively strong and effective institutions and well-articulated legal frameworks.

Sources of finance can have different degrees of stability and predictability. Taxation tied to business profits, which can fall during times of crisis, incurs greater risks than real estate taxes, because the revenues from the latter are more stable and easier to predict.

Agricultural development will require significant investments

Investment needs for primary agriculture and its downstream industries in developing countries were estimated at US$ 9.2 trillion (2009 dollars) over the 44-year period from 2005-2007 to 2050.

There are obstacles preventing higher investment in primary agriculture and especially in small farms. The insufficiency of public services limits potential returns to farmers' investments. Another issue is related to the lack of price incentives for small-scale producers, in particular when there are price controls on food products which reduce their potential net revenue. A third issue is the lack of access by smallholders to formal insurance protection against risks.

Private sector investments will be needed

Private investments in agriculture, particularly international private investments, are needed and can play an important role in boosting productivity and ensuring food security, when directed towards strategic needs. However, in order to increase the positive impact of these investments, Governments need to design policies and legislation that can create a more conducive climate for inclusive and sustainable investments. Direct incentives, for instance, such as tax incentives, can encourage investments that directly support local smallholders. Contract farming can also lead to positive investment, when small-scale farmers are assisted in contract negotiation and dispute resolution.

It is clear that public sources alone are not sufficient to address the needs in these domains. A framework for financing sustainable development needs to ensure that financing from private and public sources at the national, regional and international levels is secured. Financing has fallen short in areas that are critical for sustainable growth:

long-term investment, including infrastructure financing, research and development and investment in riskier sectors, such as small and medium-sized enterprises and innovation; and financing of international cooperation.

Further, the long time-frame necessary for infrastructure investments is outside the investment parameters of many institutional investors, even those considered to be "long-term" investors. The issue of a very long investment time-horizon arises in particular for low-carbon infrastructure projects, owing to higher risks and lower expected returns over the life of the project. In general, low-carbon technologies cannot compete with existing technologies, and this is unlikely to change unless market prices incorporate, to a much greater extent, the societal costs of using brown technologies, with their high levels of greenhouse gas emissions and other environmental risks.

Sustainable development will require significant investment from international private actors

A significant share of the investments necessary to achieve sustainable development will have to come from private sources, which nonetheless will depend on the availability of public funds to match those investments, through the provision of guarantees and/ or regulation to assure future revenue streams. Public financing, regulation and private market-based financing will therefore have to be combined, based on the specific characteristics of the newly created assets.

A framework for the financing of sustainable development will need to be supported by an enabling policy environment at national and international levels and by renewed commitments to ODA. Such a framework will need to include policy initiatives to internalize externalities, better align private incentives with public goals, and finance efforts to address global challenges. Policy coherence across domestic, regional and international initiatives is crucial, as international and regional policy agreements shape national strategies, while national policies are part and parcel of the international and regional framework.

Contents

Boxes

Figures

Tables

Explanatory notes

The following symbols have been used in the tables throughout the report:

..   **Two dots** indicate that data are not available or are not separately reported.

–   **A dash** indicates that the amount is nil or negligible.

-    **A hyphen** indicates that the item is not applicable.

—   **A minus sign** indicates deficit or decrease, except as indicated.

.   **A full stop** is used to indicate decimals.

/   **A slash** between years indicates a crop year or financial year, for example, 2013/14.

-    **Use of a hyphen** between years, for example, 2013-2014, signifies the full period involved, including the beginning and end years.

Reference to "dollars" ($) indicates United States dollars, unless otherwise stated.

Reference to "billions" indicates one thousand million.

Reference to "tons" indicates metric tons, unless otherwise stated.

Annual rates of growth or change, unless otherwise stated, refer to annual compound rates.

Details and percentages in tables do not necessarily add to totals, because of rounding.

The following abbreviations have been used:

AMIS	Agricultural Market Information System	**ILO**	International Labour Organization
BECCS	bio-energy with carbon capture and storage	**IMF**	International Monetary Fund
BMI	body mass index	**kg**	kilogram
BRT	bus rapid transit	**kWh**	kilowatt-hour
CAADP	Comprehensive Africa Agriculture Development Programme	**MAMS**	Maquette for MDG Simulations
		NNP	net national product
CCS	carbon capture and storage	**ODA**	official development assistance
CERs	certified emissions reductions	**OECD**	Organization for Economic Cooperation and Development
CF	Central Framework ((System of Environmental-Economic Accounting) (SEEA))		
		ppm	parts per million
CGIAR	formerly Consultative Group on International Agricultural Research	**PPP**	purchasing power parity
		PRSP	poverty reduction strategy paper
CLEW	climate-land-energy-water	**R&D**	research and development
CO$_2$	carbon dioxide	**ReSAKSS**	Regional Strategic Analysis and Knowledge Support System
CO$_2$e	carbon dioxide equivalent		
EJ	exajoule	**SAGCOT**	Southern Agricultural Growth Corridor of the United Republic of Tanzania
FAO	Food and Agriculture Organization of the United Nations		
		SEEA	System of Environmental-Economic Accounting
FDI	foreign direct investment	**SEEA-E**	System of Environmental-Economic Accounting for Energy
G8	Group of Eight		
G20	Group of Twenty	**SNA**	System of National Accounts
GAFSP	Global Agriculture and Food Security Programme	**SUV**	sport utility vehicle
		tCO$_2$	ton of carbon dioxide
GCARD	Global Conference on Agricultural Research for Development	**UN/DESA**	Department of Economic and Social Affairs of the United Nations Secretariat
GDP	gross domestic product		
GEA	Global Energy Assessment	**UNEP**	United Nations Environment Programme
gha	global hectare	**UN-Habitat**	United Nations Human Settlements Programme
GNH	gross national happiness	**UNSD**	United Nations Statistics Division
GNP	gross national product	**WFP**	World Food Programme
Gt	gigaton	**WHO**	World Health Organization
ICT	information and communications technologies	**WIDER**	World Institute for Development Economics Research (United Nations University)
IEA	International Energy Agency		

The designations employed and the presentation of the material in this publication do not imply the expression of any opinion whatsoever on the part of the United Nations Secretariat concerning the legal status of any country, territory, city or area or of its authorities, or concerning the delimitation of its frontiers or boundaries.

The term "country" as used in the text of this report also refers, as appropriate, to territories or areas.

For analytical purposes, unless otherwise specified, the following country groupings and subgroupings have been used:

Developed economies (developed market economies):

Australia, Canada, European Union, Iceland, Japan, New Zealand, Norway, Switzerland, United States of America.

Group of Eight (G8):

Canada, France, Germany, Italy, Japan, Russian Federation, United Kingdom of Great Britain and Northern Ireland, United States of America.

Group of Twenty (G20):

Argentina, Australia, Brazil, Canada, China, France, Germany, India, Indonesia, Italy, Japan, Mexico, Republic of Korea, Russian Federation, Saudi Arabia, South Africa, Turkey, United Kingdom of Great Britain and Northern Ireland, United States of America, European Union.

European Union (EU):

Austria, Belgium, Bulgaria, Cyprus, Czech Republic, Denmark, Estonia, Finland, France, Germany, Greece, Hungary, Ireland, Italy, Latvia, Lithuania, Luxembourg, Malta, Netherlands, Poland, Portugal, Romania, Slovakia, Slovenia, Spain, Sweden, United Kingdom of Great Britain and Northern Ireland.

EU-15:

Austria, Belgium, Denmark, Finland, France, Germany, Greece, Ireland, Italy, Luxembourg, Netherlands, Portugal, Spain, Sweden, United Kingdom of Great Britain and Northern Ireland.

New EU member States:

Bulgaria, Cyprus, Czech Republic, Estonia, Hungary, Latvia, Lithuania, Malta, Poland, Romania, Slovakia, Slovenia.

Economies in transition:

South-Eastern Europe:

Albania, Bosnia and Herzegovina, Croatia, Montenegro, Serbia, the former Yugoslav Republic of Macedonia.

Commonwealth of Independent States (CIS):

Armenia, Azerbaijan, Belarus, Georgia,[a] Kazakhstan, Kyrgyzstan, Republic of Moldova, Russian Federation, Tajikistan, Turkmenistan, Ukraine, Uzbekistan.

Developing economies:

Africa, Asia and the Pacific (excluding Australia, Japan, New Zealand and the member States of CIS in Asia), Latin America and the Caribbean.

Subgroupings of Africa:

Northern Africa:

Algeria, Egypt, Libya, Morocco, Tunisia.

Sub-Saharan Africa:

All other African countries, except Nigeria and South Africa, where indicated.

Subgroupings of Asia and the Pacific:

Western Asia:

Bahrain, Iraq, Israel, Jordan, Kuwait, Lebanon, Occupied Palestinian Territory, Oman, Qatar, Saudi Arabia, Syrian Arab Republic, Turkey, United Arab Emirates, Yemen.

South Asia:

Bangladesh, Bhutan, India, Iran (Islamic Republic of), Maldives, Nepal, Pakistan, Sri Lanka.

East Asia:

All other developing economies in Asia and the Pacific.

Subgroupings of Latin America and the Caribbean:

South America:

Argentina, Bolivia (Plurinational State of), Brazil, Chile, Colombia, Ecuador, Paraguay, Peru, Uruguay, Venezuela (Bolivarian Republic of).

Mexico and Central America:

Costa Rica, El Salvador, Guatemala, Honduras, Mexico, Nicaragua, Panama.

Caribbean:

Barbados, Cuba, Dominican Republic, Guyana, Haiti, Jamaica, Trinidad and Tobago.

---

a   As of 19 August 2009, Georgia officially left the Commonwealth of Independent States. However, its performance is discussed in the context of this group of countries for reasons of geographical proximity and similarities in economic structure.

Least developed countries:

Afghanistan, Angola, Bangladesh, Benin, Bhutan, Burkina Faso, Burundi, Cambodia, Central African Republic, Chad, Comoros, Democratic Republic of the Congo, Djibouti, Equatorial Guinea, Eritrea, Ethiopia, Gambia, Guinea, Guinea-Bissau, Haiti, Kiribati, Lao People's Democratic Republic, Lesotho, Liberia, Madagascar, Malawi, Mali, Mauritania, Mozambique, Myanmar, Nepal, Niger, Rwanda, Samoa, Sao Tome and Principe, Senegal, Sierra Leone, Solomon Islands, Somalia, Sudan, Timor-Leste, Togo, Tuvalu, Uganda, United Republic of Tanzania, Vanuatu, Yemen, Zambia.

Small island developing States and areas:

American Samoa, Anguilla, Antigua and Barbuda, Aruba, Bahamas, Barbados, Belize, British Virgin Islands, Cape Verde, Commonwealth of the Northern Mariana Islands, Comoros, Cook Islands, Cuba, Dominica, Dominican Republic, Fiji, French Polynesia, Grenada, Guam, Guinea-Bissau, Guyana, Haiti, Jamaica, Kiribati, Maldives, Marshall Islands, Mauritius, Micronesia (Federated States of), Montserrat, Nauru, Netherlands Antilles, New Caledonia, Niue, Palau, Papua New Guinea, Puerto Rico, Saint Kitts and Nevis, Saint Lucia, Saint Vincent and the Grenadines, Samoa, Sao Tome and Principe, Seychelles, Singapore, Solomon Islands, Suriname, Timor-Leste, Tonga, Trinidad and Tobago, Tuvalu, United States Virgin Islands, Vanuatu.

Parties to the United Nations Framework Convention on Climate Change:

Annex I parties:

Australia, Austria, Belarus, Belgium, Bulgaria, Canada, Croatia, Czech Republic, Denmark, Estonia, European Union, Finland, France, Germany, Greece, Hungary, Iceland, Ireland, Italy, Japan, Latvia, Liechtenstein, Lithuania, Luxembourg, Monaco, Netherlands, New Zealand, Norway, Poland, Portugal, Romania, Russian Federation, Slovakia, Slovenia, Spain, Sweden, Switzerland, Turkey, Ukraine, United Kingdom of Great Britain and Northern Ireland, United States of America.

Annex II parties:

Annex II parties are the parties included in Annex I that are members of the Organization for Economic Cooperation and Development but not the parties included in Annex I that are economies in transition.

Chapter I
Global trends and challenges to sustainable development post-2015

Summary

- The global community has made great strides in addressing poverty, but a mere continuation of current development strategies will not suffice to achieve sustainable development. Economic and social progress remains uneven, the global financial crisis has revealed the fragility of progress, and accelerating environmental degradation inflicts increasing costs on societies.

- There are a number of economic, social, technological, demographic and environmental megatrends underlying these challenges—a deeper globalization, persistent inequalities, demographic diversity and environmental degradation—to which a sustainable development agenda will have to respond.

- These trends influence and reinforce each other in myriad ways and pose enormous challenges. Urbanization is proceeding rapidly in developing countries, globalization and financialization are perpetuating inequalities, while exposing countries to greater risks of contagion from crises, and food and nutrition as well as energy security is threatened by competing demands on land and water, as well as environmental degradation.

- Most important, environmental degradation has reached critical levels. Business as usual is therefore not an option, and sustainable development will require transformative change at the local, national and global levels.

A more challenging context for global development

Significant progress has been made in the new millennium in achieving global development goals. Poverty was decreasing in all regions of the world, at least until the onset of the global financial crisis, underpinned by strong economic growth in developing countries and emerging economies. As a result, the first target of the Millennium Development Goals—halving the proportion of people living in extreme poverty globally—has already been met. Improvements in school enrolment rates and health outcomes demonstrate similar progress in the dimension of social development.

Rising inequalities, the
food, fuel and financial
crises, and the breaching of
planetary boundaries have
made clear that a mere
continuation of current
strategies will not suffice
to achieve sustainable
development after 2015

Nonetheless, a mere continuation of current strategies will not suffice to meet all the Millennium Development Goals by their 2015 deadline and to achieve sustainable development after 2015. In important areas, development is falling short and targets will be missed, including the reduction of hunger, vulnerable employment and maternal mortality, and improvements in the lives of slum dwellers, among others. Even where global goals have been reached, there are wide disparities between and within countries. Thanks in part to the remarkable growth rates in Asia, the region has made a large contribution to the achievement of global goals. Other regions, and particularly the least developed countries within them, have been less successful. Within countries, economic growth was frequently accompanied by rising income inequality, and the very poor and those discriminated against owing to their sex, age, ethnicity or disability have benefited least from overall progress (United Nations, 2011a). Income inequality is mirrored by very unequal social development and access to health services and education. Such intragenerational inequalities pose an equally important challenge to sustainable development, which is primarily associated with intergenerational equity.

The fragility of progress became apparent during the food, fuel and financial crises in 2008 and 2009. The global recession of 2009 was triggered by a global financial crisis engendered by the financial systems of developed countries, engulfing their financial and banking sectors. The resulting shock to economic activity passed through the global economy quickly, with international trade, investment and other financial flows collapsing. The recession and the slow subsequent recovery have increased unemployment worldwide and have slowed or partly reversed the decline in poverty. The fact that the global financial crisis coincided with a peak in food and energy prices aggravated its impacts in many countries. Food prices had risen rapidly since 2003, largely driven by rising energy prices and the increased production of biofuels, which became competitive owing to very high oil prices. Exacerbating factors such as extreme weather events in Australia, Ukraine and countries in other regions of the world, as well as increased speculative activity in commodity markets, highlight the intertwined risks between the three crises and the multidimensional nature of the challenges they posed (Headey, Malaiyandi and Fan, 2010).

Last, accelerating environmental degradation indicates that the world is facing a strong sustainability challenge; that is to say, there are limits to the substitutability of certain forms of natural capital, and thus to the extent to which technologies will be available to overcome environmental and planetary challenges in future (Ayres, 2007). As many forms of this natural capital are absolutely essential to human survival in the long run, its preservation is critical. A future global agenda has to address this strong sustainability challenge and facilitate transformative change at all levels—local, national and global.

Underlying global megatrends

These challenges to sustainable development are driven by broad underlying economic, social, technological, demographic and environmental megatrends. Megatrends are understood in this context as major shifts in economic, social and environmental conditions which change societies and substantially impact people at all levels.

Both the progress in development that has been achieved in recent decades and its uneven nature are tied intrinsically to changes in the global economy and globalization.

Many countries have benefited from access to global markets and the spread of knowledge and technology, but others remain marginalized. Tighter trade, investment and financial links have also increased interdependence between countries and led, particularly in combination with financialization, to greater risks of contagion in times of crisis. At the same time, economic growth has been accompanied by rising income inequalities in many countries.

In the years ahead, extremely diverse population dynamics have the potential to further exacerbate inequalities, both in developing and developed countries, and at the global level. With countries at different stages of the demographic transition, further population growth, urbanization and rapid ageing put major stresses on the national infrastructure and health and education systems. If necessary investments are not made, such demographic changes will also heighten the vulnerability of countries and populations to economic, social and environmental crises.

In addition to globalization, inequalities and major demographic changes, there is a fourth megatrend, accelerating environmental degradation, which introduces critical challenges for sustainable development. This megatrend is driven by unsustainable production and consumption patterns, and already impacts development at all levels. Extreme weather events contributed to the food crisis, and environmental problems often affect the poor disproportionally, since they are the least well equipped to deal with them. In the long run, a continuation of current trends and the breaching of planetary boundaries in particular would undermine all efforts to achieve sustainable development.

A more integrated, but multipolar and heterogeneous global economy

A deeper globalization

Globalization is not a new phenomenon. In the nineteenth century, the world economy underwent its first process of globalization, driven by technological progress in the form of lower transportation and communication costs. World trade expanded at close to 4 per cent annually on average throughout the century, much faster than in previous centuries (O'Rourke and Williamson, 2004). In addition, capital flows boomed and migration between continents occurred on a large scale. Today's globalization is therefore not entirely unprecedented in terms of trade levels, but it is qualitatively different. Beyond the mere expansion of trade and investment flows, underlying global production patterns have changed in recent decades, in particular since the turn of the millennium, driven by the rise of transnational corporations and global value chains. Instead of shallow integration, characterized by trade in goods and services between independent corporations and portfolio investments, this new phase of globalization has brought deep integration, organized by transnational corporations which link the production of goods and services in cross-border value adding networks (Gereffi, 2005).

Assembly-oriented export production in newly industrializing economies in East Asia marked the beginning of this geographical fragmentation of production. The movement of labour-intensive operations of manufactures production to low-wage locations upended the traditional international division of labour, creating opportunities for industrialization in developing countries. Successful insertion into global value chains contributed to rapid and sustained growth in numerous countries, accounting for much of the overall progress in the global fight against poverty.

Deepening globalization
is characterized by tighter
trade and investment
links and geographically
fragmented production
processes organized by
transnational corporations

The fragmentation of production was made possible by a favourable global political environment which gradually reduced barriers to trade and investment, and by major advances in transportation and in information and communication technology. The latter in particular is widely seen as the key general-purpose technology of the globalization age, driving technological progress in a wide range of sectors (Jovanovic and Rousseau, 2005). Those advances enabled corporations to manage complex global supply chains and was thus a precondition for the outsourcing and offshoring of production tasks, initially in manufacturing sectors such as apparel and simple electronics, but gradually in more and more sectors including, most recently, services and knowledge work (see, for example, Sturgeon and Florida, 2000, for the automotive industry; and Gereffi, 2005, for an overview).

Information and communications technologies have also made the diffusion of information easier, and have facilitated better access by developing countries to the global knowledge pool. Because of the critical role of science and technology in addressing the social, economic and environmental challenges faced by countries, this wider diffusion is contributing to the progress of development in a wide range of areas. At the same time, innovative activity and technology development continue to be concentrated in a small number of advanced economies. Only very few countries such as Brazil, China and India, have entered this segment in recent decades, because core research and development activities are very rarely outsourced and remain overwhelmingly centred at corporate headquarters in developed countries (Castaldi and others, 2009).

The changes in global production are reflected in changing global trade patterns. Overall trade has grown at rates much faster than those of world domestic product, and not only did developing countries expand their share in world trade, but they were able to diversify and increasingly export manufactured products (United Nations, 2010a). However, these patterns are far from uniform—diversification is largely limited to developing and emerging economies in Asia, whereas traditional trade patterns based on commodity exports and imports of manufactures and capital goods prevail in Africa and, to a lesser extent, in Latin America. The rise of China in particular has contributed to this trend, both directly owing to China's large demand for commodities and the traditional sectoral patterns exhibited by rising South-South trade, and indirectly by contributing to high commodity prices, particularly for oil and minerals (Erten and Ocampo, 2012).

The disintegration of production, and its acceleration since the turn of the millennium, is visible also in a rapid increase of trade in intermediate goods (figure I.1). As a result, the income elasticity of trade has increased as lead firms react to changes in demand and pass shocks on to their downstream suppliers more quickly (Milberg and Winkler, 2010), thus further increasing interdependence in the global economy. However, since their collapse during the 2008 and 2009 crisis, trade flows have recovered but slowly, and trade expansion is likely to remain significantly slower than before the crisis, indicating a potential weakening of globalization of trade (United Nations, 2013).

Deep globalization is also characterized by increasing foreign direct investment (FDI) and financial flows of deep globalization. FDI flows grew as a number of countries offered conducive environments for investment and served the needs of corporations competing based on the transnationalization of production. Growth in FDI has outpaced even the rapid growth in world trade. Global FDI inflows reached $ 1.5 trillion in 2011, although they have yet to reach the pre-crisis peak of 2007 (United Nations Conference on Trade and Development, 2012b). Fifty-one per cent of total FDI was destined for

Figure I.1
World non-fuel merchandise exports by type of goods, 1998-2011

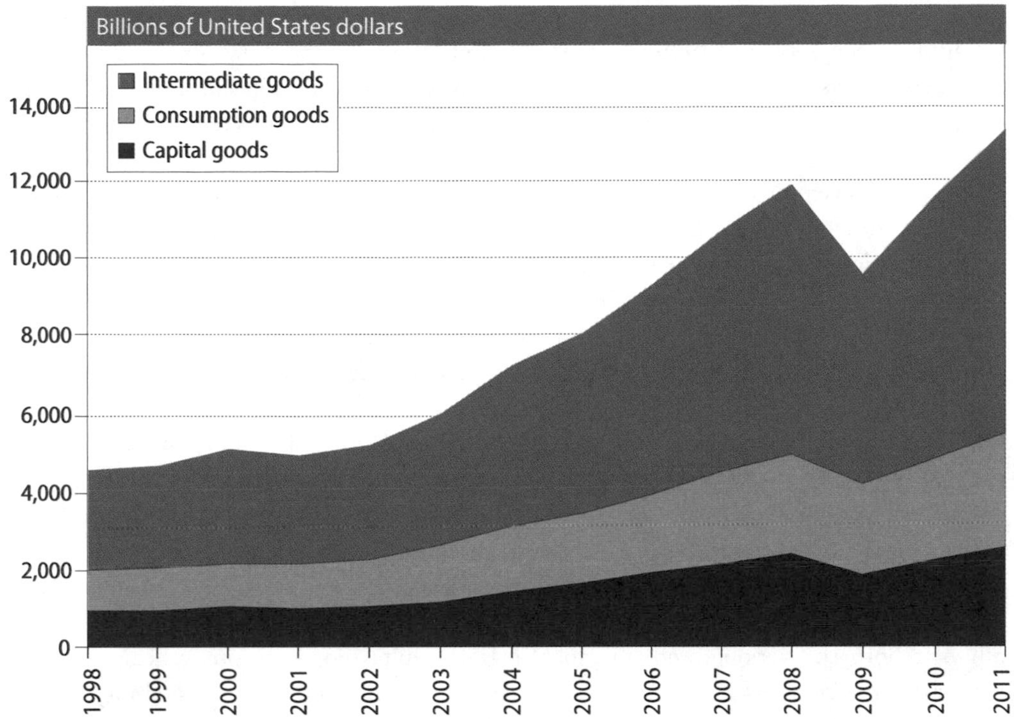

Billions of United States dollars

Legend:
- Intermediate goods
- Consumption goods
- Capital goods

Source: United Nations Commodity Trade Statistics Database (UN Comtrade).

developing countries and transition economies, which have steadily and rapidly increased their share of overall FDI owing to their dynamic development. Yet, not all developing countries benefit from this trend. The least developed countries in particular remain marginalized, having attracted only $15 billion, or less than 1 per cent of global FDI.

Financial globalization and financialization

Globalization has progressed furthest, perhaps, in finance, where the liberalization of capital markets and short-term capital flows has been promoted since the 1980s, most prominently by the International Monetary Fund (IMF). The rationale was to enable global savings to be allocated to their most productive use, and thus to provide developing countries in particular with access to scarce savings. The actual outcome of financial liberalization was quite different, however. The increased volatility of capital flows, global macroeconomic imbalances, and multiple financial crises—typically followed by severe recessions, most recently on a global level—have highlighted both the large risks and the very uncertain gains of financial globalization for development.

Capital controls and restrictions to short-term capital flows were an essential part of the post-war Bretton Woods regime. With the Great Depression and the financial crisis that had preceded it in mind, policymakers agreed to restrict international capital mobility and thus prioritize trade and production over finance and give countries greater macroeconomic policy space. However, this essentially Keynesian vision was undermined by the ascendancy of financial interests in key developed countries, a broader move towards deregulation and liberalization, and growing trade links between countries, which made it more difficult to administer capital controls (Rodrik, 2011).

Capital market liberalization proceeded first in developed economies and then in developing countries, and international capital flows did increase significantly subsequently, from an average of below 5 per cent of global gross domestic product (GDP) between 1980 and 1999 to a peak of about 20 per cent in 2007. At the same time, short-term flows—portfolio and bank-related investments—have become a much more prominent part of total capital flows, particularly in the period between 2003 and 2007 (International Monetary Fund, 2012).

Financial globalization has led to rapidly increasing and more volatile international capital flows, macroeconomic imbalances and more frequent crises. And since the global financial crisis, cross-border financial flows have declined by more than 60 per cent

Developing countries that opened their capital accounts and relied more heavily on foreign finance did not promote growth and investment, however; in fact, they grew more slowly than their peers (Prasad, Rajan, and Subramanian, 2007). At the same time, the volatility of capital flows increased, their procyclical nature exacerbated macro-economic instability, and financial crises became much more frequent. These crises generally follow a similar pattern. Capital inflows based on market optimism fuel credit bubbles, leading to increases in the values of real estate and the currency; but over-indebtedness soon undermines the capacity to repay. Once the bubble bursts, capital inflows stop and the ensuing credit crunch leads to economic contraction (Kindleberger and Aliber, 2011). The social costs of such crises are extremely high. Laeven and Valencia (2012) find that since the onset of the global financial crisis, the median output loss from systemic banking crises, which often coincide with currency crises, has amounted to 25 per cent of GDP.

Financial market liberalization has also increased macroeconomic insta-bility, at both the national and the global levels. Capital flows are procyclical and thus exacerbate the business cycle. At the same time, they limit policymakers' ability to use macroeconomic policies to smooth out the business cycle (Ocampo, Spiegel and Stiglitz, 2006). Consequently, many countries have built up their international reserves to protect themselves against the risks associated with volatile capital flows. The massive increase in reserves held by developing and emerging countries—which amounted to $7 trillion in 2011 (United Nations, 2012a)—leads to global macroeconomic imbalances however.

Tightly related to capital market liberalization is the process of financializa-tion. Broadly described, financialization entails the increasing role of financial motives, actors, markets and institutions in the economy, as evidenced in the increase in profits of financial institutions relative to non-financial corporations and the overall increase in rentiers' share of national income (Epstein, 2005). In the 1970s, starting in the United States of America followed by other advanced economies, financialization was driven by financial interests that sought profitable investments in the context of slowing economies. It led to changes in corporate behaviour in line with principles of shareholder value and shorter time horizons of corporations in their investment decisions, changes in financial markets which facilitated increased indebtedness and asset-price bubbles, and changes made in economic policy, not least of all to facilitate financial globalization (Palley, 2007).

More recently, and in parallel to the recent slowdown in trade globalization, the global crisis may have ushered in an era of weakening financial globalization. In fact, cross-border financial flows have declined by more than 60 per cent from their peak in 2007 (Lund and others, 2013). Financial regulation is being strengthened worldwide, both in major developed and emerging economies and at the international level, and major advocates of financial globalization have modified their position. Most prominently, IMF adopted a new institutional view on capital controls, highlighting the risks associated with rapid capital inflows and outflows, and embracing capital flow management measures under specific circumstances (International Monetary Fund, 2012).

Convergence, but greater vulnerability and heterogeneity in the global economy

Overall, globalization has provided opportunities for emerging economies and developing countries, and in recent years their growth rates have been consistently higher than growth rates in the developed world. There are two critical caveats with respect to this broad trend of convergence, however. It has not made developing countries immune to cyclical shocks: indeed, globalization has increased countries' vulnerabilities; and it is far from uniform, with some developing countries not only excluded from this convergence process but falling further behind. Average per capita growth also hides increasing inequalities within countries, which are also partly related to globalization. A significant part of the global population therefore does not benefit from convergence (Dervis, 2012).

Since the 1990s, per capita incomes in emerging economies have grown consistently faster than in the developed world. Since the turn of the millennium, growth in developing countries has accelerated as well, leading an overall trend of convergence in the global economy (figure I.2). Convergence is partly driven by globalization, which has facilitated access to technology and know-how through tighter trade and investment links and thus higher productivity growth in manufacturing. In fact, manufacturing sectors have experienced an unconditional convergence in labour productivity, that is to say, a convergence independent of geography or policies (Rodrik, 2012). Since this does not hold for other sectors of the economy, structural transformation—a decreasing reliance on the primary sector and a shift of resources to higher value adding manufacturing and modern services activities—will remain a necessary condition of sustained economic growth.

As a result of rapid growth in developing and emerging economies, the world economy is becoming more multipolar, which inevitably leads to the creation of a world that is more multipolar politically. These changes will have to be accommodated within a global

Deepening globalization has facilitated growth in developing and emerging economies, but has also made national economies more vulnerable to external shocks

Figure I.2
Annual growth of GDP per capita, high-, low- and middle-income countries, 1990-2011

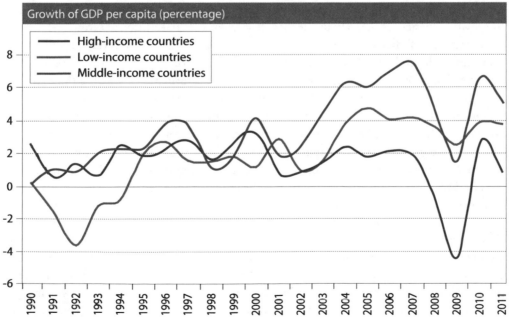

Source: World Bank World Development Indicators.

governance regime. The expansion of global trade associated with the fragmentation of production also adds to global carbon dioxide (CO_2) emissions, with the transport sector a significant source of those emissions. On average, internationally traded goods generate emissions that are 50 per cent higher than those generated by locally traded goods (United Nations, 2013). Relatedly, the vast expansion of global consumption and of changing consumption patterns in emerging economies will add to the strong environmental sustainability challenge driven originally by unsustainable consumption patterns in developed countries (see further below). Economically, continued growth in emerging economies in particular can be an engine of growth for the world economy and provides opportunities for other developing countries, but the gravity shift to China and India, the major drivers of this process, will also change the nature of end markets and is likely to pose new challenges for economic development.

Deepening globalization has also increased the cyclical interdependence of national economies. Owing to tighter links, they are more vulnerable to external shocks, and crises like the 2008-2009 global financial crisis spread quickly. Global value chains are partly responsible for this, as demand shocks in one region are passed on much more quickly through tightly integrated global value chains (see, for example, Cattaneo, Gereffi and Staritz, 2010). Reductions in consumer demand in end markets are transmitted in real time to producers, often with large and immediate effects on employment in exporting countries (Keane, 2012).

Perhaps even more important is the fact that financial globalization has increased countries' vulnerability to financial crises, as evidenced by the frequency of financial crises in recent years and the contagion effects arising from such crises. Many countries have taken the lessons learned from the crisis to heart—most notably developed economies such as the United States—and have taken steps to strengthen financial regulation. Interdependence in the global economy, however, also implies that the externalities of national economic policies are increasing and thus require better management and coordination at the global level. Again, notable first steps in this regard have been taken since the crisis, for example, through the establishment of the Financial Stability Board, and through the issuance of new rules by the Basel Committee on Banking Supervision.

There are concerns not only about external shocks, but also about heterogeneity in growth experiences, i.e., about the fact that progress is not uniform. Growth in many countries is not sufficient to enable them to be part of the overall convergence process, or they remain dependent on low value adding resource exports for growth. Yet, development strategies based on industrialization and structural transformation following the example of East Asia have become more challenging as rents for simple manufacturing and assembly procedures within global value chains have eroded and as prices for manufacturing goods typically exported by low-income countries have fallen more rapidly with the entry of China into global markets (Kaplinsky, 2006). In future, shifting end markets will also lead to shifting patterns of global import demand, with a heavier emphasis on demand for commodities and raw materials as well as unprocessed goods, likely rendering upgrading strategies within value chains more difficult (Kaplinsky and Farooki, 2010).

The 2008-2009 crisis has also accelerated the consolidation of global value chains, which began as early as the 1990s in some sectors, but can now be observed across sectors (Cattaneo, Gereffi and Staritz, 2010). Many lead firms used the crisis to end relations with marginal suppliers, relying on globally operating suppliers instead. This may preclude, or at least render significantly more difficult, the future entry of new firms, in particular those based in marginal countries, into global value chains. In combination with continuing global macroeconomic imbalances and the related pressure on countries with current-account deficits to rebalance their external positions, as well as the slowdown in trade expansion already observed, these changes will render development strategies based on export-led growth, so successfully implemented in many of the best performing developing countries in recent decades, much more difficult in the years ahead.

Persistent inequalities

The heterogeneity among countries exists side by side with persistent inequalities, of which income inequality is only one, if the most visible, dimension. While global income inequality has receded slightly in recent years, inequalities within many countries have been rising. These trends are complex and driven by many, often structural and country-specific factors, and they are tightly linked to social, environmental and political inequalities. Nonetheless, globalization has important direct and indirect impacts on inequality. Left unaddressed, these inequalities threaten sustainable development prospects in multiple ways.

Owing to the convergence of mean incomes of developing and developed economies, global income inequality has been falling in recent years, albeit to a very small degree, and from a very high level. In the wake of the great global divergence in incomes that started with the industrial revolution in the nineteenth century, location rather than socioeconomic status or class is still responsible for the overwhelming share of overall income inequality. More than two thirds of global inequality is explained by differences in income between countries, and only one third by the distribution patterns within countries (Milanovic, 2011a).

The more recent stabilization and slight narrowing of global income inequality largely reflect economic growth in China since the 1990s, and growth in India, other emerging economies and developing economies since the turn of the millennium (Milanovic, 2012). At the same time, income inequalities are increasing at the national level in most regions of the world (figure I.3; see also Vieira, 2012). While national income inequalities had for the most part decreased after the Second World War, this trend was reversed in the 1980s, when inequality started to rise sharply again, particularly in developed and emerging economies, with the largest gains going to the top 1 per cent of households. The extent of within-country inequalities, while growing in most countries, varies widely between them. In several countries in Latin America, the major exceptions to the overall trend, social programmes and improvements in labour productivity have played a major role in reducing income inequality since 2000. Distributional diversity, however, applies to the developed world as well as to developing countries, which suggests that in addition to global economic forces, institutional factors play an important role in explaining it (Palma, 2011).

Changes in the global economy—while not the only driver of trends in inequality—play an important role in the context of many of its underlying causes. In developed countries, the outsourcing and offshoring of jobs requiring mid-level skills—facilitated by changes in global production patterns and technological changes—have led to a hollowing out of labour markets from the middle and may be partly responsible for stagnating wages for low-skilled workers (Abel and Deitz, 2012). At the same time, financialization has increased executive compensation and wages at the very top of the income distribution (for the United States, see Piketty and Saez, 2003). A significant decline in the share of wages in the functional income distribution, reflecting lower bargaining power

Income inequalities within many countries have been increasing, while global inequality, although it has receded slightly in recent years, remains extremely high

Figure I.3
Income share of the top 1 per cent for a sample of developed and developing countries, 1915-2010

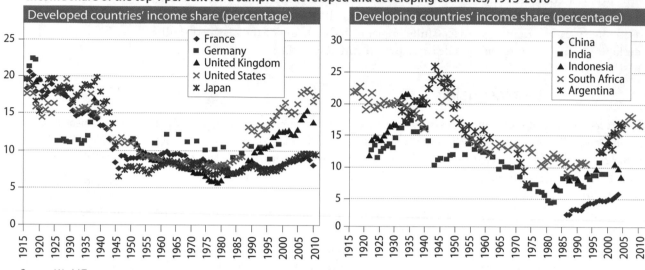

Source: World Top
Incomes Database.

of immobile labour versus mobile capital, exacerbates these trends, as capital ownership is typically highly concentrated (United Nations Conference on Trade and Development, 2012a). For this reason, the collapse in stock prices during the global financial crisis led to a temporary fall in the share of the top percentile in total income in the United States. However, during the uneven recovery from 2009 to 2011, incomes in the top percentile bounced back and grew by 11.2 per cent, while the average incomes of the bottom 99 per cent of households fell by 0.4 per cent (Saez, 2013).

In developing countries, income inequality is often due to insufficient employment generation, if, for example, growth is based on commodity exports, as was the case in some regions in Africa. In East and South-East Asia, structural change from a primarily agricultural to a modern economy—as famously described by Kuznets—is an important driver of inequality. In addition, global economic developments such as financialization and rapidly rising capital flows, as well as a global policy agenda with very different priorities, had long constrained national policymakers in their use of macroeconomic, tax and redistributive, labour-market and other policies to directly tackle inequalities (United Nations Conference on Trade and Development, 2012a).

Rising inequalities undermine prospects for sustained growth and sustainable development by threatening economic and social stability and by constraining the life choices of individuals

Not only are rising income inequalities at the national level undesirable in their own right, but they may also undermine prospects for sustained growth and broader sustainable development. Empirically, higher levels of inequality are associated with a shorter duration of growth spells. Many developing countries have been able to initiate and sustain high growth for several years, but sustaining steady growth over a longer period has proved to be much more challenging. Such longer growth spells are robustly associated with more equality in income distribution (Berg and Ostry, 2011). Potential reasons for this are inequality's negative impact on the composition of aggregate demand, investments in social services and education, and sociopolitical and economic stability.

In terms of social development, large inequalities constrain life choices for individuals and perpetuate unequal economic and social opportunities, i.e., inequality of outcome translates into inequality of opportunity. Several studies have emphasized that increasing inequalities are detrimental to child development. Beyond the psychosocial and cognitive consequences for children (Hoff and Pandey, 2004), persistent inequalities increase the chances of lower development outcomes in health, including under-nutrition and stunting, and in education, including in school enrolment and learning outcomes. These inequalities may solidify over time, as the political influence of wealthier groups increases, leading to institutional arrangements that favour their interests (World Bank, 2005). Such economic and social inequalities are strongly intertwined with and often exacerbated by horizontal inequalities, i.e., inequalities based on disability, gender, ethnicity, caste or other hereditary characteristics. Conversely, in more equal societies, better social outcomes can be expected: people are more likely to live longer and to achieve higher grades at school, and less likely to suffer from obesity and violence (Pickett and Wilkinson, 2009). For instance, there is evidence that the proportion of the population with obesity is higher in developed countries with higher income inequality (Pickett and others, 2005).

Last, income inequality can threaten economic stability (see, for example, Rajan, 2010; and Stiglitz, 2012). In the United States, stagnating real wages for the middle class lowered the purchasing power of households. Low interest rate policies were introduced to spur consumption, which contributed to the mounting of household debt beyond sustainable levels (Rajan, 2010). The increase in debt in turn generated profitable activities in the financial sector, widening wealth and income gaps, while contributing to asset-price bubbles and ultimately to the financial crisis.

Demographic changes

The global population reached 7 billion in 2011 and will continue to grow, albeit at a decelerating rate, to reach a projected 9 billion in 2050 (United Nations, Department of Economic and Social Affairs, Population Division, 2011). Beyond aggregate global population growth, demographic development is characterized by heterogeneity, as countries are at different stages of their demographic transition. While global population growth is slowing, it is still high in some developing countries, and while the world population as a whole is ageing rapidly, some countries are witnessing an increase in the proportion of youth in their overall population. Such diversity, combined with persistent inequalities, in turn creates migratory pressures both within countries and internationally. These demographic trends pose major challenges for future development strategies at all levels: local development will be shaped by further urbanization, national development strategies will have to adapt to evolving demographic structures, and migratory pressures will have to be addressed at the global level.

Population dynamics are driven by fertility rates and mortality rates—changes in which are often described as jointly constituting the demographic transition—and migration patterns. Historical patterns in developed countries suggest a demographic transition from an initial state of high fertility and high mortality to a state of low fertility and low mortality, where mortality typically declines first followed at a later stage by a more abrupt decline in fertility. At the global level, fertility rates have long been falling from their peak and the global fertility rate currently stands at 2.52 children per woman. It is expected to fall further, to 2.17 children per woman, in 2045-2050. However, these averages mask great heterogeneity between countries. Fertility is below replacement level in countries that account for almost half of the global population, namely, most developed countries, but also China. It has fallen rapidly in many developing countries as well, whereas it remains at 4.41 for least developed countries, and is projected to stay significantly above replacement level in coming decades (ibid.). The empowerment of women, better access to birth control and the postponement of marriage are immediate drivers of fertility declines, but fertility rates are also dependent on economic development, mortality declines and improvements in education levels.

Owing to improvements in nutrition and public health and social development more broadly, mortality is declining throughout the world. Life expectancy at birth is currently at 67.9 years, and is expected to increase to 75.6 years by 2045-2050, based on increases in all regions and development groups. Even though mortality trends have been more uniform, there is regional diversity nonetheless, with the impact of HIV/AIDS on life expectancy in sub-Saharan Africa particularly visible.

While mortality is declining throughout the world, fertility rates remain high for some countries, notably least developed countries, and as a result, future population growth will be extremely concentrated geographically

Migration is the third driver of population dynamics. Net migration from less developed to more developed regions has been increasing steadily from 1960 onward. Between 2000 and 2010, developed regions attracted 3.4 million migrants annually on average. While these flows dominate global migration patterns, migration between developing countries is also significant, and several of them have attracted migrants in large numbers, for example, as guest workers (in the Middle East) and as refugees (in Africa). Looking forward, migration patterns are more difficult to predict, as they are influenced by a complex interplay of economic, social, demographic, environmental and political factors; but overall migration from less to more developed regions is projected to continue, albeit at a slower pace, in the decades ahead (United Nations, Department of Economic and Social Affairs, Population Division, 2011).

These demographic drivers lead to four major global population trends: the world population will continue to grow; it will grow at a much slower pace than previously; it will become older; and it will be increasingly urban (Cohen, 2010). These global trends mask large underlying heterogeneity between countries, and they pose important challenges to sustainable development, both globally and in specific regions and countries. With regard to population growth, it reached its peak between 1965 and 1970, and has decelerated ever since. This trend will continue, and by 2050 population in developed countries is expected to almost stagnate, and population growth in developing countries other than least developed countries will be 0.50 per cent annually, while the population of the least developed countries will grow at the rate of 1.42 per cent annually, significantly below today's rate, but still high enough to enable populations to double every 49 years (United Nations, Department of Economic and Social Affairs, Population Division, 2011; see also figure I.4).

This diversity implies that future increases in world population will be highly concentrated geographically. Only eight countries—the Democratic Republic of the Congo, Ethiopia, India, Nigeria, Pakistan, the Philippines, the United Republic of Tanzania, and the United States—will account for half of the projected global population increase. More worrisome is the fact that rapid population growth continues in countries that are the least well equipped to provide the necessary investments to deal with larger populations. Populations are expected to more than double in the least developed countries between now and 2050, and short of major development progress in these countries, this is likely to challenge their sustainable development prospects in a number of ways. A vicious circle of poverty, lack of education, ill health, high fertility and high infant mortality can perpetuate inequalities. Breaking it will require further investments in health and education systems, as well as better access to reproductive health services and the protection of women's reproductive rights. At the same time, these investments have to be complemented by expanding productive employment opportunities, as a growing number of young people enter labour markets. Last, population growth, in particular in combination with climate change, can add to local environmental stresses and resource and land scarcity.

Owing to the decline in fertility and mortality rates, the global population will also become older at an accelerating pace (Lutz, Sanderson and Scherbov, 2008). The share of persons aged 60 years or over will increase to 22 per cent in 2050 globally, up from 11.2 per cent in 2011 and from only 8 per cent in 1950. However, countries are at very different stages in their demographic transition. Population ageing is most advanced in developed countries, leading to sharp increases in dependency ratios and putting a strain on those countries' health and pension systems. Developing countries are younger on average, but their populations are growing older as well. Critically, the ageing process is projected to occur at a much higher speed than was the case in developed countries, while family structures undergo major changes and family support systems consequently play a smaller role. If basic pension systems are lacking, a growing share of older persons will therefore be at risk of falling into poverty.

On the other hand, because of their continuously high fertility rates, the least developed countries will continue to see the number of youth and adolescents rising. A growing share of young people presents opportunities for reaping a demographic dividend, if a demographic transition occurs and fertility rates and dependency ratios fall, which, at this point, is projected to happen in least developed countries in Asia (United Nations Population Fund, 2011). However, this dividend will pay out only if those economies can create employment opportunities, which will be a major challenge for least developed countries in the decades ahead. Such disparities in international population dynamics, in combination with existing income disparities, are also contributing to continued migratory pressures at the global level. If addressed in a coherent manner, migration can be beneficial for both countries of origin and countries of destination, by alleviating—although by no means eliminating—problems arising from demographic trends, and contributing to

Population ageing will lead to sharp increases in dependency ratios, while global disparities in population dynamics and persistent income disparities will increase migratory pressures at the global level

Figure I.4
Projected population by development region, medium variant, 1950-2050

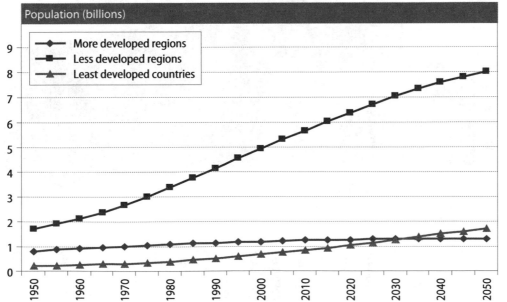

Source: United Nations, Department of Economic and Social Affairs, Population Division (2011).

transfers of knowledge and resources. Yet, at this point, there are no adequate mechanisms at the global level for addressing these concerns.

As noted above, the fourth major trend is increasing urbanization. Already, more than half of the world's population live in towns and cities, and most future population growth will occur in the urban areas of developing countries (figure I.5). In the least developed countries, the rate of growth in urban areas is 4 per cent per year, mostly driven by rural-urban migration in search of employment (United Nations Population Fund, 2011). Many of these migrants live in informal settlements and urban slums where they are exposed to environmental hazards and increased health risks. Climate change can further increase these risks, as many cities are in locations particularly exposed to its effects (Satterthwaite, 2009). On the other hand, urbanization offers opportunities to provide better access to services and employment at lower cost and with a lower environmental impact. While building the infrastructure that would allow those opportunities to be realized entails huge investment and planning needs, the reality of continued population growth will render such an undertaking critical to any sustainable development strategy.

Environmental degradation

While an unusually stable global environment has been the precondition for unprecedented human development over the last ten thousand years, this stability is now under threat from human activity. Most critically, energy consumption has skyrocketed owing to rapid population and economic growth, resulting in unprecedented concentrations of CO_2 in the atmosphere and anthropogenic climate change. If greenhouse gas emissions, global

Figure I.5
Urban and rural population growth, high-, low- and middle-income countries, 1950-1955 to 2045-2050

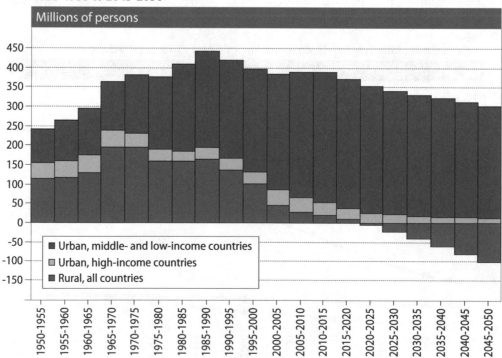

Source: Population Division, UN/DESA.

resource consumption and habitat transformation continue at or above current rates, a state shift in the Earth's biosphere is likely (Barnosky and others, 2012), irreversibly changing the environmental conditions so favourable to human development in recent millenniums.

The environmental impact of human activity and the strong sustainability challenge that it poses are tightly related to the megatrends identified above. To decompose their overall effects and shed more light on the many interlinkages, it is useful to draw on the ImPACT identity, which relates demographic, socioeconomic and technological changes to their environmental impact. More specifically, ImPACT specifies that the product of total population (P), world product per person or affluence (A), the intensity of use of GDP or consumption patterns (C) and the efficiency of producers determined by technology (T) together determine overall environmental impact (Im) (Waggoner and Ausubel, 2002).[1] These forces influence each other in important and multiple ways. Population dynamics impact on per capita income and vice versa, income levels affect consumption patterns and efficiency in production, and environmental changes in turn exert an impact on economies, to give just a few examples.

Within this framework, the contribution of the megatrends to environmental degradation can be delineated. Population dynamics determine the overall number of persons whose material needs have to be met, both at the local and national levels, and at the global level. Diverse demographic trends present highly diverse challenges to sustainable development at the local and national levels. Globally, however, population growth is slowing. More important, population growth is concentrated in countries whose contribution to global environmental challenges is comparatively small.

Economic growth lies at the heart of the global development agenda, and the persistence of large unmet material needs implies that sustainable development requires further increases in income and affluence for many. At the same time, humanity's overall demand for natural resources already exceeds Earth's bio-capacity (WWF, 2012). Contributions to this excessive environmental footprint are extremely uneven, however: the global inequalities in incomes and wealth described above translate directly into starkly differing environmental impacts (see chap. II).

The impact of per capita income on the environment is mediated by the intensity of GDP use, which is a reflection of consumption patterns, and by the efficiency of production of goods, or technology. Consumption patterns and technological progress are sometimes called sustainability levers, as they can mitigate the environmental impact of income growth (Waggoner and Ausubel, 2002). Growth itself can be a driver of such technological progress, of structural change entailing movement away from material-intensive industries towards services, and of changes in consumer preferences. An environmental Kuznets curve hypothesis suggests that for these reasons, resource use would increase in the early stages of development, but fall in later stages (Rothman, 1998). However, there is no evidence of such an absolute decoupling of growth in resource use from economic growth at the global level, and only very limited evidence for relative decoupling, where resource use grows more slowly than the economy. Most importantly, global CO_2 emissions have grown as fast as or faster than global GDP since the turn of the millennium, as large emerging economics industrialize (see below and chap. II).

The stability of the global environment is under threat from human activity, owing largely to unsustainable consumption patterns that reflect extreme inequalities

---

1   The well-known Kaya identity—expressing total global CO_2 emissions as a product of total population, GDP per capita, energy consumption per gross world product, and global CO_2 emissions per global energy consumption—is the basis of a specific exercise in decomposing overall environmental impact—in this case global emissions—into contributing driving factors P, A, C and T.

Threats to global ecosystems

In a number of areas, damage to the global environment is reaching critical levels and threatens to lead to irreversible changes in global ecosystems. Rockstroem and others (2009) have identified interlinked planetary boundaries, and found that in some areas, including most prominently climate change, boundaries have already been exceeded. There is also strong evidence for tipping points to exist for ocean acidification, the phosphorous cycle, and stratospheric ozone depletion, while in other areas, the impacts of environmental degradation may be limited to local and regional ecosystems (Nordhaus and others, 2012). Overwhelmingly, these changes are driven by the reliance on fossil fuels to power economic growth, and by industrialized forms of agriculture, necessary to feed a growing and increasingly wealthy global population.

Damage to the global environment is reaching critical levels and threatens to lead to irreversible changes in global ecosystems. Most visibly in climate change, critical thresholds have already been exceeded

The overarching environmental challenge is anthropogenic climate change. The increased concentration of greenhouse gases in the atmosphere—most importantly, CO_2—is leading to a warming of the planet. The atmospheric CO_2 concentration has increased from 260-280 parts per million (ppm) in pre-industrial times to 391 ppm in September 2012, and global mean warming is already 0.8° C above pre-industrial levels (World Bank, 2012a). Projections of future global warming depend on assumptions regarding future development pathways and demographic, economic and technological developments, and thus vary widely, but further warming is predicted in all scenarios. The business-as-usual scenario produced by the Intergovernmental Panel on Climate Change (2007a) arrives at a best estimate of a 4° C increase of global average surface temperature in 2100 as compared with the period 1980-1999.

There is also a strong scientific consensus that global warming is induced by human behaviour, predominantly by fossil fuel use and, to a smaller extent, by changes in land use and deforestation. The extent of future global warming will therefore primarily depend on successfully using the sustainability levers by reducing the energy intensity of GDP growth and the carbon intensity of energy, assuming that GDP per capita and population continue to grow. However, current trends are not favourable. While the carbon intensity of global growth decreased and thus slowed down the overall growth in CO_2 emissions up until 2000, emission growth has accelerated in the new millennium because of a reduction—and, partly, even a cessation—in the long-term decreasing trends of carbon intensity of energy and energy intensity of GDP, largely owing to the high energy requirements of intensive growth in developing and emerging economies (Raupach and others, 2007).

This challenge, in its starkness and immediacy, clearly requires a global response. Rockstroem and others (2009) propose a CO_2 concentration boundary in the atmosphere of 350 ppm, which has already been breached. Yet, reaching agreement on this global response entails addressing difficult equity questions, as contributions to global emissions have varied widely historically and continue to do so. While developed countries are responsible for almost 60 per cent of cumulative emissions and therefore bear the brunt of the blame historically, they now contribute little to emissions growth, which is driven by China, India and other developing countries (Raupach and others, 2007). In fact, China is now the single largest contributor to global CO_2 emissions, having emitted 9.7 billion tons in 2011, representing 29 per cent of all emissions (Olivier, Janssens-Maenhout and Peters, 2012). At the same time, the stabilization of emissions in developed countries can be explained in part by growing imports of emissions-intensive products from developing countries. If these emissions transfers are taken into account, developed countries have not been able to stabilize their contribution to global emissions (figure I.6). The picture is further complicated by stark differences in per capita emissions. While per capita emissions in the United States are about five times the global average, per capita emissions in least developed countries are a mere tenth of the global average (Raupach and others, 2007).

Climate change poses numerous and stark challenges for sustainable development, and its effects will be felt in all regions of the globe, although the intensity of exposure will vary. Degree of vulnerability will vary even more, with developing countries and the poor, which have contributed the least to global warming, likely to suffer the most. Coastal communities, notably in small islands and megadeltas, mountain settlements and urban communities in megacities of developing countries are particularly vulnerable (Intergovernmental Panel on Climate Change, 2012a). Agriculture will also be negatively impacted by the increasing frequency of extreme weather events such as heatwaves and droughts, and the intensification of the water cycle, further intensifying aridity of already dry zones and thus reducing the amount of arable land. Growing average temperatures and changes in precipitation trends are already having a significant negative impact on yields of global maize and wheat crops (Lobell, Schlenker and Costa-Roberts, 2011).

Arguably even more important in the functioning of the Earth system, albeit less visibly, are the world's oceans. They, too, are dramatically affected by increased CO_2 emissions, which lead, through the effects of warming and thermal expansion, to a rise in sea levels, as well as to ocean acidification. The latter would, if current trends continued, halt or even reverse coral reef growth, undermining marine ecosystems, and, in combination with sea-level rises, would endanger coastal regions worldwide (World Bank, 2012a).

Climate change is also exacerbating biodiversity loss. Biodiversity is critical for the resilience of ecosystems and thus important for the provision of often-irreplaceable ecosystem services, encompassing, inter alia, food, water and cultural services (Steffen and

Figure I.6

CO_2 emissions of developed and developing countries, as allocated to production and consumption (production plus net exports), 1990-2010

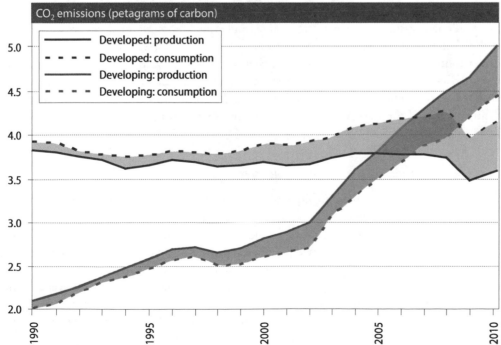

Source: Peters and others (2012).

others, 2011). While current losses in biodiversity are mostly caused by habitat destruction, climate change could soon become an even bigger threat to the survival of species and is expected to accelerate the overall trend in biodiversity loss (Bellard and others, 2012). Causal chains are complex and multiple, and include the increase in average temperatures and changes in precipitation patterns, the higher frequency of extreme weather events such as droughts and flooding, ocean acidification and further land-use changes.

The expansion and modernization of agriculture are largely responsible for interference with the planetary nitrogen and phosphorus cycle, and contribute to global land-use change. Fertilizer use, a major driver of the green revolution in agriculture, has increased by 700 per cent since 1960 (Foley and others, 2005). Fertilizer production involves the conversion of nitrogen from the atmosphere into reactive forms through which it becomes usable nutrient for plants. This has allowed for the remarkable expansion of agriculture, but at the same time it has led to the widespread dispersion and accumulation of reactive nitrogen in the environment. The same is true for phosphorus, which is mined from rock and also used in fertilizers. The excess concentration of nitrogen and phosphorus degrades water quality and threatens biodiversity and thus the resilience of marine ecosystems. Increasing nitrogen concentrations also contribute to acidification of rivers and streams, to stratospheric ozone depletion and to climate change (Galloway and others, 2003). Land-use change, which is driven not only by agriculture but also by the expansion of urban areas, further contributes to change in the global and regional climates and to biodiversity loss.

Most worrisome are the substantial risks of large-scale non-linear impacts of climate change and the breaching of other planetary boundaries. Once certain environmental thresholds are crossed, biological changes might interact in multiple ways, through feedback mechanisms which are not yet fully understood, and move the planet's biosphere irreversibly into a different state. Such state shifts have occurred multiple times in the Earth's history, most recently about thirteen thousand to eleven thousand years ago, when the planet transitioned from its last glacial into the present interglacial condition, or the Holocene, characterized by exceptionally benign conditions for human development. Planetary state shifts are irreversible, and cause dramatic changes in the global, regional and local assemblage of species (Barnosky and others, 2012). Some of the better-understood potential feedback mechanisms encompass a rapid loss in rainforest coverage and dieback, of the Amazon rainforest in particular; disruptions in the ocean ecosystem; abrupt loss of Arctic summer sea-ice; irreversible meltdown of the Greenland ice sheet; disintegration of the west Antarctic ice sheet; and melting of permafrost in the northern hemisphere (Lenton and Ciscar, 2012).

> Once certain thresholds have been crossed, there are substantial risks of large-scale non-linear impacts, which could irreversibly alter the state of the planet's biosphere

A strong sustainability challenge?

Climate change also puts pressure on natural resources that are essential for sustaining human civilization. In the past, resource scarcity was often presented as a critical challenge, but for much of the twentieth century, resource prices actually fell. The combination of rapid economic expansion, continued population growth and a changing climate raises the spectre of resource scarcities. In the medium and long term, it may lead to a strong sustainability challenge. There is significant scope for substitution in many areas, yet certain forms of natural capital including the ecological services they provide cannot be replaced by man-made capital. Their exploitation has thus to be limited so as to preserve the overall capacity of ecosystems to provide those services (Ayres, 2007).

Land, water and energy in particular are critical resources for humanity, and their availability and use are tightly interconnected, with multiple feedback channels between them. All of them have strong links to agriculture and food production. Large unmet needs at the global level require and will inevitably lead to a further expansion in their use and exploitation. Combined with the additional impact of climate change, this expansion may very well lead to much tighter supplies, and thus to price volatilities and sustained price increases. If scarcities arise and if limits to substitutability are reached, distributional conflicts will have to be addressed at the national and global levels, as well as with respect to purposes of use.

The common drivers of resource use are population growth and economic expansion and the associated lifestyle changes. The global population will continue to expand, but population growth will take place largely in the poorest countries, adding comparatively small additional pressure at the global level. Resource use is strongly correlated with income, however. Currently, per capita material and energy use in developed countries is higher than in developing countries by a factor of 5-10. Population density also appears to be a significant determinant, with densely populated areas needing fewer material resources to achieve the same standard of living (Krausmann and others, 2009). For these reasons, the major drivers of global resource demand in the decades ahead will be economic growth and changes in consumption and urbanization patterns.

Competing demands for land stem from increasing global demand for food and feed, for livestock in particular, increasing biofuel production, and the expansion of cities, and from the need to protect forests so as to meet the demand for fibre, as well as the need for carbon sequestration (Evans, 2010). Climate change may further reduce the amount of arable land, particularly in low-lying regions susceptible to flooding (World Bank, 2012a). Increasing pressure on land is already occurring worldwide, as evidenced by the dramatic increase in land deals. The Global Commercial Pressures on Land Research Project estimates that 203 million hectares of farmland worldwide have been sold or leased since 2001, with the pace of acquisitions accelerating markedly since 2008. Africa is the biggest target for these land deals, accounting for reported sales of 134 million hectares. (Anseeuw and others, 2012; see also chapter IV).

Stresses in water supplies arise from the increase in consumptive use and pollution of freshwater, for which agriculture is overwhelmingly responsible. The consumption of agricultural products accounts for 92 per cent of the global freshwater footprint, an indicator for humans' appropriation of freshwater resources (Hoekstra and Mekonnen, 2012). Different commodities and types of food in particular differ dramatically in their water intensity; therefore, going forward, changes in food consumption patterns will have a major impact on global water stress.

In addition, energy production is likely to become thirstier in coming years, as biofuels become a more prominent part of the energy mix. The International Energy Agency (2012) estimates that water consumption for energy production will increase by 85 per cent between now and 2035. Overall, global energy demand is projected to increase by about one third in this time period. While technological advances are unlocking previously inaccessible fossil fuels for extraction, their exploitation is at odds with global emissions reduction goals. In fact, only a third of proved reserves of fossil fuels can be consumed by 2050, if CO_2 concentration in the atmosphere is to be limited to 450 ppm (ibid.).

All three factors—land, water and energy—have a direct impact on agriculture and food production. Food prices have already increased and become more volatile

Economic growth and changes in consumption and urbanization patterns are the main drivers of rising global resource demand, which— in combination with climate change—could lead to increasing pressure on arable land and water supplies in recent years, partly driven by higher prices and tighter supplies of those factors. By 2050, global food production will have to further expand by 70 per cent, in order to feed a growing world population and simultaneously address existing malnutrition and hunger (Food and Agriculture Organization of the United Nations, 2011a). Competing demands for land, water and energy, and the impact of climate change, are exacerbating the scale of this challenge. At the same time, the expansion of food production has to be achieved in an environmentally sustainable way, so as not to contribute to further degradation of the environment. This will entail dramatic improvements in food production, processsing, and distribution (Godfray and others, 2010).

The implications of resource scarcities are manifold. Increasing prices and price volatility will not only heighten the vulnerability of poor and net food consuming households, but also raise issues of food and energy security for countries, and globally as well. Poor households are particularly vulnerable to rising food prices, at least in the short run, as they spend a much larger proportion of their total income on food. For this reason, they are also less well equipped to deal with price volatility and sudden price spikes, which, by possibly requiring them to sell assets, can exert permanent effects (Evans, 2010).

At the national level, higher food and energy prices dampen growth prospects for food-deficit countries and net energy importing countries. Globally, higher expenditure in resource-exporting countries is unlikely to compensate for the fall in aggregate demand in importing countries (Dobbs and others, 2011a). At the same time, tighter trade links and lower buffers associated with more integrated production patterns cause local or regional shocks triggered by resource scarcities to reverberate more quickly in other regions of the world. Lastly, the prospect of scarcity could also increase concerns about the security of supply of food, energy and water and lead to more "resource nationalism". The recent spike in cross-border land acquisition can be interpreted in this light, as can export restrictions on crops or mineral resources, which have increased in recent years (ibid.).

Huge investments will be necessary to increase the food and energy supply in an environmentally sustainable manner

To address these issues, huge investments will be necessary to increase supply in an environmentally sustainable manner. Securing long-term financing at an adequate scale to finance these investments will be a major challenge. Yet, expansions of supply, technological progress and efficiency gains at all levels may not be sufficient. In this case, distributional questions will inevitably arise. Access to resources is already extremely unequal, even in an age of relative plenty, as evidenced by the large number of people who go hungry or remain without access to modern forms of energy. With scarcity, distributional conflicts over access to natural resources will become much more pressing, both within and between countries (Evans, 2011).

Sustainable development in a more interdependent world

Achieving sustainable development post-2015 will entail progress in its four dimensions—inclusive economic development, inclusive social development, environmental sustainability and effective governance and peace and security (United Nations System Task Team on the Post-2015 UN Development Agenda, 2012). The megatrends discussed above raise multiple challenges which threaten our ability to achieve such progress in the decades ahead. They also reinforce each other in myriad ways, and therefore have to be addressed in a broad and holistic manner, by achieving transformative change in production and consumption patterns, natural resource management, and mechanisms of governance.

Mutually reinforcing trends and challenges

Global socioeconomic, demographic and environmental megatrends have increased interdependence among countries, but without any commensurate strengthening of global governance. As a result, global macroeconomic imbalances, migratory pressures and environmental challenges are insufficiently addressed, and crises occur with increasing frequency. At the same time, countries with growing exposure and interlinkages become more vulnerable to such external shocks, and crises spread more quickly, threatening development progress.

At the national and subnational levels, these tighter links have facilitated socioeconomic progress, but not everybody is benefiting to the same degree. Rather, inequalities both within and between countries persist. While growth has accelerated in many developing countries, often it has been non-inclusive, failing to create sufficient employment opportunities and exacerbating inequalities. The consolidation of value chains and the related deceleration of trade growth may render the implementation of export-based growth strategies even more difficult in the years ahead, at the same time as demographic developments make accelerated employment generation an imperative in countries with large youth cohorts. Population dynamics will also impose additional stresses on local governments and rapidly growing cities and national health and education systems. Rapid ageing in numerous countries, in particular, will require further investments in social protection systems. The persistence of inequalities, whether in incomes, or in access to services, decent jobs, land or technology, also hints at their entrenched structural causes. Discrimination and exclusion, based on gender, age, disability or ethnicity, have to be tackled directly in order that greater inclusiveness and transformative change may be achieved.

These challenges are exacerbated in multiple ways by accelerating environmental degradation. The poor are most vulnerable to environmental hazards and, owing to the unequal distribution of assets, will also suffer the most from resource scarcities. In terms of the medium and long run, threats to the stability of the global climate overshadow all other challenges, as they would fundamentally undermine the preconditions for human development.

> Megatrends have increased interdependence among countries without any commensurate strengthening of global governance, while heterogeneity has increased both within and between countries

Strategies for sustainable development

World Economic and Social Survey 2013 discusses the changes required in local, national and global policies to achieve sustainable development post-2015. The transformative change necessary to address the challenges set out above will be driven mainly by actors at the local and national levels. Coherence between local and national strategies will therefore remain critical. Policy decisions in one country have regional and often global repercussions, but currently such externalities—be they positive or negative—are not taken sufficiently into account in decision-making processes.

Coherence in national development strategies implies most fundamentally that socioeconomic development strategies aim to avoid further environmental distress. Developed countries in particular have to address unsustainable consumption and production patterns and their continuously rising environmental impact, while emerging and developing economies need to pursue the goal of greening their catch-up growth. At the global level, the human development agenda and the goal of environmental protection have to be jointly pursued. Developed countries in particular would make moves towards sustainable production and consumption, while developing countries would offer greater cooperation in meeting climate and other global challenges. Such a global consensus on sustainable development will be based on solidarity, with human development and environmental protection as integrated and universal goals for all countries (chap. II).

Meanwhile, many specific measures will be designed and implemented at the local level and in towns and cities in particular (chap. III). Urbanization offers the opportunity to achieve socioeconomic progress in a more environmentally sustainable manner; but for that opportunity not to be wasted, enormous investments will be necessary.

Many of the major trends and challenges reinforce each other, as was starkly revealed by the 2008-2009 global food, fuel and financial crises. Therefore, policy coherence between areas is equally important. The availability and use of land, water, and energy, in particular, are tightly interconnected. They all impact on agriculture and food production, and that impact, in combination with the additional impact of climate change, will require a rethinking of food and nutrition security strategies (chap. IV). Achieving food security while minimizing the environmental impact will require increasing agricultural productivity, particularly in developing countries. At the same time, reductions in food waste and less resource-intensive diets could make a remarkable contribution to food and nutrition security.

A transformation of the energy system will be necessary to achieve near universal access to energy in an environmentally sustainable manner (chap. V). Current emissions trends of greenhouse gases will likely lead to further increases in global temperatures, with potentially catastrophic consequences. To avert further warming, major investments in energy efficiency are critical, while industrial policies and technological innovation, transfer and adaptation can support a low-carbon inclusive growth path to facilitate a global energy transformation that is compatible with economic and social inclusion in developing countries.

To achieve this energy transformation together with food and nutrition security, sustainability of cities and other development goals after 2015, large-scale investments will be needed. Such investments will require sufficient levels of supply of long-term financing, and they will have to be carried out both by public actors through increased public expenditure and by the private sector, which will depend critically on creating the right incentives for investments in sustainable development.

Chapter II
Strategies for development and transformation

Summary

- While technology will play an important role in the transition to sustainable consumption, conscious efforts will still have to be made to move away from more resource-intensive to less resource-intensive consumption, from a private to a public mode of consumption, from use of non-biodegradable to use of natural and biodegradable material, and from unequal to more equitable consumption.

- Sustainable and equitable consumption patterns, with appropriate reorganization of the economy and society, including a redefinition of output and the sharing of productivity gains, can ensure income and employment and a better quality of life for all.

- Human development will remain the main focus of developing countries post-2015. In this regard, the transition of developed countries to equitable and sustainable consumption will make it easier for developing countries to pursue their human development goals in a more environmentally sustainable way.

- Some developing countries have been implementing initiatives directed towards sustainability that, so far, are more advanced than those of developed countries, which suggests that developing countries can provide real leadership in the transition to sustainability.

Process tracks of implementation of Agenda 21 and its consequences

As the period for the Millennium Development Goals expires in 2015, the world community faces the challenge of implementing strategies to address the concerns that have become more global and more pressing. The international community faced a similar situation when it gathered at the United Nations Conference on Environment and Development, held in Rio de Janeiro, Brazil, in June 1992. One outcome of the Conference was Agenda 21 (United Nations, 1993), which constituted a comprehensive and integrated programme encompassing all three dimensions of sustainable development.

Implementation of
Agenda 21 proceeded
along different tracks

The actual implementation of Agenda 21, proceeded, however, along different tracks (figure II.1). On the one hand, during the 1990s, some of the concerns regarding economic and social development took the form of advocacy for "human development", which crystallized in the Millennium Development Goals through the adoption of the United Nations Ministerial Declaration[1] (Nussbaum, 2011; Sen, 1999). On the other hand, concerns regarding the environment (global warming, for example) were reflected in the United Nations Framework Convention on Climate Change,[2] which was opened for signature at the 1992 Rio Conference. This was followed by the adoption, in 1977, of the Kyoto Protocol to the United Nations Framework Convention on Climate Change,[3] by the Conference of the Parties to the Convention at its third session. Another response to environment-related concerns was the Convention on Biological Diversity,[4] which was also opened for signature at the Rio Conference. Yet another example of global environmental protection effort is the United Nations Convention to Combat Desertification. Also, the United Nations Environment Programme (UNEP) has been working on environmental issues since 1972.

The Millennium Development Goals focused on some aspects of economic and social development, which are both dimensions of sustainable development.[5] However, they were weak on environmental protection.[6]

The above-mentioned separate tracks of the implementation process of Agenda 21 were also associated with very different domain configurations. For example, the domain of action of the Millennium Development Goals was confined to developing countries. By contrast, the Kyoto Protocol, following principle 7 on common but differentiated responsibilities of the Rio Declaration on Environment and Development (United Nations, 1993), required only developed countries to undertake greenhouse gas emissions reduction targets, while exempting developing countries from the requirement of undertaking such targets.

---

1   See General Assembly resolution 55/2.

2   United Nations, *Treaty Series*, vol. 1771, No. 30822.

3   Ibid., vol. 2303, No. 30822. In fact, the Kyoto Protocol may be regarded as having set out the first major sustainable development goal, not counting that contained in the 1987 Montreal Protocol on Substances that Deplete the Ozone Layer (United Nations, *Treaty Series*, vol. 1522, No. 26369).

4   United Nations, *Treaty Series*; vol. 1760, No. 30619.

5   It should be noted that the Millennium Development Goals did not exhaust the United Nations development goals, which have a broader range. The latter, often referred to as constituting the United Nations development agenda (United Nations, 2007) or the internationally agreed development goals, represent all of the development goals adopted at various international conferences held under the auspices of the United Nations. Also, economic development goals are not explicitly encompassed by the Millennium Development Goals. Instead, they are implicit, in the sense that achievement of the Millennium Development Goals would require an increase in per capita income, the traditional indicator of economic development. However, since an increase in per capita income is not sufficient for poverty reduction and other social goals, the Millennium Development Goals have focused directly on those goals, omitting conventional indicators of economic development.

6   The Millennium Development Goal directly related to the environment is Goal 7, which focused originally on reduction of slums and greater access to clean drinking water. Later on, biodiversity protection targets, among others, were added. However, these targets did not achieve prominence and were not pursued vigorously within the Millennium Development Goals framework. For example, although the expanded list of Goal 7 targets included a carbon dioxide (CO_2) emissions reduction, the main international effort to reduce CO_2 proceeded under the auspices of the United Nations Framework Convention on Climate Change.

Figure II.1
Different tracks of the implementation process of Agenda 21 and the consequences

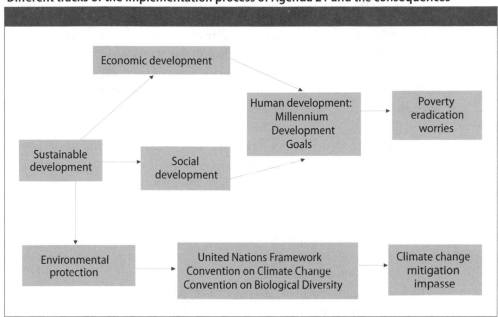

Source: UN/DESA, Development Policy and Analysis Division.

The impasse with regard to climate change mitigation

The eighteenth session of the Conference of the Parties to the United Nations Framework Convention on Climate Change held in Doha in November and December 2012 again illustrated that climate change mitigation efforts are insufficient to achieve the goal of holding the global temperature increase below 2° Celsius above the pre-industrial level. In Doha, countries agreed and launched the second commitment period for the Kyoto Protocol that was to commence from 1 January 2013 and end on 31 December 2020. However, several countries that had ratified the Kyoto Protocol for its first commitment period withdrew from it and decided not to join the second commitment period. The remaining states parties to the protocol with obligations to reduce greenhouse gas emissions currently account for only 15 per cent of global emissions (Toye, 2012).

Second, the greenhouse gas reduction goals set out in the Kyoto Protocol remain largely unachieved. If the economies in transition are not taken into account, most of the developed countries (Annex B to the Protocol) have failed to achieve their reduction targets. Countries that apparently have achieved their targets have often done so mainly through offshoring greenhouse gas-intensive production operations to developing countries (chap. I; Li and Hewitt, 2008; Peters and Hertwich, 2008). Meanwhile, since production technologies in developing countries are generally more greenhouse gas-intensive, offshoring has led to an increase rather than a decrease in the total (global) volume of emissions, thus frustrating the very purpose of the Protocol.

Third, although countries agreed to continue the Kyoto Protocol via the second commitment period through 2020, the post-2020 comprehensive regime, which is to be universal and applicable to all countries, is yet to be negotiated and concluded by 2015.[7]

---

7   See, FCCC/KP/CMP/2012/13/Add.1, decision 1/CMP.8.

Worries regarding poverty eradication and other human development goals

Worries regarding poverty eradication emanate from the weaknesses with respect to poverty reduction achievement so far. First, although the world as a whole is on track towards achieving Millennium Development Goal 1, this has been largely due to China, which succeeded in raising about 600 million people out of poverty. By contrast, South Asia and sub-Saharan Africa have been less successful, and the absolute number of the poor in these regions has in fact increased. Chen and Ravallion (2010) indicate that "the developing world is poorer than we thought", reporting that the number of poor in 2005 was 1.4 billion (using $1.25/day as the poverty line). They further indicate that if the higher, $2/day definition is used, the number of the poor in developing countries in 2005 increased to 2.6 billion (representing 47.6 per cent or almost half, of the developing world's population).

Second, those who have risen above the poverty level still remain very close to it, so that negative shocks can easily wipe out the poverty reduction gains, which was what occurred during the recent food price spike.

Third, despite progress, the overall rate of poverty reduction is proving too slow to be satisfactory. For example, recent calculations by Woodward (2013) show that based on the average growth rate of income of the lowest decile of population during 1993-2008 (leaving out China), eradication of poverty, as measured by the $1.25/day line, would require another century; and it will take even longer if a higher income threshold (such as $5/day) is used (figure II.2). It is difficult to see how the world can wait that long to eradicate poverty without meanwhile becoming embroiled in major social conflicts, both internal and external.

Relying on the poverty reduction trends that held during 1990-2010, Ravallion (2012) suggests that an "optimistic" target would be to reduce the poverty rate (poverty line of $1.25/day) to 9 per cent in the next 10 years. Woodward (2013), however, points out that progress in poverty reduction during that period was dominated by China's exceptional performance, and that it is difficult to believe that this record can be replicated with China largely out of the world poverty picture post-2015. It is therefore not by chance that Ravallion himself deems this target "optimistic".

Meanwhile, projections (see discussion below) show that decreasing marginal returns to additional public interventions over time increase the marginal costs of achieving the Millennium Development Goals. In addition, there are concerns with regard to quality. For example, while progress has been made in school enrolment rates (goal 2), concerns remain regarding the quality of schooling. Thus, significant human development challenges persist.

More importantly, the current course of the human development effort appears to be on a collision course with the environment protection goal. The reduction in forest cover, biodiversity, stock of various mineral and other natural resources, etc., and the huge increase in various types of waste (including non-biodegradable plastic waste) have also been unintended consequences of the current type of human development effort.

Thus, proceeding along different tracks to implement Agenda 21 has also led to problems with regard to both human development and environmental protection.

Figure II.2
Income of the poorest decile, World (excluding China), 2000-2250

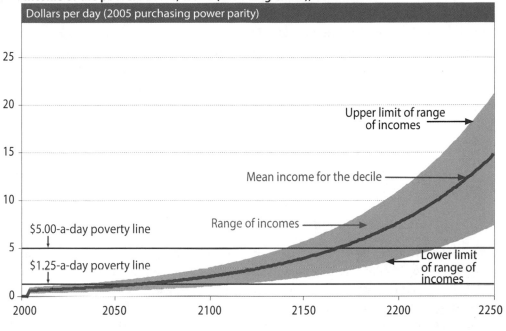

Source: Woodward (2013).

Source: Woodward (2013).
Note: The graph shows a projection of incomes for the lowest decile of the world population excluding China, based on extrapolation of the trend of mean per capita income in this decile between 1993 and 2005. The upper limit of the range of incomes is the income marking the division between the 9th and 10th deciles ($0.85 per day in 2005). The lower limit is a conservative (high) estimate of the lower band, set at half the mean income for the tenth decile ($0.30 per day in 2005) and corresponding with the upper bound of the 100th percentile.

Millennium Development Goals and Sustainable Development Goals

Discussions on the Millennium Development Goals track have been prompted by the impending expiry of the Millennium Development Goals deadline in 2015. A large literature—including AIV (2011), Institute of Development Studies (2010), Kenny and Sumner (2011), Melamed (2012), Vandemoortele (2012) and World Vision (2011)—has emerged concerning this track. The report of the United Nations System Task Team on the Post-2015 UN Development Agenda (2012) carries forward this discussion.

The other track is represented by the outcome document of the United Nations Conference on Sustainable Development entitled "The future we want",[8] pursuant to which a process of formulation of sustainable development goals was initiated. This has led to the establishment of the Open Working Group of the General Assembly on Sustainable Development Goals (see Assembly decision 67/555 of 22 January 2013).

These two tracks often present two different perspectives. Some of the publications associated with the Millennium Development Goals track were written before the Conference and hence did not consider the concept and the process of formulation of Sustainable Development Goals. They generally continued to assign environmental goals a rather limited role in the post-2015 extension of the Millennium Development Goals, similar to what has been the case in the context of the existing Millennium Development Goals.

Discussions on the Millennium Development Goals and the Sustainable Development Goals reflect different tracks of the Agenda 21 implementation process, but the two sets of goals need to be integrated

---

8   General Assembly resolution 66/288, annex.

There is a view that these two tracks, under which discussion is proceeding, need to converge so that the international community can emerge with one integrated set of goals. This conviction was reflected by the call, in the report of the United Nations System Task Team on the Post-2015 UN Development Agenda (2012), for a rebalancing of the post-2015 agenda by giving more importance to the goal of environmental protection (and to peace, security and governance issues). Similar feelings were reflected in the recommendation of the inter-agency technical support team of the Open Working Group that technical input be sought from the Task Team.

Means of achieving an integrated post-2015 agenda

Causes of the climate change mitigation impasse

It is well known that one reason for the climate change mitigation impasse is the demand by some developed countries that large, fast-growing developing countries, such as China, India, Brazil, and South Africa, also accept greenhouse gas emissions reduction goals. Those developed countries argue that developing countries as a whole currently produce more greenhouse gas emissions than developed countries (chap. I) and that large, fast-growing developing countries have now become major emitters of greenhouse gases. As a result, effective climate change mitigation is no longer possible without the agreement of those developing countries to reduce the growth of their greenhouse gas emissions.

In response, developing countries point out that their per capita greenhouse gas emissions are still very low and of recent origin. By contrast, developed countries have been emitting at a high per capita level for several centuries (Raupach and others, 2007). Accordingly, it is unfair to impose restrictions on developing countries' greenhouse gas emissions, which need to increase as these countries try to reduce poverty and raise the material standard of living of their populations. Reconciling these two opposing viewpoints has so far proved difficult.

Causes of human development concerns

One main reason for the concerns regarding poverty eradication is unequal distribution of wealth and income (figure II.3). Within-country inequality has generally increased across the world in recent decades (United States of America, Congress of the United States, Congressional Budget Office, 2011; Galbraith, 2012; Milanovic, 2012; Stiglitz, 2012; Wilkinson, 2005; Wilkinson and Pickett, 2008). Owing to this inequality, the elasticity of poverty reduction with respect to increases in total or average income (of the country) is very low. For small improvements in poverty, large increases in the income of people in upper income groups are necessary. According to Simms, Johnson and Chowla (2010, p. 18) and Woodward and Simms (2006, pp. 16-17), of every $100 worth of growth in world per capita income, the poor received only $2.20, during 1981-1990. This figure decreased to $0.60 during 1990-2001, because in the meantime, inequality had increased and the poor's share of income decreased further (figure II.4). As a result, to reduce poverty by $1, it was necessary to raise global production and consumption by $166 during the latter

Figure II.3
Distribution of global absolute gains in income, 1988-2008: more than half of those gains went to the top 5 per cent

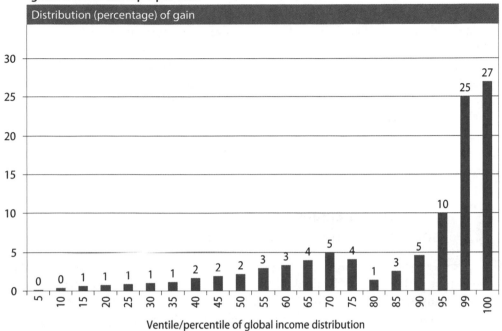

Source: Milanovic (2012).

Figure II.4
Share of the poor in per capita growth, 1981-2008

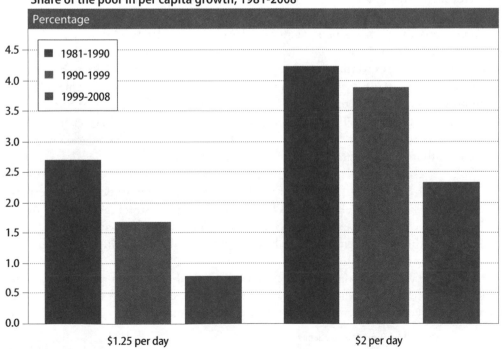

Source: Woodward (2013).

decade. Furthermore, the fact that poverty is now concentrated in middle-income countries, instead of low-income ones, also shows the limits of the current approach to reducing poverty (through raising total and average output).

The low elasticity of poverty reduction is problematic from another angle. It exacerbates the current conflict between the human development (e.g., poverty reduction) goal and the environmental protection goal. According to Simms, Johnson and Chowla (2010), human beings are already consuming nature's services 44 per cent faster than nature can regenerate (to replenish resources consumed) and reabsorb (the waste generated). Ironically, the poor suffer the most from the environmental stress resulting from this process.

The climate change impasse, the continuing challenge of human development and the tension between current human development and environmental protection efforts all demonstrate the pressing need for the integration of human development and environmental protection goals in the post-2015 agenda.

Towards reintegration of human development and environment protection goals

Integration of the Millennium Development Goals and the Sustainable Development Goals is possible through a consensus under which developed countries would genuinely move towards sustainable consumption and developing countries would assume a more proactive role in dealing with global environmental problems

The process may start with the movement of developed countries towards sustainable consumption with equitable distribution (figure II.5, step (a)).[9] How to determine what constitutes sustainable consumption is an issue, and there is no consensus criterion in this regard. However, given that, of current challenges, climate change has emerged as the most destabilizing, one may use per capita greenhouse gas emissions as the criterion of sustainability. This criterion is objective and has been well accepted as a relatively accurate measure.

Pre-industrial data suggest that the atmosphere's sustainable CO_2 absorption capacity (i.e., the absorption that does not cause a rise in CO_2 concentration) is about 5 gigatons. According to the United Nations Population Division projection (medium-fertility variant), the world population will stabilize at about 10 billion by 2080 (United Nations, Department of Economic and Social Affairs, Population Division, 2011). This suggests a little over 0.5 ton of CO_2 (tCO_2) as the sustainable level of annual per capita emissions. However, expecting the per capita greenhouse gas emissions level to be brought down to about 0.5 tCO_2 may appear unrealistic at this stage. Therefore, some scholars, based on the generally accepted goal of 450 ppm (parts per million) (instead of the pre-industrial level of about 270 ppm), have put forward 3 tCO_2 as the per capita annual emissions level that needs to be achieved by 2050, assuming that the population will have reached 9 billion in that year.

These sustainable levels of greenhouse gas emissions may be contrasted with the current per capita emissions level of the United States (about 19 tCO_2) and of most other developed countries (about 10 tCO_2). The differences illustrate the enormity of the challenge faced by developed countries in climbing down to sustainable levels of CO_2 emission. Yet, this is a challenge that needs to be accepted, if sustainability is to be attained (figure II.5, step (b)).

Another often-suggested criterion of sustainability relies on the concept of the ecological footprint, which measures the biological space (expressed in terms of area) required to produce the resources that a person consumes and to absorb the waste that his

---

9   See Islam (2012) for details.

Figure II.5

Framework for integrating human development and environmental protection goals and making them universal

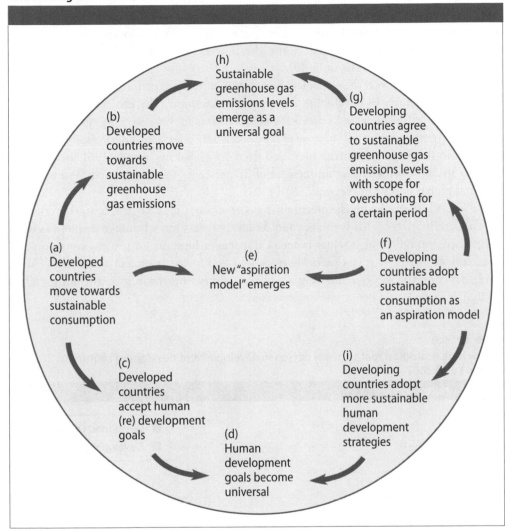

(h) Sustainable greenhouse gas emissions levels emerge as a universal goal

(b) Developed countries move towards sustainable greenhouse gas emissions

(g) Developing countries agree to sustainable greenhouse gas emissions levels with scope for overshooting for a certain period

(a) Developed countries move towards sustainable consumption

(e) New "aspiration model" emerges

(f) Developing countries adopt sustainable consumption as an aspiration model

(c) Developed countries accept human (re) development goals

(d) Human development goals become universal

(i) Developing countries adopt more sustainable human development strategies

Source: UN/DESA, Development Policy and Analysis Division.

or her consumption generates (Global Footprint Network, 2010; Rees, 1992; Wackernagel, 1994). According to this measure, the bio-capacity of the earth is limited to 11.5 billion hectares of biologically productive space (Woodward and Simms, 2006, p. 3). With the current population standing at 6.4 billion, this implies only 1.8 hectares (often referred to as global hectares (gha)) of "environmental space" per person. Yet, the ecological footprint (also measured in gha) per person has already exceeded this limit and continues to increase.[10]

There is an enormous difference between the ecological footprints of developed

---

10   Put in another way, humanity's total ecological footprint for 2007, for example, was equivalent to 1.5 planet Earths, implying that humanity uses ecological services 1.5 times as quickly as the Earth can renew them. See the Global Footprint Network website (http://www.footprintnetwork.org/en/index.php/GFN/page/data_sources/).

and developing countries (figure II.6). The average ecological footprint (per person) in Europe in 2007 was 4.7 gha, compared with an actual availability of 2.9 gha, implying that people in Europe are using up bio-space of other parts of the world. The same is true for the United States, where the average ecological footprint is 8 gha, compared with available bio-capacity of 3.9 gha. In comparison, the average ecological footprint in developing countries is 1.8 gha, which is equal to the global average (Woodward and Simms, 2006, p. 3; Global Footprint Network, 2010).

Furthermore, the ecological footprint in developed countries seems to be rising at a faster pace than in developing countries. For example, the ecological footprint in developed countries increased from 3.8 global hectares in 1961 to 5.3 global hectares in 2007, representing an overall increase of 39 per cent. By contrast, the per capita ecological footprint in developing countries increased from 1.4 global hectares in 1961 to 1.8 global hectares in 2007, representing an increase of 28 per cent (Woodward and Simms, 2006, p. 3, and global Footprint Network, 2010).[11]

Compared with the greenhouse gas criterion, the ecological footprint criterion of sustainability has both advantages and disadvantages. One advantage is that it is more comprehensive, reflecting a wider range of impacts of humans on the environment. The disadvantage is that it is less precisely measured and hence is subject to disputes (Toye, 2012). In contrast, the greenhouse gas criterion is more narrowly focused, but more accurately measured and hence less controversial.

Figure II.6
Average ecological footprint per person in developed and developing countries, 1961 and 2007

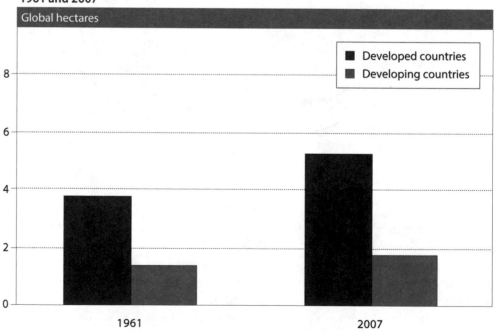

Source: Woodward and Simms (2006); Global Footprint Network, "Ecological Footprint Atlas" (Oakland, California, 13 October 2010).

11   In fact, between 1981 and 2001, the ecological footprint per person in developing countries actually decreased (Woodward and Simms, 2006, p. 3).

However, both the greenhouse gas criterion and the ecological footprint criterion reflect the same facts. First, the impact of human activities has already exceeded the capacity of the Earth to absorb it. Second, this breach has been due mainly to unsustainable consumption in developed countries. Third, as developing countries try to emulate the consumption patterns and levels of developed countries, the breaches in the Earth's planetary boundaries are becoming larger. For example, under current production technology, if the whole world wanted to consume at the 2001 level of the United States, resources equivalent to that of 15 planets like the Earth would be required (Simms, Johnson and Chowla, 2010, p. 5).

Thus, genuine movement by developed countries towards sustainable consumption will require sweeping changes in these countries. Until now, human development has generally been understood to consist in reduction of poverty, mortality rates, gender disparities in education, etc. The concept has therefore been perceived to be relevant to developing countries only. However, a shift towards sustainable and equitable consumption will require significant changes in lifestyles and reorganization of the economy and society in developed countries too. Taken together, these changes will make up another phase of human development (figure II.5, step (c)). Understood in this way, human development will become a universal goal, instead of something applicable to developing countries only (figure II.5, step (d)).

Meanwhile, genuine moves towards sustainable and equitable consumption by developed countries may give rise to a new "aspiration model" for developing countries (figure II.5, step (e)), invoking a reciprocal response from the latter (figure II.5, step (f)). With regard to climate change, the new context may make it possible for developing countries to accept sustainable greenhouse gas emissions levels as the ultimate goal, with the scope for overshooting those levels for a while (figure II.5, step (g)). It may be expected that the overshooting will not be as large in extent or for as long a period as has been the case for currently developed countries. Thus, sustainable greenhouse gas emissions levels may become a universal goal shared by both developed and developing countries (figure II.5, step (h)). A similar process may unfold with regard to other environmental goals.

On the human development side, the conventional goals of reduction of poverty, mortality, gender disparity, etc., will continue to be very much a part of the agenda for developing countries. However, these goals would now be pursued in a more sustainable way (figure II.5, step (i)). To the extent that the new aspiration model promotes equitable distribution in developing countries, it will become easier to achieve poverty reduction and other human development goals.

Overall, figure II.5 presents a framework within which both human development and environmental protection can become universal goals and be integrated, ending the current separation between their domains of application. This framework can provide the basis for the post-2015 agenda.

The ideas and the causal linkages presented in figure II.5 are abstract and very general. It is necessary to make them more concrete. By considering in some detail the changes that are necessary in developed and developing countries in order for the proposed framework to be effective, the next two sections attempt to provide that concreteness.

Strategies for transformation in developed countries

Role of technology in ensuring sustainability

While technology has a key role to play in transiting to sustainable consumption, developed countries need to make conscious shifts from material to non-material consumption, from a private to a public mode of consumption, from one-time to multiple use of products, and from use of non-biodegradable to use of biodegradable material

The fact that the consumption pattern in developed countries is unsustainable has been known for quite some time. However, efforts to move away from this unsustainable pattern have so far focused mainly on technology.

The technological route to sustainability was supported by the concept of "decoupling" of economic growth from resource requirements (Pearce, Markandya and Barbier, 1989; Ocampo, 2009). The concept has in turn been interpreted in two ways. "Relative decoupling" implies an increase in output with a "less than proportionate" increase in the inputs required. "Absolute decoupling" implies an increase in output with "no" increase in inputs required. While there has been some progress in achieving relative decoupling, there is no evidence to support absolute decoupling (United Nations, 2011b). The aggregate volume of both resources used and waste generated continues to rise (Meadows and others, 1972; Meadows, Randers and Meadows, 2002; Turner, 2008).

The evidence, however, does not suggest that the importance of technology is to be discounted. Earlier predictions of resource exhaustion have been invalidated by technological progress; and the advent of new technologies can serve as a "game changer" in future, too. For example, breakthroughs in hydrogen fuel technology and in technologies allowing extraction of carbon from the atmosphere to produce fuel can greatly reduce the greenhouse gas content of consumption. However, simply waiting for such technologies to arrive on the scene cannot be deemed a strategy (Brookes, 1990; Huesemann, 2003, 2004; Stern, 2007; United Nations, 2009). More importantly, the pace of development and adoption of new technologies depend on societal demand. Once the society decides on the kind of transformations that it wants to achieve, necessary technologies can develop in response to the demand. On the other hand, without such societal demand, even technologies feasible in principle may remain undeveloped and unused (Jackson, 2010). It is therefore important to ascertain the ways in which consumption patterns need to change in order to achieve sustainability.

Shifts in consumption patterns

It may be anticipated that necessary changes in consumption patterns would move in some general directions.[12] One desirable change would entail movement away from material towards non-material consumption. For example, reading e-books may be less greenhouse gas-intensive than cutting down forests and filling up wetlands in order to construct large houses, and commuting to work in sport utility vehicles (SUVs). It is instructive to note that some shift towards non-material consumption is occurring even within the current order of things, owing to the impact of Internet-based communications technology and as a result of increased awareness of the environmental impact of human activities. However, it is necessary to accelerate this shift through implementation of policies.

---

12   It should be noted in this regard that considerable variations across countries need to be accepted, as a reflection of their different physical and social conditions.

Another desirable change would entail movement away from private to public modes of consumption. For example, use of public modes of transportation is less greenhouse gas-intensive than use of private cars. Similarly, use of a community pool is less energy- and resource-intensive than use by individual families of the private pool in their backyard.

Movement in a third direction of desirable change would consist in the reversal of the "one time use" mode of consumption. While this mode of consumption has its usefulness in certain spheres, such as health care, questions of overuse may be raised even here. In most other spheres, utilization of this mode of consumption is often unjustifiable, as it leads to overuse of resources and over-generation of waste.

A fourth direction of desirable change would entail discouraging development of spurious new models of essentially the same product, leading to unwarranted obsolescence of products and hence to wastage of resources and to generation of excessive waste.

Another important direction of desirable change would require movement away from non-biodegradable materials to either natural or biodegradable materials. While much of the discussion of sustainability focuses on greenhouse gas emissions, the threat posed to the environment by increased use of non-biodegradable plastic materials also deserves attention. As figure II.7 demonstrates, while the weight per unit GDP of conventional materials such as steel, timber and paper has decreased, that of plastic has increased sharply. Easy availability of plastic has been one reason for the spread of the one time use mode of consumption and also for the "spurious new models" phenomenon.

Most of the plastics in use are non-biodegradable. Even the ones that purport to be biodegradable will take centuries to decompose and be absorbed by the Earth's natural elements. Until then, plastic wastes will exert their harmful physical and toxic

Figure II.7
Increased share of plastic in gross domestic product, 1900-2000

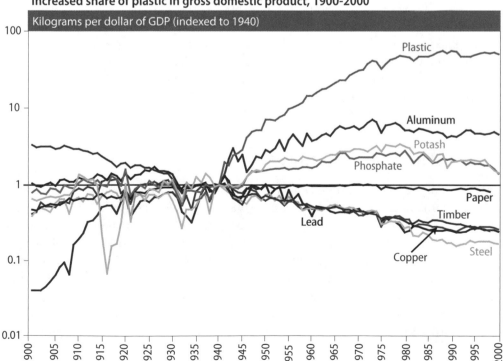

Source: United Nations (2011b).

chemical influence on the Earth's soil and water (Kaeb, 2011). Plastic waste has become a serious threat to inland water bodies, such as rivers and lakes, and even to the oceans and marine environment. Hence, substitution of plastic by natural fibre and production and use of rapidly decomposing plastic (in cases where natural substitutes are not available) would represent an important direction of change in consumption and production practices post-2015.

The above discussion of desirable directions of change in consumption patterns is certainly not exhaustive. However, the general idea is clear: the changes have to be such that fewer resources are required and less waste is generated. The question is how such changes can be brought about.

Means of bringing about shifts in consumption patterns

Means of bringing about desirable changes in consumption include price corrections, taxes, subsidies, environmental-economic accounting, and emphasis on the strong concept of sustainability

In a market economy, prices can play an important role in moving consumption towards sustainability. It is well known that in the presence of externalities, market prices do not ensure efficient resource allocation and need to be corrected so as to internalize the externalities. Thus, commodities and services involving high levels of greenhouse gas emissions need to be priced in such a way as to reflect the cost they impose through climate change. Similarly, products and services having a high plastic content need to be priced so as to reflect the cost that the disposal of plastic waste imposes on the environment. In most cases, necessary price corrections will have to take the form of taxes and subsidies.

There is strong evidence of the influence of price corrections on consumption behaviour. For example, high gasoline taxes in European countries and Japan have played a role in creating an environment where urbanization is more compact and public transportation is more important than in the United States, for example, and, currently, in China.

The necessity and importance of price correction are generally not denied. The challenge lies in determining which prices are to be changed and by how much, and in making these changes politically feasible. This in turn requires calculation of the damages and benefits from a particular product or activity to nature and society that are not captured by market prices. Environmental accounting therefore becomes important (Burritt, Hahn and Schaltegger, 2002; Nordhaus and Kokkelenburg, 1999; Owen, 2008; Pemberton and Ulph, 2000; Schaltegger and Burritt, 2000).

Environmental accounting

The report of the World Commission on Environment and Development (the Brundtland Commission) entitled *Our Common Future* (1987), had defined sustainable development as the process that "meets the needs of the present generation without compromising the ability of future generations to meet their own needs" (World Commission on Environment and Development, 1987). The concept inherent in this definition led to two versions of sustainability: "strong sustainability", which does not allow substitutability between natural capital and produced capital (either physical or human), and "weak sustainability", which allows such substitutability. In either case, proper accounting (quantification and valuation) of natural capital and the services that it provides is a precondition for determining whether sustainability is ensured. The United Nations Environment Programme (UNEP) (2010a; 2011) has rightly noted that the world's natural capital "deserves a seat at the table".

Preservation of capital for future generations also requires paying more attention to depreciation, in particular of natural capital (Kates, Parris and Leiserowitz, 2005). In fact, economists have shown that net concepts of output, such as net national product (NNP), are better measures of welfare than the corresponding gross measures, such as gross national product (GNP) (Asheim and Weitzman, 2001; Dasgupta, 1994; Dasgupta, Kristrom and Maler, 1997; Weitzman, 1976, 2000, 2003). One reason for the lesser prominence of the net measures of output, despite their theoretical optimality, is the difficulties encountered in the computation of depreciation (Hartwick, 1990; Weitzman, 1997). These difficulties are more salient in the case of natural capital, which itself has yet to be properly quantified and valued (United Nations Environment Programme, 2005).

Fortunately, considerable progress has been made in this regard by the United Nations Statistics Division (UNSD), the Division for Sustainable Development of the United Nations Secretariat, UNEP and other organizations, and individual scholars. Through its System of Environmental-Economic Accounting (SEEA) project, UNSD has formulated guidelines for the quantification and valuation of natural capital and the various non-marketed services that it offers (box II.1). An important post-2015 goal may be to implement those guidelines and to make an estimation of natural capital and its depreciation part of national income accounts.

The fact that, initially, many difficulties and disagreements will remain with respect to the estimation of natural capital and its non-marketed services, is one reason why the concept of strong sustainability needs to be upheld. Otherwise, natural capital will quite possibly be underestimated and the decrease in natural capital will appear to be more than compensated by growth in produced capital. It is therefore important, within the context of encouraging implementation of environmental-economic accounting, that such undesirable unintended consequences be prevented.

Shifts in consumption and quality of life

There is concern that efforts to make consumption sustainable will lead to a decline in the quality of life. However, recent research indicates that the opposite may be true. Surveys of citizens of developed countries show that life satisfaction does not necessarily increase with increase in material consumption and that the non-material aspects of life, such as family and community relationships, play a more important role in ensuring subjective well-being (figure II.8). Since the relentless drive to increase production and consumption of material goods has affected family and community relationships adversely, the increase in material consumption has failed to increase life satisfaction and instead, has resulted in a "social recession" (Thompson and others, 2009).

Thus, shifts away from material to non-material, from private to public, and from unequal to more equitable consumption, may actually improve the quality of and satisfaction with life and provide a win-win solution to problems of both environmental unsustainability and social recession (Lyubormirsky, Sheldon and Schkade, 2005).

It is sustainable consumption, instead of a relentlessly increasing material consumption, that can ensure greater life satisfaction and, through a redefinition of output and the sharing of profit and employment, can promote greater stability of the economy and society

Figure II.8
Factors influencing subjective well-being

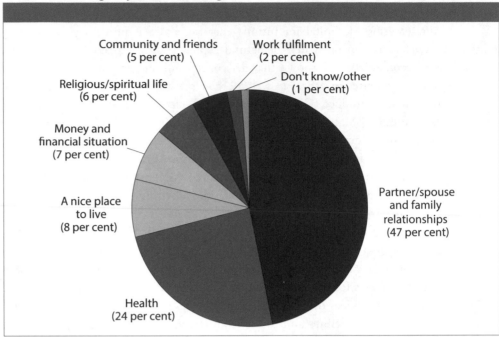

Source: Jackson (2009).

Shifts in consumption patterns and the implications for employment and income

Concerns remain, however, with regard to the impact of the transformation proposed above on the economic growth, employment and income of populations. Some scholars have coined the expression "growth dilemma" to capture these concerns (Jackson, 2009). This expression encapsulates the fact that, on the one hand, relentlessly increasing output and consumption is not environmentally sustainable and that, on the other hand, without growth, employment and income are likely to suffer and thus prove socially unsustainable. Active research is under way on this issue (Simms, Johnson and Chowla, 2010; Jackson, 2009. However, several observations can already be made.

First, as the "transformation" of consumption is not the same as its "reduction", the focus needs to be on the "pattern" of consumption and not necessarily on its "level". Accordingly, the move towards sustainable consumption may not necessary imply a fall in income and employment even in a conventional setting, which is not, however, to ignore the fact that there are limits to material consumption arising from the very real physical limitations of human beings. For example, there is a limit to the amount of food a person can consume, the number of items of clothes he or she can wear, and the amount of dwelling space he or she can effectively use. Beyond a certain point, an increase in consumption along these lines may prove unnecessary or even harmful. Non-material consumption has its limits as well, inasmuch as there are only 24 hours in a day. The number of e-books that a person can read, the number of films downloaded from the Internet he or she can view and the amount of time he or she can spend with family and friends are all limited. Thus, the issue of reorganization of the economy and society to deal with a situation where relentless quantitative growth of consumption is no longer desirable cannot be entirely sidestepped (Daly, 1991, 1996; Patel, 2010).

Second, the above considerations also point to the fact that the current measures of output and income are not absolutes but rather social constructs of somewhat recent origin. As they reflect a particular arrangement of the economy and society, it is quite possible that those measures will be modified in the light of changing contexts and demands (Layard, 2005; Stiglitz, Sen and Fitoussi, 2010).[13]

Third, it may be noted that a shift of consumption towards non-material items may be complementary to an increase in productivity, because non-material consumption may require more leisure time.

The answer to the question of the potential impact of proposed changes in consumption on income and employment may therefore depend to a great extent on how distribution and the organization of the economy and society are carried out. If productivity gains are shared widely, people may experience an increase in leisure time (to be devoted to non-material consumption, and family, friends, community and society) without suffering from a diminished income or unemployment. Thus, institutional changes facilitating sharing of employment and profit may be helpful in this regard. Weitzman (1984; 1985) and others have created models showing that a shared economy (where workers share profits of enterprises) produces better outcomes with regard to both employment and productivity. Many business leaders are calling for a move away from profit and towards making "three P" (namely, people, planet and profit) the driving force behind business activities (Rahman, 2012). There is also a rising call for "social business", under which entrepreneurs will be motivated by the desire to earn social recognition rather than private profit (Yunus, 2007; 2010). Implementing some of these concepts might be part of the post-2015 agenda. Strengthened political egalitarianism may be helpful in achieving wider distribution of productivity gains and in facilitating the move towards more socially motivated business operations.

Finally, it may be noted, in this connection, that transition to sustainable development will require development and diffusion of many new technologies, and that developed countries can provide leadership in this regard. Thus, the transition to sustainable consumption may lead to the expansion of employment and income even within the traditional framework.

Having examined the broad directions of transformation necessary in developed countries for sustainability, we now turn to a discussion of the directions of changes necessary for sustainability in developing countries.

---

13 In fact, some shifts from work and time devoted to the market to work and time devoted to non-market pursuits (family, community and society) can be helpful in improving life satisfaction. Devotion of more time to non-market activities may not imply unemployment per se but rather a more satisfying use of time. Redefining GDP to include non-marketed output with imputed values may ensure that the shifts mentioned above do not appear to signal a fall in a nation's output level (see below).

Box II.1

The United Nations Statistics Division has developed a System of Environmental-Economic Accounting (SEEA), which helps to reveal connections between the environment and the economy. The SEEA Central Framework is ready for use by all countries. SEEA has now been extended to include Experimental Ecosystem Accounting

System of Environmental-Economic Accounting 2012*

The System of Environmental-Economic Accounting 2012 (SEEA) provides a measurement framework within which to integrate environmental data in physical and monetary terms with economic data. SEEA organizes environmental information adopting a systems approach to stocks and flows, using definitions and classifications that are consistent with those of the System of National Accounts (SNA).[a] The strength of the framework lies in the derivation of high-quality aggregates, which are comparable across countries, consistent over time and go beyond gross domestic product (GDP).

The *System of Environmental-Economic Accounting 2012 Central Framework*[b] (SEEA Central Framework (CF)) provides the statistical framework for categorizing and analysing stocks of individual environmental assets such as water, mineral and energy resources, timber, fish, land and soil, the flows of resources into the economy, the exchanges of products within the economy and the return of residuals from the economy. At its forty-third session in 2012, the Statistical Commission adopted the SEEA Central Framework as the initial version of the international statistical standard for environmental-economic accounts, on a par with the SNA, and encouraged a flexible and modular approach to its implementation, depending on country priorities and policy demands.[c]

Regional and global CO$_2$ emissions per capita, from the production and consumption perspectives, based on data compiled for 27 European countries in 2006

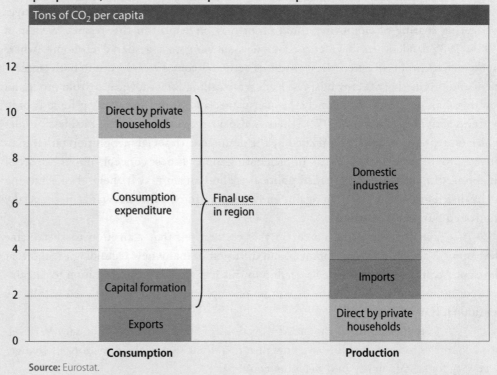

Source: Eurostat.

* Prepared by the United Nations Statistics Division.

** Available from http://unstats.un.org.

a *System of National Accounts 2008* (United Nations publication, Sales No. E.08.XVII.29).

b United Nations publication, forthcoming. The pre-edited text, issued as a white-cover publication.**

c See *Official Records of the Economic and Social Council, 2012, Supplement No. 4* (E/2012/24), chap. I, sect. B, decision 43/105. See also the background document, entitled "Implementation strategy for the System of Environmental-Economic Accounting (SEEA)".**

d See the background document, entitled "System of Environmental-Economic Accounting: SEEA Applications and Extensions".**

SEEA Applications and Extensions describes many indicators that may be generated through use of the SEEA Central Framework.[d] For example, the SEEA Central Framework may be used to calculate environmental efficiency (e.g., tons of CO$_2$ generated per unit of GDP) and its evolving pattern over time so as to evaluate decoupling trends. Through its defined system for incorporating use of resources by industry, SEEA also permits evaluation of resource use over time by different industries and may be used to evaluate the generation of wastes discharged into the environment, by industry or sector. The figure above presents an application of data analysis through the SEEA

Box II.1 (cont'd)

for 27 countries of the European Union in 2006, using data obtained from Eurostat. It shows the decomposition of CO_2 emissions from the perspectives of production and consumption. Information derived from this exercise can be helpful in studying many policy questions.

Water and energy have been identified as two priority areas in many countries. The System of Environmental-Economic Accounting for Water (SEEA-Water)[e] and the System for Environmental-Economic Accounting for Energy (SEEA-E)[f] are subsystems of the SEEA Central Framework and provide a more in-depth discussion of the statistical framework for water and energy. These subsystems also provide examples of indicators that can assist in tracking progress towards national policy goals in these areas.

The SEEA Central Framework is accompanied by the SEEA Experimental Ecosystem Accounting, which provides a robust statistical framework for countries seeking to measure the contributions of ecosystems to economic activities and human well-being as well as track the condition of ecosystems, changes in conditions, and the impact of those changes on the provision of services.[g] The SEEA Experimental Ecosystem Accounting builds on well-established disciplines, including national accounting, economics and ecological sciences. A research agenda designed to advance the methodology based on testing and practical experimentation in several countries was approved by the Statistical Commission.[h] Selected modules of ecosystem accounts, in particular those focusing on the measurement of biodiversity, flows of ecosystem services and ecosystem conditions, will provide, in due course, useful indicators for policy analysis.

SEEA accounts and resulting indicators can provide information to decision makers on progress in meeting goals and targets, including the movement towards sustainable consumption and production. Those accounts and indicators will therefore be helpful in monitoring the achievement of progress towards meeting the sustainable development goals that may be adopted through the post-2015 consultation process.

e United Nations publication, Sales No. E.11.XVII.12.**

f United Nations publication, forthcoming.

g See the background document entitled "System of Environmental-Economic Accounting (SEEA) Experimental Ecosystem Accounting".**

h See *Official Records of the Economic and Social Council, 2013, Supplement No. 4* (E/2013/24), chap. I, sect. C, decision 44/104. See also the background document, entitled "Research agenda for SEEA Experimental Ecosystem Accounting".**

Sustainable development strategies in developing countries

A heterogeneous developing world

Developing countries have become more heterogeneous than they were when Agenda 21 was formulated. Some of them have proved successful in achieving industrialization and have reached per capita income levels close to those of developed countries. Others have not been so successful, and the difference between their per capita income levels and those of developed countries has increased further. This diversity among developing countries can be seen with regard to the achievement of the Millennium Development Goals as well. While some countries have made remarkable progress in achieving the Goals, others have lagged behind. These varied performances with regard to achievement of the Goals could be a point of departure in discussions concerning future efforts for sustainable development.

Human development will remain the pre-eminent goal of developing countries, and further progress along existing dimensions of the Millennium Development Goals will require a more equitable distribution of endowments and income

Further progress in achieving the current Millennium Development Goals

An important priority for developing countries post-2015 is therefore to consolidate the progress made, to overcome the weaknesses that remain and to strive to achieve further progress along the dimensions encompassed by the current Millennium Development Goals. With regard to Goal 1, as noted earlier, even countries that have done well in terms of the $1.25/day poverty line need to raise the income of their poor population further; otherwise, they may easily fall back into poverty, particularly because $1.25/day is a very low threshold for measuring poverty.

Second, in the post-2015 phase, it will be necessary to pay more attention to quality issues than was possible during the current phase. For example, as noted earlier, in an effort to achieve Millennium Development Goals 2 and 5, many countries made significant progress in raising school enrolment. However, less attention was paid to the quality of schooling. Quality issues are also important with regard to several other Goals, targets and indicators.

Third, more attention must be paid to coherence and compatibility of achievement made along different dimensions. For example, improvement in schooling enrolment rates needs to match job creation rates. Thus, greater policy coherence at the national level must be an important characteristic of post-2015 development strategies.

The above discussion also suggests that it will be important in post-2015 strategies to pay greater attention to variations in temporal characteristics (such as duration, gestation lag, etc.) of various dimensions of human development efforts. For example, cash transfer programmes can exert rapid effects on poverty rates, and enrolment rates may also respond quickly to investments. However, for investment in education and health to be reflected (through human capital development) in a country's economic (growth) performance, more time is required. It will therefore be important that a lack of return to investment in education and health in the short run not become a source of frustration. This also implies that much of the investment made by developing countries in health and education during the current Millennium Development Goals period may actually yield returns post-2015. The issues of policy coherence and gestation lags will be discussed in more detail later in this chapter.

Human development through more equitable distribution post-2015

An important lesson for post-2015 strategies learned from the current Millennium Development Goals experience is that equitable distribution of income, wealth and access to opportunities and resources helps greatly in achieving human development goals. This lesson was clear from the low elasticity of poverty reduction with respect to the increase in average and total income of a nation. Cross-country evidence provides additional support for this lesson. For example, among Latin American countries, Brazil has been more successful in poverty reduction in part because it also succeeded in reducing inequality, countering the general trend in most other countries of an increase in inequality.

Research shows that redistribution of only 1 per cent of the income of the richest 20 per cent can provide as much additional income to the bottom 20 per cent of the population as would be derived from per capita income growth rate of between 8 and 25 per cent in the majority of developing countries, including almost all countries of Latin America and sub-Saharan Africa (Woodward and Simms, 2006, p. 19).

The fact that inequality in China rose as it succeeded in reducing the poverty rate does not negate the importance of equitable distribution for human development. It is well known that China and several other East Asian countries started off with a highly egalitarian distribution of physical and human capital which allowed the growth benefits to be distributed more widely and led to poverty reduction. A comparison with India illustrates the point more clearly. Since India did not begin with an egalitarian distribution of its initial endowment, the impact on poverty reduction of its recent growth has been less dramatic than in China. Furthermore, the experiences of both China and India show that a highly unequal distribution is socially unsustainable. According to many observers, rising inequality is one reason behind the spread of insurgency in some parts of India.

The unequal distribution observed in developing countries is often the result of the imitation of the economic model and policies of developed countries. Moves towards more equitable distribution by developed countries will therefore be helpful in facilitating the switch towards greater equality in developing countries, too.

Development in a more environmentally constrained post-2015 world

While emphasis on further progress along existing dimensions of Millennium Development Goals is necessary, it is important to recall that unless human development and environmental protection goals are integrated, they will remain in competition, jeopardizing both sets of goals. It is therefore important that post-2015 strategies of human development internalize and reflect more thoroughly the environmental protection goal.

First of all, developing countries cannot ignore global environmental problems, such as climate change. As a whole, they are no longer minor contributors to these problems. Without their playing an effective role, it will no longer be possible to solve global environmental problems.

At the same time, it is important to recall the heterogeneity of the developing world. There are now vast differences across developing countries with regard to their contribution to environmental problems and their potential role in resolving them. In particular, fast-growing large developing countries, such as China, India, Brazil and South Africa, currently assume an important role in dealing with global environmental as well as other problems. Their inclusion in the Group of Twenty (G20) reflects recognition of this changed reality.

On the other hand, a vast number of developing countries remain as marginal as before with regard to their role in creating global environmental problems and their potential for resolving them. Yet, many of them are, ironically, the worst sufferers from global environmental problems. Thus, many small island developing States, such as Maldives, face submergence due to the sea-level rise caused by climate change. The same situation is found in many least developed countries, such as Bangladesh, which is the world's seventh largest country in terms of population (about 160 million inhabitants).

Industrialization causes not only global environmental problems but also severe local environmental problems. The processes that increase greenhouse gas emissions also lead to other types of air pollution whose impact is more local. Similarly, countries that engage in large-scale deforestation not only increase greenhouse gas emissions, but also suffer from landslides, the filling up of water bodies, and the diminution of biodiversity, etc. Rampant use and inappropriate disposal of plastic waste clog local drainage systems. Chemicalization of agriculture damages local water bodies, fish stock and the aquatic environment. Local adverse impact is another reason why developing countries may pay more attention to the environmental problems in their post-2015 strategies, within the framework of "common but differentiated responsibilities".

Intense local consequences are another reason why developing countries may foster environmental protection

The South's initiatives towards sustainable development

Many countries of the South are going beyond developed countries in promoting sustainable consumption and protecting the environment. The cooperation of developed countries can make these initiatives of developing countries more successful

In fact, in recent years, many developing countries have been implementing initiatives that are more advanced than those of developed countries. For example, Ecuador has included the "rights of nature" in its 2008 constitution, thereby recognizing the inalienable rights of ecosystems to exist and flourish. Under this initiative, individual citizens and organizations can petition and seek remedy in case of the violation of those rights, and the Government is obliged to offer such remedy (box II.2). Nature is thus considered a "subject" rather than, as in the traditional view, an "object", to be conquered, occupied and exploited—or, at best, managed. Ecuador's declaration of the rights of nature is part of the general initiative towards fostering *buen vivir* (the good life), which encompasses an alternative view of development—one that, instead of focusing on material wealth, emphasizes harmony in the community and with nature. On the basis of this alternative philosophy of development, Ecuador has decided not to exploit the oil reserves in its Yasuni National Park in order to protect the forests of the Amazon. Many other developing countries have come forward with pioneering initiatives aimed towards sustainable development. Several developing countries, such as Bhutan, Costa Rica, Maldives and Tuvalu, have announced their goal of becoming carbon-neutral.[14]

The economics historian Alexander Gerschenkron coined the phrase "advantages of backwardness" to conceptualize the phenomenon whereby late industrializing countries benefit from technologies that were already developed by early industrializing countries.[15] This concept may also be used in arguing for the leapfrogging of developing countries to more sustainable post-industrial consumption patterns and lifestyles.

There are several directions in which developing countries can go in making use of these advantages. One option is related to the fact that, in many cases, developing countries face the task of "building anew" rather than modifying what has already been built. A clear example in this regard is provided by urbanization. Many developing countries need to create new urban spaces. In doing so, they can "plan from scratch" and make their cities environmentally more sustainable. Many developing countries are indeed doing just that. For example, China is creating brand-new "eco-cities", which rely on public transportation and renewable energy, achieve high degrees of conservation and recycling and minimize carbon emissions and other waste. Similar initiatives can also be seen in Brazil, Cameroon, the Republic of Korea, the United Arab Emirates, etc.

Another direction along which such leapfrogging may be possible is that of promoting sustainable life practices. Members of the more environment-conscious segments of society in industrialized countries often revert to the practices of pre-industrial societies, albeit upgraded to a new level. They are returning to organic agriculture, non-motorized modes of transportation (walking and biking), use of non-fossil fuels as a source of energy, vegetable-oriented diets, use of natural fibres instead of non-biodegradable ones, etc. Developing countries can make creative use of their pre-industrial heritage to promote these features of sustainable living. This does not mean, however, that sustainable development has to be a throwback to the past. Indeed, sustainable development has to be a forward-looking post-industrial goal which builds on the positive achievements of the industrial revolution.

14 Other countries and areas that have pledged carbon neutrality include Iceland, New Zealand, Norway, the Holy See and British Columbia.

15 Economists later used this conceptualization to explain the faster growth rates of many developing countries compared with richer economies.

Box II.2

Sustainable development initiatives from the South

Many developing countries have been implementing significant initiatives aimed at promoting sustainable development. Ecuador, for example, has included the "rights of nature" in its constitution, adopted in 2008. In declaring that nature and ecosystems have the right to exist and flourish, Ecuador empowers its citizens to petition whenever those rights are violated, and obliges the Government to remedy such violations.

Recognition of the rights of nature reflects the concept of *buen vivir* (the good life) which is now gaining popularity in many countries of South America. The concept, which originated among the indigenous peoples of South America, focuses on social, environmental and spiritual rather than material wealth. It recasts the relationship between humans and nature as a bio-pluralistic one, and emphasizes harmony with other people and nature. *Buen vivir* is, in a sense, a response to conventional development efforts, which often failed to improve the conditions of the common people and damaged the environment. It constitutes an alternative concept of development, suggesting that the good life can be achieved only in a community that includes nature. The constitution of Ecuador embodies *buen vivir* in a set of rights, including the rights of nature. Proceeding from the concept of the rights of nature, Ecuador has decided to leave the oil reserves (valued at approximately 3.5 billion United States dollars) in its Yasuni National Park untapped in order to protect the forests of the Amazon.

In a similar vein, the King of Bhutan, Jigme Singye Wangchuck, coined the term "gross national happiness (GNH)" in 1972 as a more holistic measure of quality of life and social progress than the conventional gross domestic product (GDP). Inspired by the idea, the Centre for Bhutan Studies developed a survey instrument to measure the well-being of the population, and policies in Bhutan must pass a GNH review.

The four pillars of GNH are the promotion of sustainable development, preservation and promotion of cultural values, conservation of the natural environment, and establishment of good governance. Support for the concept of GNH is not limited to Bhutan. In fact, so far, five international conferences have been held on GNH, in Japan, Canada, Thailand, Brazil and Bhutan itself.

These initiatives show that developing countries are not waiting for developed countries to provide initiatives that promote sustainable development. Instead, based on their own heritage and experience, they themselves are offering "aspiration models" of sustainable development.

> Many developing countries have been implementing advanced initiatives aimed at promoting sustainable development and protecting the environment. Ecuador's initiative to include the "rights of nature" in its constitution and Bhutan's initiative to develop the gross national happiness index are good examples

Success in leapfrogging of the above types will depend, to some extent, on the cooperation of developed countries. First, as shown in figure II.5, by presenting a new "aspiration model", developed countries can encourage the leapfrogging process. Second, developed countries can provide technologies and market opportunities necessary for this process to be successful. For example, developing countries are eager to expand and switch to non-renewable sources of energy. Developed countries can develop large-capacity and cost-effective wind-power and solar-power technologies and make them available to developing countries on favourable terms. Similarly, developed countries can open their market for organic produce from developing countries.

Diffusion of new energy technologies and expansion of organic agriculture in developing countries may also help developed countries switch to sustainable consumption. Thus, a virtuous cycle may unfold, confirming that achieving sustainable development has to be a joint task of both developing and developed countries. However, as shown above, the new aspiration model (based on sustainable consumption) does not necessarily have to be derived from developed countries. Based on their heritage and experience, developing countries are themselves offering aspiration models of sustainable development (box II.2).

Challenges of financing human and sustainable development

As noticed above, overcoming the weaknesses in the achievement of the Millennium Development Goals on which apparent progress has been satisfactory and accelerating the pace with regard to the Goals on which progress so far has not been satisfactory remain important tasks for developing countries and the world community. Research shows that considerable financial challenges will have to be overcome if these tasks are to be accomplished. Evidence drawn from country-level economy-wide modelling analyses for 27 developing countries (with 18 from Latin America and 9 from Africa) suggests that achieving the Millennium Development Goals by 2015 will require a significant increase in public spending in developing countries.[16] The analyses started with the establishment of a "business as usual" scenario which projected the progress towards targets of the Millennium Development Goals that would be achieved under the currently expected pace of economic growth and existing public spending priorities and budget financing policies. This baseline scenario allows non-linearities in the effectiveness of social spending in achieving various targets of the Goals. The results showed that, although all 27 countries would make substantial progress towards achieving the Goals even under the business-as-usual scenario, only two countries (Chile and Cuba) would fully meet by 2015 a set of targets for primary school completion, reduction of child and maternal mortality rates, and expanded coverage of drinking water and basic sanitation.

The modelling analyses also probed a number of policy scenarios under which public spending was stepped up as much as needed to create a path towards meeting the human development goals by 2015. From a comparison of these policy scenarios and the business-as-usual scenario, it was found that 18 countries would need to raise their public spending by 2 percentage points of GDP on average for each year until 2015. For some countries, many of them least developed countries, this figure increases to about 7 per cent.

The modelling analyses were redone for six countries of Latin America and the Caribbean to take into consideration the effects of the recent global financial crisis which caused a growth slowdown in many countries, thereby requiring changes in the baseline assumptions (see Sánchez and Vos, 2010). It was found that the additional public spending requirements specifically owing to the crisis would range between 1.6 and 3.4 per cent of GDP per year between 2010 and 2015. These spending requirements are on top of those that were estimated for those six countries (table II.1).

---

16   These analyses were conducted by national researchers and government experts with technical support from UN/DESA and the World Bank. At the core of the economy-wide modelling framework used is a dynamic computable general equilibrium (CGE) model called Maquette for MDG Simulations (MAMS). This model was developed originally at the World Bank and was subsequently improved in numerous country-specific applications in collaboration with UN/DESA and national experts (Lofgren, Cicowiez and Diaz-Bonílla, 2013). The main results of the modelling analyses have been reported in Sánchez and Vos, eds. (2013) and Sánchez and others, eds. (2010) who covered, respectively, 9 case studies of countries of Africa and Asia and 18 case studies of countries of Latin America and the Caribbean.

Table II.1

Additional public spending requirements for meeting human development targets under two alternative financing scenarios,[a] 2010-2015

Percentage of GDP		Additional public spending requirements	
	Baseline public spending[b]	Foreign financing scenario	Domestic direct taxation scenario
Argentina	3.71	1.30	1.40
Bolivia (Plurinational State of)	4.30	2.00	2.80
Brazil	7.32	1.70	2.20
Chile	2.33	0.00	0.00
Colombia	6.48	1.40	1.70
Costa Rica	7.30	1.10	1.40
Cuba	11.40	0.00	-
Dominican Republic	2.50	3.30	3.70
Ecuador	3.38	1.30	1.50
Egypt	1.50	0.26	0.28
El Salvador	5.09	2.60	2.80
Guatemala	3.11	4.80	6.10
Honduras	6.83	4.30	4.60
Jamaica	5.21	1.30	1.40
Kyrgyzstan	4.88	7.83	8.21
Mexico	3.37	2.90	5.50
Nicaragua	5.65	3.60	4.70
Paraguay	4.92	2.00	2.10
Peru	1.18	0.90	0.90
Philippines	2.00	6.30	7.41
Senegal	7.18	8.04	-
South Africa	3.07	-	9.08
Tunisia	5.09	5.56	6.09
Uganda	4.24	6.73	9.21
Uruguay	5.34	2.50	3.30
Uzbekistan	6.28	4.76	4.62
Yemen	16.04	10.39	17.39

Source: UN/DESA, based on studies presented in Sánchez and others, eds. (2010) for countries of Latin America and the Caribbean; and Sánchez and Vos, eds. (2013) for all other countries.

a Referring to the difference between the estimate for public spending in primary education, health, and water and sanitation under each of the financing scenarios and the estimate for the same spending under the baseline scenario. Targets are set for net (on time) primary completion rate, child and mortality rates, and access of the population to drinking water and basic sanitation.

b Lack of detailed information on public spending in primary education, health, and water and sanitation, as required to set up the modelling analyses' accounting framework, may have caused baseline public spending to appear low for some countries (Chile, Egypt, Peru and the Philippines).

The modelling analyses also yield results that help in examining and comparing the implications of alternative ways of financing the additional spending requirements mentioned above. The implications were gauged by the differential impact on GDP growth. It was found that domestic financing, using, for example, direct taxation, tends to yield a less positive impact on GDP growth than does foreign financing (except for Uzbekistan). This result is due to the fact that increased government taxation decreases private disposable incomes and hence aggregate domestic demand. Investors may foresee lower net profits for the future and therefore choose to reduce investments. The crowding out of private consumption and investment is what reduces GDP growth and employment, hurting in the process private provisioning of, as well as the demand for, social services. This feedback effect requires the government to invest more to compensate for the loss of private spending in social sectors in order to ensure achievement of the human development goals, thereby incurring even more public spending.[17] The "crowding in" from using tax revenues to finance public expenditures and investments may not take full effect in a short period of time, as explained further below.

There are trade-offs associated with foreign financing too. It is well known that the inflow of foreign currency, whether from borrowing or from receiving grant aid, may lead to real exchange-rate appreciation, harming the tradable sector. This will be particularly the case when the amounts are spent on non-tradable social services, as would be required to achieve the Millennium Development Goals. The appreciation of the real exchange rate may result in what is often labelled as Dutch disease if it leads to resource allocation away from export industries, resulting in an undesirable structural change entailing the move away from dynamic production activities.[18] This shift would typically be difficult and time-consuming to reverse should other neutralizing and coherent policies not be put in place at the same time.

Regarding investments made to achieve the Millennium Development Goals, another important issue concerns the gestation lag for the fruition of these investments in terms of higher GDP growth. This is particularly true for investments in the education and health sectors. For example, children need to go through one or more educational cycles and there needs to be improved child and maternal health care today for there to be a pay-off in terms of healthier students and workers several years from now. Countries will require more rapid and sustained economic growth to reduce the costs associated with stepping up upfront public spending.

Important insights in this regard have also surfaced from another update of the modelling analyses for 4 of the 27 developing countries (Bolivia (Plurinational State of), Costa Rica, Uganda and Yemen) (see Sánchez and Cicowiez, 2013). These updates also extended the time frame of simulated scenarios to determine long-term pay-offs of Millennium Development Goals-related investments. First of all, it was found that, because of the trade-offs discussed above, the growth effects of the increased Millennium Development Goals-related investment remain limited during the period up to 2015. The GDP growth rate in these countries was found to increase by 0.6-1.8 percentage points

---

17   The scenario analyses also indicate that tax financing would still be less costly as compared with the case where the government resorts to domestic borrowing in most cases, excluding countries where the "demand compression" effect of higher direct taxation appears to be particularly strong.

18   Repayment of newly acquired loans under a foreign borrowing scenario may offset some of the appreciation of the real exchange rate in the long term. The most important resource allocation effects from the relative price shift will occur, however, in the short term before the economy has had enough time to adjust.

per year. One possible explanation of this low growth effect is the long gestation period required for education- and health-related investment to bear fruit. To examine this hypothesis, the modelling analysis was used to trace growth effects over the period 2015-2030, assuming that the public investment levels associated with the Goals (as a percentage of GDP) reached in 2015, when a number of Goals are set to be achieved, remain unchanged for future years.

It was found that GDP could experience an additional percentage point growth of 0.2-1.0. This growth effect beyond 2015 is explained by the delayed impact of human capital investments made before 2015. Enough time would have elapsed for children to have gone through one or more educational cycles and for better education and better health to have led to an improvement of human capital. As a consequence, the employment of newly available human capital, which is also more productive, generates additional GDP growth.

Furthermore, whether or not these potential additional GDP growth effects were realized would depend on whether commensurate investments had been made in other areas of the economy, creating enough employment opportunities for the better-educated graduates entering the workforce. Lack of those investments may translate into higher levels of unemployment for the most skilled workers, as shown in the figure below, using two country cases as examples. This negative result points to the importance of complementary investments in different dimensions and the policy coherence that can ensure it.

One additional challenge stands out, besides the cost in terms of additional public spending requirements and the macroeconomic trade-offs associated with financing it. This challenge arises from the issue of whether there is real access to, and the macroeconomic feasibility of using, a particular source of finance. First of all, domestic financing through taxation is not an easy option, because existing tax burdens on taxable parts of the economy in many developing countries are already considered high. Second, the foreign financing route is also becoming problematic. On the one hand, if this financing comes in the form of loans, then it increases the debt burden. On the other hand, a continued financial crisis in developed countries is making prospects of aid and concessional financing for developing countries increasingly limited and uncertain.

In sum, the challenges of financing human development (and sustainable development in a broader context) are based on the following concerns: (a) pursuing development goals might demand the investment of significant public resources and have macroeconomic consequences; (b) future potential crisis and sluggish growth could slow down development progress, especially if expected long-term pay-offs of past development investments are offset; (c) commensurate investments should take place in other areas of the economy, creating enough employment opportunities for the better-educated graduates entering the workforce, in order for the past development investments to bring about additional productivity improvement effects in the long term; (d) countries will need fiscal space to pursue human (as well as sustainable) development goals and will have to carefully assess their options in order to establish the feasibility or optimality of a financing strategy.

Unfortunately, the world confronts a highly constrained financing situation—one where developing as well as developed countries require a huge amount of upfront investment in order to realize the sustainable development emphasized at the United Nations Conference on Sustainable Development in 2012. As indicated in chapter V, mitigation policies designed to curb carbon emissions through the adoption of renewable sources of energy will also require substantial stepping up of new investments. And, given existing financing constraints and challenges, accelerated investments for human and sustainable development could overstretch countries' public finances, with potentially pernicious macroeconomic consequences.

Probably, most developing countries will have to consider a mixed financing strategy for their human and sustainable development goals. In most cases, the balance in this mix should be tilted towards broadening the domestic tax base, in view of the fact that public debt levels are already high (restricting the scope for domestic borrowing) and prospects regarding foreign aid are not bright. For a number of countries (particularly least developed countries), foreign financing will be needed because they have no real scope for further raising tax revenues. As a consequence, developed countries and the world community will have to arrange adequate international financing for these countries so as to ensure that they make further progress in achieving human development in a sustainable way.

A new type of global cooperation

A new type of global cooperation, based on solidarity, is needed

Global cooperation in the post-2015 era has to switch from the current framework, which is based predominantly on the donor-recipient relationship, and move to a new foundation of solidarity. Accordingly, global governance must become more democratic.

The role of the Millennium Development Goals in national development efforts depended to a large extent on the degree of a country's dependence on ODA (Toye, 2012; Vandermoortele, 2012). Over time, however, the importance of ODA for developing countries has been decreasing. As a result, there is now less scope for adapting the post-2015 agenda to the donor-recipient framework (Vandermoortele, 2012). Instead, the

Figure II.9

Unemployment rate of the most skilled labour under the baseline scenario and Millennium Development Goals-financing scenario,[a] Costa Rica and Yemen, 2005, 2015 and 2030

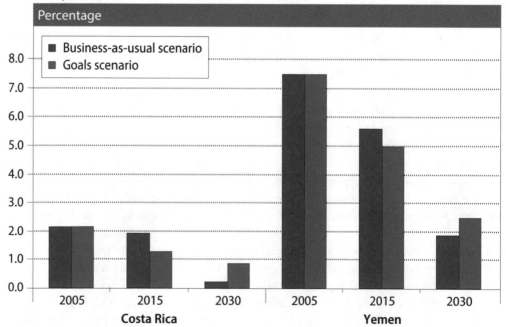

Source: Sánchez and Cicowiez (2013).

a Public spending is scaled up as necessary to meet a set of Millennium Development Goals targets and is financed through foreign sources in the Goals-financing scenario.

framework has to be one of "solidarity". The framework proposed in figure II.5 shows how this solidarity may be generated and utilized.

The traditional imbalances between various groups of countries are shifting with changes in economic strength (Toye, 2012). Often, as noted above, more of the advanced initiatives for achieving sustainable development are created by developing countries. Perhaps, through this changed reality, the old ways of thinking will ultimately be overcome, which will pave the way for cooperation among all countries of the world on the basis of solidarity.

Chapter III
Towards sustainable cities

Summary

- Numerous challenges threaten the ability of cities to become viable pillars of sustainable development. Unequal access to, and inefficient use of, public services, as well as financial fragility and the harm inflicted by natural hazards, demand an integrated and coordinated response at the local, national and international levels.

- The predominance of small- and medium-sized cities provides an opportunity to invest in green infrastructures, bypassing old energy technologies, and in social development, before social inequities become unsustainable.

- Rural development is critical for an integrated approach to sustainability and for reducing poverty. Ensuring wider and inclusive access to public services can reduce rural/urban inequalities, disaster risk and food insecurity, as well as strengthen networks between cities and villages.

- Building sustainable cities requires investment in (a) renewable energy sources, (b) efficiency in the use of water and electricity, (c) design and implementation of compact cities, (d) retrofitting of buildings and increase of green areas, (e) fast, reliable and affordable public transportation and (f) improved waste and recycling systems. Cities in poor countries need resources to support green technology transfer, and capacity development, and to improve access to soundly constructed housing, water and sanitation, electricity, health and education.

Introduction

Cities and towns have become the primary human living space. Since 2007, more than half of the world's population has been living in urban areas and the figure is estimated to exceed 70 per cent by 2050. This is a hallmark of the transformation of humans' economic base and social structure, inasmuch as, previously, populations lived and worked primarily in rural areas.

Cities can provide many socioeconomic benefits. By concentrating people, investment and resources (a process known as agglomeration), cities heighten the possibilities for economic development, innovation and social interaction. More specifically, cities also make it possible to lower unit costs so as to provide public services such as water and sanitation, health care, education, electricity, emergency services and public recreational areas (Polèse, 2009; Satterthwaite, 2010). However, this requires a functioning city government able both to ensure that such benefits are realized, and to adopt a sustainable framework that encourages the city's growth within ecological limits. Along these lines, cities also face challenges that threaten their efforts to achieve sustainability, for example, through improvement of access to, and efficiency in the use of, public services, as well as reduction of their ecological footprint and financial fragility, and the building of resilience against the adverse impact of natural hazards.

The present chapter recommends an integrated strategy for making cities thriving centres of sustainable development and innovation. It starts by assessing what a city is, the scale and speed of urbanization in recent decades, and the main trends and projections of urban growth across regions. The trends and projections analysed serve as an introduction to the conception of future urbanization as a process that can enhance the benefits of cities, while reducing the threats to a more balanced and sustainable development. The evolution of the concept of urban sustainability is described and a framework is proposed based on four pillars: economic development, social development, environmental management and effective urban governance. The following section examines relevant challenges associated to the fulfilment of those objectives by different groups of countries. The last section examines urbanization through the lens of the investment opportunities that addressing those challenges involves. A proposal put forth for an integrated set of investments in infrastructure, public services and capacity development is complemented by an examination of relevant world experiences associated with urban sustainability at the sectoral level (e.g., disaster risk reduction, housing and green infrastructure) as well as a policy framework for a sustainable financing of cities.

The city and main urbanization trends

There is no uniform definition of what constitutes a city, given the diversity of urban realities around the world. Every country defines cities according to its own criteria. It should also be noted that gaps in and measurement issues connected with urban data limit the accuracy of projections and international comparisons of levels of urbanization and sizes of city populations. Box III.1 discusses the different criteria used in defining cities and data issues.

Cities are diverse in terms of their size, structure, spatial form, economy, wealth, local resources availability and ecological impact. According to population size and conditions, urban centres can be, e.g., small, medium, large or mega. The population of an urban centre can range from a few thousand to over 10 million people or more. According to relevant studies, "small urban centres" have a population less than or equal to 500,000 people; medium urban centres, a population between 1 million and 5 million people; and mega urban centres, a population of 10 million or more (United Nations, Department of Economic and Social Affairs, Population Division, 2012; Dobbs and others, 2011b). For statistical comparison of urban centres' sizes and development, this chapter uses the categories along with "large urban centres" defined as agglomerations with 5 million inhabitants or more.

The scale and scope of urbanization

By 2050, the world urban population could reach 6.25 billion, 80 per cent of whom would live in developing regions, and concentrated in cities of Africa and Asia

At the start of the twentieth century, just 16 cities had 1 million or more people, with the majority located in advanced industrialized countries (Montgomery and others, 2004). By 2010, there were 449 cities with 1 million people or more, of which three quarters were

Box III.1

Definition of a city and data issues

The majority of countries use a single characteristic or a combination of administrative, population size or density, economic and urban characteristics (e.g., paved streets, water-supply systems, sewerage systems and electric lighting) to define a city. The lower limit above which a settlement can be considered urban varies greatly, between 200 and 50,000 inhabitants, which can give rise to error when comparing urban populations (and urban areas) in different countries. For example, if India's national authorities would classify populations of 5,000 or more as urban, the country would be considered predominantly urban and not rural. In Angola, Argentina and Ethiopia, all settlements with 2,000 people or more are classified as urban. In Benin, only areas with 10,000 people or more are considered urban. In Botswana, an agglomeration of 5,000 people or more where 75 per cent of the economic activity is non-agricultural can be considered urban (Cohen, 2006). Certain countries define the urban population as comprising people who live within certain administrative centres or *municipios* (El Salvador) or under the jurisdiction of municipality councils (Iraq). Others define cities as places with a municipality, municipal corporation, town committee or cantonment board (Bangladesh and Pakistan).

The population of any urban centre is influenced by how its boundaries are set—for instance, are they determined by the built-up area or are peri-urban areas which have little or no urban development included within them? The size of a city can be made significantly larger if fringe populations are included in official statistics; many cities have boundaries set to include the city and large areas around the city which may include small towns and large rural populations. Most large cities have more than one boundary—boundaries for the central city, for instance, for an entire metropolitan area, or for a wider planning region which often includes many rural settlements. In general, countries' urban populations are defined as the residents whose main source of income is not from agriculture or forestry (Satterthwaite, 2010).

Inadequate attention paid to data limitations has led to misconceptions regarding urban trends which can ultimately distort urban policies. Urban population projections often do not include high- and low-variant estimations, which are typical of world population projections published by the United Nations (Satterthwaite, 2007; United Nations, Department of Economic and Social Affairs, Population Division, 2012). Moreover, the traditional urban/rural dichotomy has become increasingly inadequate for distinguishing between urban and rural settlements. Increased trade, labour mobility and innovation in communications have spread urban functions and influence over wide geographical areas, including rural ones. In parts of Asia and the Pacific, for example, intense economic activity in the intersection between urban and rural areas has blurred differences (Cohen, 2006). Yet, in the case of countries in Latin America and the Caribbean, censuses and surveys that consider the urban/rural dichotomy are still valid since they persistently indicate social inequalities subsisting between rural and urban areas (United Nations, Economic Commission for Latin America and the Caribbean, 2012). Still, some of the most profound social inequalities are seen within cities or within nations' urban populations.

To improve the consistency and comparability of data on urban populations across countries and over time, the United Nations, Department of Economic and Social Affairs, Population Division (2012) uses two auxiliary concepts: (a) urban agglomeration, which refers to "population contained within the contours of contiguous territory" inhabited by, e.g., 750,000 inhabitants or more and (b) metropolitan region, which includes both the contiguous territory and "surrounding areas of lower settlement density" which are under the direct influence of the city through frequent transport, roads, commuting and so forth (p. 7). In addition, there is a potential for research on urban databases and data-collection mechanisms to support local policy, planning and investment decisions.

In general, caution is recommended regarding the interpretation and comparison of urban population statistics between nations, owing to different official criteria for defining urban areas, and setting city boundaries, and, in some cases, to the lack of census data.

Source: UN/DESA.

located in developing countries (United Nations, Department of Economic and Social Affairs, Population Division, 2012).

Pursuant to the caveats associated with urban population projections noted in box III.1, the following estimations should be interpreted as guidance only. During 2000-2050, developing regions could add 3.2 billion new urban residents, a figure larger than the world population in 1950 and double the urban population added during 1950-2000. By 2050, the world urban population could reach a total of 6.25 billion, 80 per cent of whom may be living in developing regions, and concentrated in cities of Africa and Asia. It is possible that African urban centres would house over 1 billion people by 2050, which would be about 3 times the figure for the urban population of North America, twice the figure for the urban population of Latin America and the Caribbean or Europe, and comparable to the figure for China's urban population at that time. These trends would challenge the institutional capacities of many of these cities to provide decent employment, public services and a clean environment, especially for those that already have sizeable—and growing—numbers of underserved residents living in slums, under unsafe conditions (Satterthwaite, 2007).

> In the next 10-15 years, for the first time in history, the rapid pace of urbanization would also usher in the absolute decline of the world rural population

Urban population growth is expected to continue setting the pace of world population growth, and in the next 10-15 years, for the first time in history, the world rural population is expected to decline (figure III.1).

Globally, a net 1.3 billion people was added to small urban centres during 1950-2010, more than double the number of people added in medium (632 million) or large urban centres (570 million).[1] This trend is important, since different sizes of urban

Figure III.1
Population trends and projections, 1950-2050

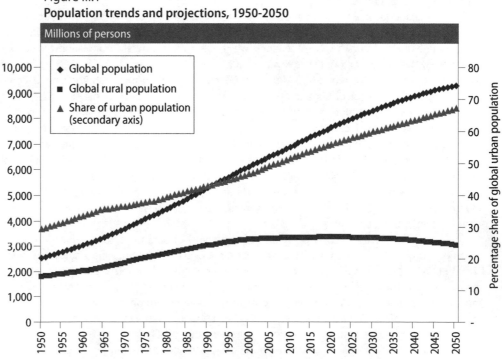

Sources: United Nations, Department of Economic and Social Affairs, Population Division (2011; 2012).

---

1   During a similar period, only 40 million people were added to urban settlements with populations between 500,000 and 1 million people.

settlements can affect the levels of provision of services needed to sustain growing populations. The challenges and policy implications of the likely continued predominance of small urban centres and the rising significance of middle and large urban centres in the next 15 years are noteworthy and will be further analysed below.

Diverse paths and paces of urbanization

There is considerable regional diversity in the patterns of urbanization and an even greater variation in the level and pace of urbanization of individual countries. For example, on average more than three quarters of the Latin America and the Caribbean region is highly urbanized, whereas least developed countries and landlocked developing countries are still predominantly agricultural—although their path towards urbanization is expected to accelerate in the next decades (table III.1). The case of the small island developing States is worth mentioning because they have been able to achieve a balance through a mid-level urbanization path (60 per cent share) with economies that are based on industry and services.

On average, nearly 80 per cent of the population in developed regions resides in urban centres, contrasting with an average share of urban populations in Asia and Africa of less than 50 per cent. At the country level, while urbanization in some African nations such as Burkina Faso, Burundi, Ethiopia and Malawi can be as low as 20 per cent, the urban population represents over 60 per cent of the total population in South Africa. Moreover, urban populations in low-income nations are highly concentrated in a very small number of cities, which also contrasts with the urbanization pattern in developed regions. For example, 75 per cent, 60 per cent and 47 per cent of the urban populations in Sierra Leone, Kenya, and Guinea are concentrated in Freetown, Nairobi and Conakry, respectively (Grübler and Buettner, 2013; United Nations, 2010b).

The patterns and paces of urbanization have been diverse within developing regions and between developing and developed regions

By and large, urbanization in developing countries has followed a brisker pace and has often been concentrated in capital cities

Table III.1
Regional figures for share of urban population, 1975, 2000, 2012, 2025, 2050

Percentage					
Country/region	*1975*	*2000*	*2012*	*2025*	*2050*
World	37.7	46.7	52.6	58.0	67.2
More developed regions	68.7	74.1	78.0	81.1	85.9
Less developed regions	27.0	40.1	47.1	53.6	64.1
Africa	25.6	35.6	39.9	45.3	57.7
Asia	25.0	37.4	45.7	53.1	64.4
Europe	65.2	70.8	73.1	76.1	82.2
Latin America and the Caribbean	60.7	75.5	79.4	82.5	86.6
North America	73.8	79.1	82.5	85.0	88.6
Australia and New Zealand	85.4	86.9	88.9	90.3	92.4
Oceania	71.9	70.4	70.7	71.1	73.0
Least developed countries	14.7	24.3	28.9	35.2	49.8
Small island developing States	45.8	55.5	59.5	62.4	67.3
Landlocked developing States	22.2	26.1	28.3	32.6	45.6

Source: United Nations, Department of Economic and Social Affairs, Population Division (2012).

Yet, "late urbanization" in Asia and Africa is expected to gain speed and concentrate the majority of the additional 3 billion urbanites during 2010-2050. Similarly, the number of urban agglomerations (750,000 inhabitants or more) and the number of inhabitants per agglomeration are expected to grow significantly in Asia and Africa by 2025 (United Nations, Department of Economic and Social Affairs, Population Division, 2012). It is expected that over 80 per cent of the urban population added in the next 15 years will be found in middle-income countries such as China, India, South Africa, Nigeria, Indonesia and Pakistan (ibid.).

Changing patterns of urban settlements

Even though small urban settlements will still retain their predominance in 2025, the importance of medium and large urban settlements will continue to grow at the global level

Over 50 per cent of the world's urban populations lived in settlements with 500,000 people or less by 2010. Although their significance will remain, the share will have been reduced to 42 per cent by 2025 (United Nations, Department of Economic and Social Affairs, Population Division, 2012). Medium cities (those with 1 million - 5 million people), on the other hand, will increase their share of the urban population, from 21 to 24 per cent over a similar time interval. The share of the urban population in large cities (those with more than 5 million people), including megacities, will grow the most, from 17 to 22 per cent, with an absolute increase of more than 410 million people. By 2010, megacities of 10 million inhabitants or more contained only 10 per cent of the global urban population (ibid.).

All of the types of growing cities will be located largely in low- and middle-income countries. In many developing countries, the main challenge is to provide underserved urban residents, including populations in large cities, with affordable access to adequate public services and job opportunities. Inhabitants in poor urban settlements typically reside on the outskirts as well as within large cities without adequate access to piped water, waste disposal, electricity and good schools. Evidence also suggests that rates of poverty and infant and child mortality can be high in small and large cities, often indicating an inadequate access to public-health facilities and the lack of political will to invest in them (Mitlin and Satterthwaite, 2012).

Cities in low-income countries may often lack the institutional capacity to manage growing populations. Although some national Governments in developing countries have begun to decentralize service delivery and revenue-raising to regional and local levels of government, lower tiers of urban government often do not have enough resources and adequate capacity to manage, e.g., health, education and poverty programmes (Montgomery and others, 2004).

Is there a twin path between urbanization and economic growth?

The economic strength of countries lies in cities; in fact, urban gross domestic product (GDP) represents about 80 per cent of world GDP (Grübler and Fisk, 2013). Cities have been pivotal centres for economic growth, employment creation, innovation and cultural exchange. Cities in many developing countries (e.g., Bangladesh, Brazil, China, Honduras, India, Nigeria, Peru and South Africa) concentrate the core of modern productive activities and are the areas par excellence where income-earning opportunities are to be found (Satterthwaite, 2007). Cities are also the centres where women enjoy the highest labour participation, health access, literacy rates and upward social mobility (Cohen, 2006).

Nonetheless, urban population growth has outpaced economic growth as well as the needed improvement of competence and institutional capacity of city governments in many developing countries, which contrasts with the closer correlation found in developed countries (figure III.2). Thus, for an equivalent level of urbanization, the level of income per capita in developing regions is several times lower. This trend, which might be explained partly by different criteria used for defining urban centres, has implications for the actual capacities of poor countries to build sustainable cities. Figure III.2 illustrates this trend in relation to the urbanization of the region of Latin America and the Caribbean.

Figure III.2

Urbanization and economic growth, developed regions and Latin America and the Caribbean, 1970-2010

Developed regions, 1970-2010

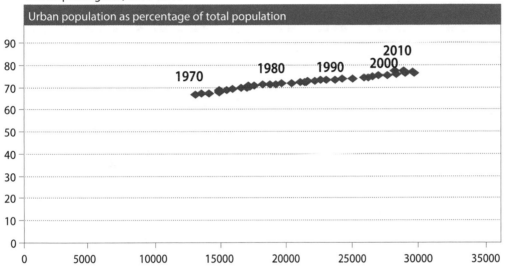

Latin America and the Caribbean, 1970-2010

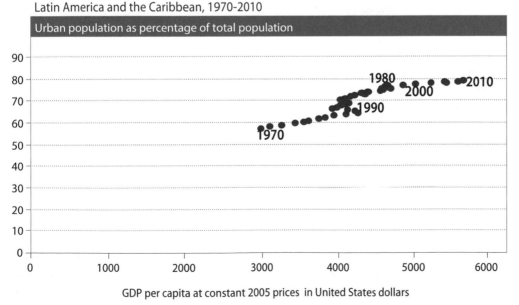

Sources: UN/DESA; United Nations (2012a; 2012b).

Note: Data for each country have been aggregated to obtain regional figures.

In particular, the urbanization process in least developed countries or countries of sub-Saharan Africa may have occurred with negative or almost no economic growth (figure III.3), which ultimately implies an increased precariousness of urban life. Population in slums almost doubled in sub-Saharan Africa between 1990 and 2010, rising from 103 million to 200 million (United Nations Human Settlements Programme (UN-Habitat), 2010). Even so, Satterthwaite (2010) recommends caution in the interpretation of the negative correlation between economic growth and urbanization in sub-Saharan countries because of data shortcomings, which can prevent accurate measurement of urbanization patterns (see, also, Potts, 2006).

Figure III.3

GDP per capita and urban share of total population, sub-Saharan Africa and least developed countries, 1970-2010

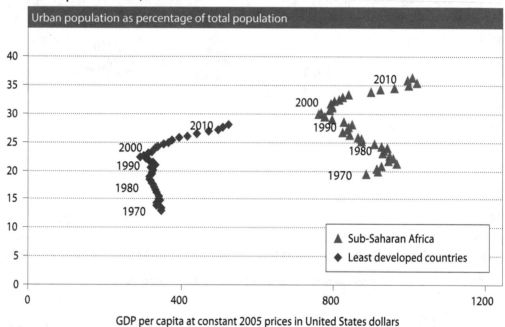

Sources: UN/DESA; United Nations (2012a; 2012b).
Note: Data for each country have been aggregated to obtain regional figures.

Cities are constantly evolving as a result of dynamic processes heightened by population mobility, natural population growth, socioeconomic development, environmental changes and local and national policies. The trends and projections described above serve as the basis for an introduction to the concept of future urbanization as a process that can enhance the benefits and synergies of cities, while reducing the threats to a more balanced and sustainable development.

Within a framework of four pillars, effective urban governance can be combined with the achievement of social and economic development and effective environmental management

A framework for sustainable cities

It has been suggested that the building of a "green" city is equivalent to the building of sustainability (Beatley, ed., 2012). Many countries are planning and engaged in building green cities and "eco-cities" as starting points for the building of sustainable development. Yet, it is important to understand cities' sustainability as a broader concept which integrates social development, economic development, environmental management and urban governance, which refers to the management and investment decisions taken by municipal authorities in coordination with national authorities and institutions. In this regard, chapter II provides guidelines for possible sustainable development paths for countries at different stages of development.

The 1987 report of the World Commission on Environment and Development, also known as the Brundtland Commission, defined sustainable development as development that meets the needs of the present, without compromising the ability of future generations to meet their own needs. The report included a chapter on urban issues. In 1991, the United Nations Centre for Human Settlements (UNCHS) Sustainable Cities Programme attempted to define a sustainable city as one "where achievements in social, economic and physical development are made to last" (United Nations Human Settlements Programme (UN-Habitat), 2002, p. 6). However, this definition was still too general and neglected the fact that a sustainable city must have a low ecological footprint and reduce risk transfer (economic, social and environmental) to other locations and into the future (Rees, 1992).

The concept of sustainable cities and its links with sustainable development have been discussed since the early 1990s.[2] Sustainable cities should meet their "inhabitants' development needs without imposing unsustainable demands on local or global natural resources and systems" (Satterthwaite, 1992, p. 3). In this sense, consumption patterns of urban middle- and high-income groups as indicated in chapters I and II are responsible for the use of a significant portion of the world's finite resources and contribute significantly to the production of polluting wastes. Sustainable development should focus on better living and working conditions for the poor, including affordable access to, and improvement of, housing, health care, water and sanitation, and electricity.

The first approximations to a concept of city sustainability noted above were reflected in the 1992 Rio de Janiero Conference on Environment and Development (United Nations, 1993) attended by more than 178 Governments. The 1992 Rio Declaration integrated the economic, social, environmental and governability dimensions of sustainability and argued for the eradication of unsustainable patterns of production and consumption, the eradication of poverty, and the role of the State, civil society and international community in protecting the environment.

Another outcome of the United Nations Conference on Environment and Development was Agenda 21 (United Nations, 1993), which aimed at preparing the world for the challenges of the twenty-first century. Agenda 21, which was built upon at subsequent United Nations conferences, defined sustainability in the context of economic, social, environmental and governance issues, noting the decisive role of authorities and civil society at the local, national and international levels for the implementation of sustainable development policies. Yet, Agenda 21 did not explain how the concept of sustainability could become the basis for the creation of sustainable cities.

The Habitat Agenda (United Nations, 1997), adopted by the United Nations Conference on Human Settlements (Habitat II), held in Istanbul from 3 to 14 June 1996, echoed the concerns expressed in Agenda 21 with respect to the multidimensionality of development, and discussed urban sustainability as requiring a harmonious integration of economic, social and environmental issues. At this summit, nations reported on the progress towards achieving the sustainability of their cities. Yet, this Agenda still needed to include climate change as one of the main threats to building sustainable cities and to development in general.

---

2   See, for example, *Environment and Urbanization*, vol. 4, No. 2 (October 1992).

At the first session of the World Urban Forum convened at the headquarters of the United Nations Human Settlements Programme (UN-HABITAT) in Nairobi from 29 April to 3 May 2002, an in-depth discussion was held on urbanization in the context of sustainable development. The Forum affirmed that addressing economic, social, environmental and governance issues was integral to the creation of sustainable cities, and that the inability to address those issues would prevent the achievement of sustainable development (United Nations Human Settlements Programme (UN-HABITAT), 2002). The main messages of the Forum were comprehensively discussed and reaffirmed at the World Summit on Sustainable Development, held in Johannesburg, South Africa, from 26 August to 4 September 2002. More recently, this approach to sustainable cities has been echoed the the Rio+20 Declaration (United Nations, 2012b, p.26) and by the United Nations System Task Team on the Post-2015 UN Development Agenda (2012), which includes governance under the broader umbrella of peace and security issues. In an increasingly urbanized world which demands more sustainable ways of living, urban governance entails the fostering of urban planning and environmental management, which includes the reduction of ecological footprints, and the decentralization of decision-making, and resource allocation, as well as enhanced policy coordination between local and national authorities.

In this context, achieving the sustainability of cities can be conceived as entailing the integration of four pillars: social development, economic development, environmental management, and urban governance. Figure III.4 presents the four pillars for achieving urban sustainability encompassing the balanced accomplishment of social and economic development, environmental management and effective governance. Yet, the ways in which a city is able to build sustainability will reflect its capacity to adapt, within the context of its particular history, to the policy priorities and goals defined by each pillar.

Figure III.4
Pillars for achieving sustainability of cities

Sustainable cities

Social development	Economic development	Environmental management	Urban governance
◆ Education and health	◆ Green productive growth	◆ Forest and soil management	◆ Planning and decentralization
◆ Food and nutrition	◆ Creation of decent employment	◆ Waste and recycling management	◆ Reduction of inequities
◆ Green housing and buildings	◆ Production and distribution of renewable energy	◆ Energy efficiency	◆ Strengthening of civil and political rights
◆ Water and sanitation	◆ Technology and innovation (R&D)	◆ Water management (including freshwater)	◆ Support of local, national, regional and global links
◆ Green public transportation		◆ Air quality conservation	
◆ Green energy access		◆ Adaptation to and mitigation of climate change	
◆ Recreation areas and community support			

Source: UN/DESA, Development Policy and Analysis Division.

The integration of the four pillars can generate synergies, for example, between waste and recycling management (environmental management) and access to water and sanitation (social development); between air quality conservation and green public transportation; and among production and distribution of renewable energy sources, green energy access, and adaptation to and mitigation of climate change, as well as between the goal of reducing inequities (urban governance) and that of ensuring adequate access to green housing, education and health (social development). Investment is the catalyst behind the realization of each of the component goals of urban sustainability.

To build upon the four pillars can be a challenge for many cities and countries. Cities are often at different stages of development and have their own specific responses to policy priorities at the local and national levels. In this sense, the sets of sustainability challenges to be overcome by cities are diverse.

The challenges associated with building sustainable cities

The present section analyses the main social, economic and environmental challenges associated with building sustainable cities in developing and developed countries.

For city governments, the challenges include securing the necessary resources for investment in disaster-proof public infrastructure, and renewable sources of energy, and providing incentives to the private sector to create decent employment for large urban populations that are underemployed and have limited access to good housing conditions, clean water, sanitation, drainage and schools (table III.2).

Upper middle income and high-income countries with urban populations that already have access to basic public services face the challenge of becoming more efficient in the use of energy and water, reducing the generation of waste, and improving their recycling systems. Growth of cities has often gone hand in hand with an increased use of natural resources and ecological systems, driven by economic growth and changes in the economic structure—in terms of a shift from agriculture to manufacturing and then to services. While wealthier cities and people, in particular, may have well-managed resource systems, they also have a greater ecological impact through drawing resources from larger areas. For example, wealthier residents in New York City, Los Angeles and Mexico City contribute greatly to the demand for freshwater from distant ecosystems, whose capacities are consequently affected and whose use generates significant levels of pollution and greenhouse gas emissions at the national and global levels (McGranahan and Satterthwaite, 2003). Thus, urbanization can be an important contributor to high resource use and waste generation, both with ecological effects at the local, regional and global levels.

Some of the most significant challenges associated with building sustainable cities are discussed more extensively below.

Social, economic and environmental challenges exert direct and indirect effects on cities and the lives of people in both developing and developed nations

Socioeconomic inequalities

Inequalities between rural and urban areas as well as within urban areas have been features of development and urbanization in developing countries (Cohen, 2006; Baker., ed., 2012). The gap between rich and poor neighbourhoods can imply significant differences in access to job opportunities and basic public services such as water and sanitation, electricity,

Inequalities in access to basic services between rural and urban areas as well as within urban areas have been typical features of urbanization in developing countries

Table III.2

Challenges to and opportunities for building sustainable cities

Main urban trends	Developing countries		Developed countries	
	Challenges	Opportunities	Challenges	Opportunities
Social				
By 2025, urban population will live mainly in small cities (42 per cent) and medium-sized cities (24 per cent)	Improve access to housing, water, sanitation; improve public infrastructure; foster institutional capacity	Investment in public infrastructure (including transportation); construction of compact buildings in middle-income countries; strengthen links between cities and rural areas	Social cohesion	Investment in *compact* urban development and decentralization
Number of urban people living in slums continues to grow	Reduce number of urban poor and disease risk; improve social cohesion; reduce youth unemployment	Investment in universal access to affordable water and sanitation; establishing public transportation, and creation of jobs to reduce growth of slums; employment of the "youth" dividend in low-income countries	Reduce urban unemployment due to economic crises (of youth in particular); provide adequate housing in poor neighbourhoods	Strengthening and widening social safety nets; upgrading investment in social protection for an effective response to crises and their aftermath
Inefficient use of public services (water, electricity)	Improve waste and recycling management; support consumption of local produce; change overconsumption patterns of high-income households	Subsidies to households and small firms to reduce non-saving water systems and waste; incentives to local communities to improve recycling systems	Change overproduction and overconsumption styles; improve waste and recycling management	Investment in retrofitting of buildings; in water- and energy-saving devices; upgrading of public infrastructure
Ageing	Create productive employment for older persons	Investment in universal pensions; extension of working age; support for family networks	Fiscal pressure to reduce health costs; improve productivity	Investment in retraining older persons, and extending the working age
Economic				
Inequality and financial fragility	Create policy space for inclusive development; reduce underemployment; promote economic diversification	Investment in green industry, adaptation to climate change, structural economic change (industrial and service *leapfrogging* for least developed countries); strengthening regional cooperation	Reduce unemployment; boost economic growth; strengthen international cooperation	Investment on green infrastructure; policy coherence and coordination
Food insecurity	Improve access to food; increase productivity	Investment in urban agriculture, local crops, storage facilities; R&D	Reduce food waste	Investment in storage infrastructure; reducing food subsidies; policy coordination
Environmental				
Energy access	Provide access to clean energy and reduce use of "dirty" energy in poor households (e.g., least developed countries); discourage high-energy consumption in high-income households	Investment in capacity development, energy-saving devices, production and use of renewable sources of energy; subsidies and incentives for efficient energy use and water use for middle- and high-income households	Reduce overproduction and overconsumption to sustainable levels	Investment and incentives to produce and use renewable energy sources; decentralization of energy production
Climate change	Reduce impact on livelihoods; reduce carbon emissions; generate financial resources for adaptation	Investment in health and education infrastructures and facilities; adaptation and mitigation technology, early warning systems, green public transpor- tation; strengthen regional cooperation for green technology transfer	Upgrade disaster risk prevention systems; reduce carbon emissions to sustainable levels	Investment in mitigation, industrial green transformation; retrofitting of buildings; policy coordination

Source: UN/DESA, Development Policy and Analysis Division.

education and health, housing and communications. As a consequence, many urban residents in developing countries suffer to varying degrees from environmental health issues associated to inadequate access to clean water, sewerage services, and solid waste disposal. In many cities of developing countries, adequate water and sanitation services are primarily channelled to upper- and middle-class neighbourhoods, while low-income neighbourhoods often depend on distant and unsafe water wells and private water vendors who charge higher prices than the public rate for water delivery (Cohen, 2006). The poor often live in highly overcrowded dwellings in shacks which lack basic infrastructure and services. On the whole, less than 35 per cent of cities in developing countries have their waste water treated, while globally, 2.5 billion and 1.2 billion people lack safe sanitation and access to clean water, respectively (United Nations Human Settlements Programme (UN-Habitat), 2012). For a broader overview and assessment of the impact of social and economic inequalities, see also chapters I and II.

Wider urban access to public services, income-earning opportunities and broader social interaction in cities has driven rural-urban internal migration in many developing countries for the past 60 years (Beall, Guha-Khasnobis and Kanbur, eds., 2012). The speed of urbanization has ultimately outstripped the limits of the economic opportunities provided by cities, making poverty a salient feature of urban life. Cohen (2006) suggests that congestion costs in large cities might be high, since the well-being advantage has declined in many cities of developing countries since the 1970s. Moreover, the rising urban inequalities in, e.g., Brazil, China and the Philippines in the 1990s is consistent with the existence of highly heterogeneous urban labour markets, which are in part the result of their high level of exposure to world markets.

Mitlin and Satterthwaite (2012) indicate that 1 out of 7 persons in the world lives in poverty in urban areas, mainly in informal settlements of the developing world, with inadequate provision of water, sanitation, health care and schools. Yet, urban poverty is still underestimated mainly owing to inadequate methodologies used to define and measure poverty. For example, the $1.25-per-day poverty line does not necessarily capture higher costs of food and non-food items in large cities, while indicators of improved water provision include public taps and standpipes which often do not provide safe and regular water.

About 1 billion people, lacking basic infrastructure and services, currently live in slums, whose number may multiply threefold by 2050 if no policy framework is in place to reduce their growth (United Nations Human Settlements Programme (UN-Habitat), 2012). More than half of urban dwellers in countries of sub-Saharan Africa and 40 per cent in Asia lack access to basic sanitation (Baker, ed., 2012). The growth of cities in least developed countries, in particular, often results in a rise in the number of people living under precarious conditions in respect of their livelihoods and employment, whose effect on the environment is harmful through their use of "dirty" energy, e.g., wood and charcoal, to meet basic energy needs.

At the regional level, data provided by the United Nations Human Settlements Programme (UN-Habitat) (2010) indicate that 62 per cent of urban populations in sub-Saharan Africa live in slums, a proportion that is expected to rise in the next decades. Slums in Latin America and the Caribbean and regions of Asia house about 24 per cent and 30 per cent of the urban populations, respectively.

Further, international migrants working in low-skilled occupations have increasingly joined the ranks of the poor in the main cities of both developed and developing countries. Key industries and trades such as food production and processing, construction and repairs, buildings maintenance, taxi driving, the garment industry, household services, and agriculture often engage a significant share of immigrant workers.[3] Frequently living in insecure and low-quality conditions in terms of housing and public services, many immigrants are undocumented and disenfranchised. In New York City and other cities in the United States of America, for example, unsafe labour conditions for many immigrant workers include working schedules of up to 60-72 hours per week and no social benefits such as health care and social security (Orrenius and Zavodny, 2009; Passel, 2006).

Sprawl and weakened capacities

Many large cities have also experienced rising sprawl over the past 50 years, challenging urban planning. Wealthier citizens have chosen to reside on the outskirts of cities where they enjoy greater privacy, have bigger homes and better schools for their children, and are spared having to use public transportation and endure the frenzied atmosphere of urban downtowns. As a consequence, the carbon footprint of wealthier inhabitants, households and neighbourhoods is often much higher than that of the rest of urban inhabitants (McGranahan and Satterthwaite, 2003).

Small cities with less than 500,000 inhabitants experience a different type of vulnerability. Although there is much diversity in their economic structure, many small cities in developing countries have very weak economies and inadequate communication with more economically dynamic cities. These cities tend to have inadequate infrastructure for provision of basic public services, which may be of low quality. Access may be time-consuming, costly and risky (in the case, for example, of public transportation). Poor land management and weak urban planning capacities are part of the problem. The deficiencies in urban governance, institution-building and adjustment to changing land development conditions have reduced real possibilities for improving urban planning (Cohen, 2006).

Energy access

The present section highlights the differences between the energy needs of poor urban households and countries and rich ones. Access to cleaner sources of energy is intrinsically linked to development, and vice versa. Countries with higher gross domestic product (GDP) per capita (e.g., above US$ 4,000) are associated with the use of electricity by above 60 per cent of the urban population, and the use of wood and charcoal for cooking by a low proportion of urban households (e.g., 20 per cent or less).[4] In fact, cities in the majority of middle-income countries have access to electricity, including Amman, Bogota, Buenos Aires, Cairo, Caracas, Jakarta, Rabat, Rio de Janeiro and Santo Domingo (Satterthwaite and Sverdlik, 2013).

Similarly, while only 18 per cent of urban dwellers in developing countries use wood and charcoal for cooking, the proportion for least developing countries is almost four times higher. Overall, there are about 680 million people in developing countries with no access to modern fuels (table III.3). Lack of access to electricity is associated with

---

[3]   At the same time, some of the "best and brightest" immigrants make up an increasing proportion of scientists, engineers, computer specialists and medical doctors in cities of developed countries (Kapur and McHale, 2005)

[4]   In countries with GDP per capita of US$ 6,000 or more, 95-100 per cent of their urban population have access to electricity.

Table III.3

Proportion of urban population lacking access to electricity and modern fuels, and proportion using particular fuels for cooking, developing and least developed countries, circa 2003-2007

Percentage		
Lack of access to:	*Developing countries*	*Least developed countries*
Electricity	10[a]	56[b]
Modern fuels (mostly gas)	30[c]	63[d]
Fuel(s) used for cooking	*Developing countries*	*Least developed countries*
Wood, charcoal, and dung	18	68
Coal	8	3
Kerosene	7	4
Gas	57	20
Electricity	6	4

Source: UN/DESA, based on Satterthwaite and Sverdlik (2013).

a Comprising 226 million people.
b Comprising 116 million people.
c Comprising 679 million people.
d Comprising 130 million people.

informal urban settlements where dwellers typically have high transportation costs and poor-quality housing. The use of cheap fuels implies increased deforestation, pollution, health risks, energy cost and time burden. Poor people often have to spend a lot of time for travelling to purchase or gather those fuels. In contrast, regular electricity supplies would often be cheaper and safer, and could be used for household appliances (e.g., lights needed by children when doing their homework and for reading) and home enterprises.

Common and differentiated impacts of natural hazards

The adverse impact of social inequalities on human health and the environment is multiplied when we factor in the adverse effects of "natural" disasters. Natural hazards linked to climate change events have also increased in intensity and frequency. Most disasters tend to occur in developing countries and the human cost in terms of both the number of persons affected and the loss of human lives is much higher in these countries. Yet, some developed countries have also started to be affected despite their generally greater resilience (United Nations, 2011b). Mutizwa-Mangiza (2012) indicates that 40 per cent of the world's urban population, many of them poor and vulnerable to storms, floods and sea-level rise (e.g., southern Brazil, China, Viet Nam and Honduras), live less than 100 kilometres from the coast (see also World Bank, 2009).

The combined impact of sea-level rise, floods, heatwaves and storms have adversely affected millions of livelihoods, homes and lives in different countries, with projections indicating that the trend will continue and, in some cases, worsen (United Nations, 2011b). Middle-income countries such as China, India, Indonesia, the Philippines and Viet Nam had the highest number of floods and storms combined during 2000-2009. Cities located along the west Coast of Africa and the coastlines of South, East and South-East Asia have been affected by sea-level rise, flooding and salt intrusion in river flows and groundwater, compromising the quality of clean water. Endemic morbidity and mortality due to diarrhoeal disease are projected to increase in these regions. The reduction of the Andean

Effects of climate change deepen the vulnerabilities of cities in poor nations and threaten the resilience and adaptation capacities of cities in richer nations glaciers and the melting of the Himalayan glaciers have disrupted the regular production of hydroelectric plants and reduced water supply in many cities (World Bank, 2010a).

In fact, the likelihood of mega-disasters has seized the attention of policy-makers, particularly in countries that have long coastlines, including Australia, China, France, Indonesia, the Philippines and the United States. Coastal developments in urban centres are likely to sharpen disaster risks from sea-level rise and increased intensity and frequency of storms and floods (Lee and others, 2012). Although disaster risks such as droughts disproportionately affect rural areas, there have been recent disasters in urban areas—such as earthquakes in Japan (2011), Haiti (2010), Chile (2010) and China (2010); flooding in China (2010), Pakistan (2010), Brazil (2010, 2011) and Bangkok (2012); and the extensive damage wrought across cities along the East Coast of the United States following Hurricane Sandy (2012)—which highlights the fact that urban disaster risk is also a reality. The concentration of people and economic activity in areas at risk from extreme weather events or earthquakes can interrupt global supply chains, reduce economic output, reverse development gains, and affect the livelihoods of the poor who often live in those areas (Baker, ed., 2012; United Nations Office for Disaster Risk Reduction, 2013).

Stronger storms and saltwater intrusion in water systems have weakened adaptive capacities in coastal cities of both developed and developing countries. The damages to infrastructure in the former and the weakening of resilience in the latter threaten their policy space for taking effective adaptation measures and developing capacities for rebuilding.

The integrated effects of the challenges described above threaten the economic resilience of cities and heighten their vulnerabilities. Cities have to start perceiving those challenges as opportunities for investment and building cities to serve as the main pillars for a sustainable world.

Opportunities for building sustainable cities

Challenges also offer a strategic opportunity for an integrated approach to urban planning and investment in industrial transformation, infrastructure, social development and environmental management

As demonstrated above, there are both challenges and opportunities associated with building sustainable cities. The multidimensional impact of megatrends represents a strategic opportunity for taking an integrated approach to urban planning and a major opportunity for investment in industrial transformation, improved infrastructure, social development and environmental management. Sustainable development in growing cities, of poor countries in particular, implies investment in infrastructure such as roads, water, sewers, electricity and services such as schools, public transportation and health-care. Leapfrogging investment in green industrial transformation can generate employment for the "youth bulge" dividend experienced by those countries. In cities of middle- and high-income countries, investment in the production and use of renewable sources of energy, as well as in the renovation of infrastructure, retrofitting of buildings and improved efficiency in the use of electricity and water, is important. At the same time, investment in strategies for the reduction of waste production and improvement of waste collection and recycling systems are needed in most cities across the world. Inevitably, there will be trade-offs between investments yielding benefits in the short term, e.g., infrastructure for development, and those with benefits in the long term, such as environmental protection and disaster risk reduction.

Cities' contribution to sustainable development can be multiplied if more countries are committed to that goal and when people are able to produce, consume and govern their behaviour in a sustainable manner. Thus, urban sustainability defined within the framework of a global integrated approach must include both developed and developing countries.

An integrated and coordinated approach

An integrated approach to urbanization will be based on a holistic view of its social development, economic development, environmental management (at the local, national and global levels) and governance components. It will entail the coordination of objectives and programmes among different city stakeholders (e.g., citizens, government and the business sector), as well as the development of linkages between and within socioeconomic sectors and activities. In economic terms, the integrated approach tries to improve synergies and efficiencies among activities such as public transportation, energy consumption, biodiversity and human health.

Further, under an integrative approach, city administrations would integrate investment in various types of infrastructures with the development of institutional and management capacities and the active participation of all stakeholders in the process of building sustainable cities. The city of Curitiba in Brazil has gained worldwide recognition for having successfully developed that kind of integrated approach to sustainability over the past 40 years. A description of the relevant process involved in Curitiba is offered in box III.2.

At the national level, the integration of the rural and urban sectors is critical. Wider access to public services and development of linkages with industrial development can leverage rural sector capacities to exchange resources and information, and engage in social interaction, with urban areas.

Investment in economic and social infrastructure in rural settlements can be a catalyst for reducing rural-urban migration. Although every area is characterized by a different configuration of land use, resources and potentials, the systemic integration of different villages, towns and cities in the context of their particular specializations and strategic locations can bring sustainable development to both urban and rural areas. Box IV.2 illustrates the positive effects of investment in rural infrastructure on Uganda's food sustainability.

Empirical evidence suggests that for the drivers of sustained development in some newly industrialized countries of South-East Asia (Cambodia, Indonesia, Malaysia and Viet Nam) within the past 50 years included improved social development in the rural sector, increased agricultural productivity, and food supply, and support of decision-making capacities of peasant farmers. In fact, macroeconomic stabilization was important insofar as it was directed towards reduction of poverty, which was understood to be concentrated in rural areas (Kees van Donge, Henley and Lewis, 2012). Henley (2012) argues that the economic success of South-East Asia was due to pro-poor agricultural development and historical consistency in respect of investment in agriculture, as was the case for Malaysia over the period 1956-1990. Pro-rural sector policies are not the same as pro-poor policies; for example, investment in land redistribution is not necessarily pro-poor when the money is allocated to purchase land and not to implement poverty-reduction programmes, as was the case in Kenya during the 1960s and 1970s.

The road towards building sustainable cities covers two types of investment, namely:

(a) Investment in infrastructure and capacity development to close social development gaps linked to the issue of access to good-quality public transportation, water and sanitation, health, education, housing and energy services in urban and rural areas;

(b) Investment in urban resilience, including industrial transformation towards the use of renewable energy sources, creation of decent employment in green productive activities, and adoption of adaptation and mitigation strategies.

Cities and nations need to engage in investment in public infrastructure, renewable energy, energy efficiency, adaptation, retrofitting of buildings, and better waste and recycling systems

Box III.2

How Curitiba became a reference point for sustainable development

Curitiba, a city in southern Brazil, has approximately 3 million residents (including in the metropolitan area). The implementation of the Curitiba Master Plan began during the first administration of Mayor Jaime Lerner in the early 1970s. The plan relied on the physical integration of a public transport system, land-use legislation and a hierarchized road network. The urban growth structure is characterized by a linear expansion across five "structural geographical sectors" which are served by "express buses". It links the city centre with the periphery and other neighbour municipalities, with priority given to public transport.

The implementation of the Master Plan was conducted incrementally, consonant with the perception of sustainable urban design as a long-term process. Curitiba first developed a modest express route system with dedicated bus lanes. It then sought out ways to improve and extend the system. The result was a surface networked system which provides high-quality service comparable with that of well-known underground systems but at a capital cost that is about 200 times less. As a result, mass transit is almost entirely financed by passenger fares.

The systematic approach to urban transportation has reduced travel times and increased convenience for commuters and other travellers. Private companies operate public buses whose intensive use continues despite the fact that Curitiba has one of the highest automobile ownership rates in Brazil. Rider surveys suggest that at least 20 per cent of the new bus passengers previously commuted by automobile. The city has replaced several downtown streets with broad pedestrian malls and shopping areas. Reduced traffic appears to result in substantial fuel savings as well as reduced carbon emissions. Estimates based on information from URBS, the public-private company that manages the system, suggest that the reduction in automobile traffic has saved 27 million litres of fuel per year.

While Curitiba is best known for its innovative public transport system, this is only one among many initiatives that have improved the environment and reduced resource use. For example, residents of subsidized low-income housing have easy access to public transportation whose route is in the direction of the Curitiba Industrial City, where polluting industries are not allowed. Curitiba has 60 square metres of green area per inhabitant, one of the highest rates among all cities in the world. Curitiba's green spaces are integrated with flood control; and artificial lakes in many public parks provide a flood control system for the entire city. A strictly enforced citywide policy ensures that rivers and streams are protected and rainwater is collected and recycled.

Curitiba has also implemented relevant solid waste programmes. The "Garbage that is not garbage" initiative, created in 1989, promotes domestic recycling through the separate collection of more than one thousand tons of metal, plastic, glass and paper per month. Additional benefits of this programme have included the positive change in the attitude of the population towards recycling and the extension of the life of landfills through the conservation of considerable space. The goal of the "Garbage purchase" programme is to clean up dense areas in low-income communities (favelas), where garbage collection vans do not have space to circulate. The community sells garbage to the city in exchange for bags of food, bus tokens, notebooks and tickets for soccer matches and plays. The innovative feature of these programmes is the integration of environmental improvement with social inclusion.

City planning is an ongoing challenge. Curitiba has grown more than fourfold in the last 30 years, which has resulted in social issues and the environmental challenges associated with traffic and transportation, land use, waste management and housing. Yet, Curitiba continues to stand out as a visible point of reference for integrated urban development based on sustainability principles. The most important lesson is that Curitiba has taken control of its own destiny by embracing a sustainability approach which has brought important benefits. At the same time, it has become an inspiration for thousands of small and medium-sized cities worldwide which are about to make crucial choices for their future and the future of the planet.

Source: Jonas Rabinovitch, Senior Adviser on Governance, Public Administration and e-Government Issues, United Nations Secretariat.

The first area of investment applies mainly to cities located in low-income countries and should be part of a development agenda that is supported by the international community with a view to spurring sustainability. In particular, support should be directed towards infrastructure investment efforts made by poor countries in order to reduce poverty (see box III.5 for an example of investment in waste processing infrastructure (Dhaka)). The second area of investment applies mainly to cities located in middle- and high-income countries. In the case of economies with fast growth, for example, resources generated by sustained economic growth in the past decade can serve as a means of financing the production and use of renewable energy as well as building resilience against natural hazards.

All things considered, building sustainable cities requires an integrated approach to investment in (a) rural development and affordable access to public services by the urban poor, (b) rapid, reliable, accessible and affordable public transportation in all its forms, (c) industrial transformation based on the production and use of renewable energy sources and the creation of decent jobs, (d) retrofitting of buildings and increase in the number of green areas, (e) improved efficiency in the use of water and electricity and (f) effective management of waste and recycling systems.

A study of urban households in the United States by Holian and Kahn (2013) indicates that investment and effective measures to reduce air pollution and crime in downtown areas have resulted in higher urban population density and reduced per capita carbon emissions. The Plan Verde of Mexico City is also making positive strides in reducing urban air pollution and carbon emissions (box III.3).

Green investment in poor countries would enable them to leapfrog from dirty/high-carbon energy use to a low/zero-carbon development path. Investment is needed in the renovation of infrastructures of transportation as well as in education programmes that value efficiency in the use of public services. Households and businesses in cities of middle- and high-income countries would need to continue investing in improving the quality of life in urban centres and to create incentives to retrofit buildings and subsidies for producing and consuming clean energy sources. Box III.4 lists 10 essentials for investments and measures to reduce disaster risk, including investment in critical infrastructure, and early warning systems, and direct involvement of communities in designating prevention and reconstruction priorities.

Trade-offs between investments?

Cities with a growing number of informal settlements are trying to meet basic urban infrastructure needs, such as for public transportation, clean piped water, drainage systems and waste management. As a result, investment in adaptation to climate change may take a back seat to investment in development. Moreover, building resilience has been constrained by poor infrastructure, weak institutions and lack of enforcement of planning regulations, e.g., in Pakistan. Similarly, in Narok and Kisumu (Kenya) and Moshi (United Republic of Tanzania), the municipalities' limited capacity, knowledge and coordination, and competing priorities, have prevented the adoption of disaster risk reduction strategies (United Nations Office for Disaster Risk Reduction, 2013).

Post-disaster reconstruction is another area where cities often face trade-offs between investing in sustainable development and re-establishing services. As observed by the Intergovernmental Panel on Climate Change (2012b), tensions frequently arise as a result of competing demands for speed of delivery and sustainability of outcome. Response and reconstruction funds tend to be time-limited, often requiring expenditure within 12 months or less from the time of disbursement, with disregard for long-term pay-offs. Such pressure is compounded by the fact that multiple agencies work with limited resources and coordination. Indeed, trade-offs are often a by-product of short-sighted approaches versus long-term investment in win-win sustainable development solutions.

In fact, trade-offs between investments are often associated with whether or not formal established incentives exist for a particular type of investment. Wu and others (2013) argue that, in China, investments in transportation infrastructure, e.g., roads and electrification, tend to attract more incentives and therefore more rewards than investments in the environment. For these reasons, local urban authorities often prioritize the former type of investment based on its higher correlation with real GDP growth, career promotion and cities' revenues from land lease sales. As a result, investments in the environment tend to be negatively affected.

Box III.3

Plan Verde of Mexico City

In 1990, Mexico City had had 333 days in which the ozone level rose above Mexico's national standard. In 2006, the city developed a 15-year Plan Verde which included the goal of reducing greenhouse gas emissions by 7 million metric tons during 2008-2012, which was accomplished in a timely manner. The Plan also has a business and citizens education component. Nearly 20 city agencies have worked together to optimize the use of the $1 billion-per-year investment, which represents about 7 per cent of the city's yearly budget. By 2009, the number of days with an ozone level above the standard had fallen to 180. Moreover, the average number of hours per day during which the ozone standard was above the norm fell from 4.9 in 1990 to just 1.5 in 2009.

In addition to improving air quality, the plan includes other "pillars" encompassing: land conservation; public spaces; waste management and recycling; water supply and sanitation; climate action planning; and transportation and mobility. The city's efforts to control atmospheric pollutants have included replacing ageing taxis, microbuses and government fleets with lower-emissions vehicles, introducing a bike-sharing programme, and building a bus rapid transit system. The city offers a tax incentive of 10 per cent of the value of a building for promotion of green roofs. By December 2011, 21,000 square metres of green roofs had been installed in public buildings and private establishments. The city has also implemented 22 programmes on 11,000 hectares of conservation land for improving water management by reducing soil loss due to water and wind erosion.

To reduce the effects of population growth and the increase in vehicle fleets, the city has plans to replace official Government vehicles with fuel-efficient and low-polluting units. By 2012, four lines of a bus rapid transit system which used clean-burning, ultra-low sulphur diesel fuel had been inaugurated. The city is investing $2 billion in constructing a twelfth metro line and is providing subsidies for replacing ageing taxis. By December 2011, 75,000 taxis had been replaced with more efficient vehicles and 12,695 taxis had been scrapped. The city has restricted vehicle usage on certain days and in certain high-traffic zones as part of the *Hoy no circula* programme which is designed to reduce both traffic and emissions. The city has also introduced a bicycle mobility strategy (EcoBici), which includes free bike rentals and the creation of 21 kilometres of new bicycle paths. The city has also built bicycle-parking infrastructures at major metro subway stations. By December 2011, EcoBici had made 1,200 bicycles available at 90 bike stations and had 35,000 registered users, who had taken a total of 3 million trips.

By focusing on improving air quality across multiple dimensions including land use, transportation, waste management and climate action planning, the city has produced effective programmes in seemingly unrelated areas such as water use and supply.

Sources: United Nations (2010b); and http://www.mexicocityexperience.com/green_living/.

Learning by doing in building sustainable cities

Building sustainable cities entails integration and coordination among sectors. For example, a land plan would need to include space for industry, residential housing, and green areas, to be integrated with adequate space for access to public transportation. Some overlaps would exist since investment in green infrastructure, for example, can imply a reduction of CO_2 emissions, while protection of green areas can include management of groundwater sources.

Similarly, integration within sectors such as transportation would include the development of linkages between various transportation modes (e.g., bus, tram, metro, bicycle and walking) in order to reduce travel time, gas emissions and the use of private cars. China, Hong Kong Special Administrative Region, for example, has an extensive network of privately owned minibuses; maintains a low-fare tram system in the traditional downtown; and has effective pedestrian connection links with commercial buildings which double

Building sustainable cities entails integration and coordination among social, economic and environmental sectors as well as within sectors such as transportation

---

Box III.4

The 10 essentials for urban resilience

1. Put in place the organization and coordination needed to promote the understanding and reduction of disaster risk, based on participation of citizens groups and civil society. Build local alliances. Ensure that all departments understand their role in disaster risk reduction and preparedness.

2. Assign a budget for disaster risk reduction and provide incentives for homeowners, low-income families, communities, businesses and the public sector to invest in reducing the risks they face.

3. Maintain up-to-date data on hazards and vulnerabilities. Prepare risk assessments, to be used as the basis for urban development plans and decisions, and ensure that this information and the plans for your city's resilience are made readily available to the public and are fully discussed with them.

4. Invest in and maintain critical infrastructure which reduces risk, such as flood drainage, adjusted where needed to cope with climate change.

5. Assess the safety of all schools and health facilities and upgrade them, as necessary.

6. Apply and enforce realistic risk-compliant building regulations and land use planning principles. Identify safe land for low-income citizens and upgrade informal settlements, wherever feasible.

7. Ensure that education programmes and training on disaster risk reduction are in place in schools and local communities.

8. Protect ecosystems and natural buffers to mitigate the impact of floods, storm surges and other hazards to which your city may be vulnerable. Adapt to climate change by building on good risk reduction practices.

9. Install early warning systems and emergency management capacities in your city and hold regular public preparedness drills.

10. After any disaster, ensure that the needs of the affected populations are placed at the centre of reconstruction, with support for those populations and their community organizations in designing and helping to implement responses, including rebuilding homes and livelihoods.

Source: United Nations Office for Disaster Risk Reduction (2012), chap. 4.

pedestrian capacity, directing people away from the noise and fumes generated by motorized traffic. Similarly, Bangkok has adopted the bus rapid transit (BRT), "a transportation system that mobilizes high-capacity buses along routes with limited stops" (Lim, 2012, p. 36).

In respect of water management, cities face access and efficiency challenges. Phnom Penh and Cape Town have been able to meet challenges by providing clean water at affordable rates to all people, including the poor living on the outskirts. Singapore has overcome its long-term water dependency with multi-pronged actions which included the installation of desalination plants and the recycling of waste water (Lim, 2012).

The annex to this chapter sets out the different profiles and policy experiences of a sample of cities in respect of building urban sustainability. Independent of its size or its breadth of experience, each city has started on its own road towards urban sustainability. Cities such as Curitiba, Copenhagen and Freiburg have greater experience in building sustainability, and a few of their accomplishments have already served as models for other cities; for example, Curitiba's integrated bus system has been emulated by the TransMilenio bus system of Bogotá, Metrovia in Guayaquil, and Metrobús in Mexico City. Other cities have just started to design and implement a sustainability plan. As stated earlier, cities are poised to become pillars of sustainable development. In this sense, urban governance (figure III.4) can promote a more balanced and inclusive development as well as ensure a more effective use of local and national resources.

As policy areas, the sectors indicated in the annex capture the economic, social and environmental aspects of urban sustainability. The specific measures and activities listed in each cell do not necessarily constitute all of the actions taken by each city; rather, they reflect mainly the relevant information found and some of the agreed priority initiatives that cities have begun to carry out. In particular, some cities have been quite actively supporting green infrastructure (in buildings and transportation); renewable energy and reduction of CO_2 emissions; and management of waste and recycling.

The sustainability challenges faced by each city are diverse and reflect the size of its economy, technology capacities and population (e.g., Shanghai has 21 million residents, while Ilo has 53,000 residents), as well as its development priorities. Information and communications technologies (ICT) can increase efficiencies, reduce costs and enhance quality of life; however, the adoption of ICT depends on the capacity to scale up and on flexibility for implementation in different urban settings. Indeed, ICT also offers an opportunity to integrate cities' infrastructures, including utilities, real estate, transportation and other public services (Falconer and Mitchell, 2012).

Cities' priorities are determined by their own urban planning capacities and by the pressing development challenges that they face. Different stakeholders, coming, e.g., from the business, professional, government and political sectors, often gather to discuss how to build a particular city's sustainability. Their individual views on urban sustainability have to be synthesized to yield common denominators, e.g., a common language and a unified approach to implementation. The survey presented in the annex reveals the existing gaps and the diversity of policy priorities adopted in different cities. For example, housing in Kampala is a priority owing to the fact that 60 per cent of its inhabitants reside in slums, while in Paris one priority is to ensure the implementation of insulation programmes for old buildings in order to improve households' energy efficiency. On the other hand, it is the Clean Air Project that is of foremost importance in Ilo, a city whose mining activities have produced "one of the world's highest levels of air pollution" (Boon, Alexaki and Herrera Becerra, 2001, p. 215). The improvement of water infrastructure is essential to improving the quality and efficiency of water use in a large urban area like Mexico City, while protection of groundwater to ensure a supply of safe drinking water and reduction of water consumption per capita are main priorities in Shanghai and Freiburg.

In this context, the fact that cities differ in their complexities militates against a "one size fits all" approach towards sustainability, since such differences render their priorities, objectives and paths diverse as well. Thus, measures of progress will be tailored to the particular challenges and opportunities determined and prioritized by the cities' main stakeholders. Yet, establishment of stakeholder roles must precede development of a sustainability plan. For example, Governments should develop technical standards, e.g., building codes while working closely with the private sector; in its turn, the private sector should develop processes for partnering with government, academia and non-governmental organizations "to ensure solutions that are both functional and economically feasible" (Falconer and Mitchell, 2012).

It is important to underscore the significance of ambitious housing plans and successful integration of public transportation infrastructures in some cities. In this regard, it is worth mentioning that China plans to build up to 36 million subsidized flats by 2015 for low-income people, mainly for the rural workers who come to work temporarily in the city and cannot afford decent housing. Similar subsidized housing projects are planned in Bangkok and Kuala Lumpur in order to reduce slums and squatter settlements (Lim, 2012). Of course, the quality of the housing to be built in terms of sustainability (based, for example, on the materials used and energy efficiency) will need to be assessed. The challenges faced by these cities in respect of providing adequate housing are enormous. For example, a vast floating population circulating among most of the cities in China, which is important for their economic success, do not have access to Government services (Mitlin and Satterthwaite, 2012).

In general, the integration and coordination of different infrastructures and modes of public transportation save travel time and energy and reduce congestion and carbon emissions; the success of these measures has been reported in cities like Copenhagen, Curitiba, Freiburg and Paris. Other cities, like Bangkok, Lima, Mexico City and Singapore, are also working on integrating different forms of public mobility. In many of these cities, the goal is to reduce the transportation time between home, the city and the workplace, so as to reduce energy consumption and ensure that people have more time to be productive and enjoy urban life.

Copenhagen's Finger Plan 2007 includes protection of its green belt and limitation of sprawl development through better use of city land, with new compact buildings located near public transportation and other services. The protection of green belts are important for reducing carbon emissions and supporting urban agriculture, which can provide employment to local farmers, bring fresh produce to urban residents, and stabilize food prices, since transportation and packaging costs are thereby reduced. More important, direct public participation has been vital for planning legislation in Copenhagen, through, for example, the Citizen's Dialogue Project, which is being financed through the city's annual budget.

Freiburg promotes the integration and mixing of functions within compact buildings and neighbourhoods which encompass shops, medical offices, schools, churches and children's playgrounds, including nearby green spaces. Renewable energy production is encouraged through the tax credits from the federal Government and subsidies from the regional utility Badenova; grass-roots financing schemes also allow citizens to invest directly in renewable energy sources.

It is important to note the level of awareness that some cities have attained with respect to waste reduction and recycling for urban sustainability. Waste is treated as a raw material and energy source in Freiburg, while cities like Copenhagen, Curitiba, Kampala, Shanghai, Singapore and Stockholm, have made significant progress in recycling and reducing waste. Private-public partnerships have often been the key to financing and improving waste collection and transformation. Although by many accounts, Dhaka exemplifies a city with an unsustainable growth pattern, box III.5 indicates that, even under those circumstances, it is possible to build up an effective partnership on solid waste management.

Lastly, in many cities, the use of the bicycle is becoming an essential part of public transportation. Education and initiatives to discourage car circulation (e.g., through the imposition of higher tariffs during rush hours in Singapore and the *Hoy no circula* programme in Mexico City), and the provision of adequate infrastructure, such as bike parks near metros and bike lanes, free bike rentals, and bike-sharing, have facilitated the rapid adoption of bicycles as a means of transport and the rapid spread of their use in cities of both developed and developing countries.

Act locally with national support and global coordination

To strengthen the financial and decision-making capacities of cities, national Governments need to adopt an inclusive and decentralized approach towards the use of resources and development. Issues such as rapid ageing in developing countries pose a real challenge to urban authorities, which often do not have sufficient resources to respond and therefore need long-term sources of finance. National authorities need to enhance decentralization and share the resources needed for economic growth to increase the policy space of local administrations. Effective dialogue between urban and national authorities on development priorities can be a means of identifying synergies and areas of development for national, regional and global coordination.

National sustainable strategies of development should explicitly consider cities as main pillars for building sustainability. Some countries have already begun to build sustainable cities in country capitals such as Copenhagen, Oslo and Stockholm and in a selected group of cities including Tianjin, Chongqing and Shenzhen (eco-cities) in China.

A coordinated international response is necessary. Sustainable national strategies should reflect development priorities that are consistent with cities' priorities. For example, food security and adaptation to climate change are two of the most immediate priorities in poor countries, while recovery from financial fragility and measures for reducing the impact of ageing can be pressing priorities in rich countries. In both cases, upfront investment in green productive activities, infrastructure and efficient use of public goods is essential for building thriving and sustainable cities.

Urbanization will be truly sustainable only when it engages the commitment of the global community. To overcome the challenges to building sustainable cities, the identification of common and differentiated urban development priorities should itself be prioritized and those priorities should be consistent with common and differentiated responsibilities for addressing the impact of climate change among countries. Further, binding commitments between countries to confront cross-border challenges such as climate change can greatly improve the effectiveness of urban sustainability strategies.

Box III.5

A partnership in Dhaka to convert organic waste to a resource and generate carbon credits

Economic development, population growth and urbanization have generated rising volumes and diverse streams of municipal solid waste in Dhaka, a city with limited urban infrastructure and capability. The city generates 3,500 metric tons of municipal solid waste daily, which is transported to a sanitary landfill. However, uncontrolled land filling has become a common practice in the city, which does not have adequate facilities for treatment, recycling and disposal of hazardous waste, a common problem in many cities of poor countries. Eighty per cent of municipal solid waste generated in Dhaka is organic in nature, with a moisture content ideal for recycling into compost.

Waste Concern, a local non-governmental research organization, works in partnership with the Government, the private sector, international agencies and local communities to implement community-based composting. Its services include waste collection, separation and composting. Since its launch of solid waste management projects in 1998, Waste Concern has served 30,000 people in Dhaka and 100,000 in 14 other cities and towns in Bangladesh, including low- and middle-income communities. The project has led to new job opportunities and better livelihoods in the communities.

Innovative financial arrangements have included community involvement and public-private cooperation. Communities utilize a door-to-door collection service and share the cost of waste collection by paying a monthly fee based on affordability. The private sector stakeholder has joint venture partners which include Waste Concern and banking institutions. The investment required for the project was 12 million euros and the mode of financing was made up of equity (38 per cent), a soft loan (45 per cent) and a loan from a local bank (17 per cent).

A private company ensures the sale of compost by enriching the compost with nutrients and effecting its subsequent distribution to the market (e.g., farmers). As a result, 75 per cent of the project's revenue comes from the sale of compost. The partnership was also registered as a Clean Development Mechanism project under the United Nations Framework Convention on Climate Change;[a] as a result, the remaining 25 per cent of the revenue comes from community contributions in the form of a user fee and the sale of certified emissions reductions (CERs).

The project had several positive effects: (a) reduction of the landfilling budget of the city; (b) creation of assured revenue for 10 years through the sale of compost and CERs; (c) creation of 800 jobs for poor urban residents; (d) production of 50,000 metric tons of compost for sustainable farming; and (e) achievement of knowledgeability by urban communities about the resource value of waste.

Source: United Nations (2010b).

a United Nations, *Treaty Series*, vol. 1771, No. 30822.

Financing sustainable cities

The scale and scope of needed finance

Building sustainable cities poses significant financial challenges to national and municipal authorities. It entails commanding enough resources to finance the cost of infrastructure and the provision of a wide range of public services, within the context of major challenges such as ageing of populations and climate change threats. Urban authorities have to prioritize competing financing requirements, usually without sufficient budget resources to address the challenges of sustainable development simultaneously.

The nature of the trade-offs between economic development and climatic priorities varies from city to city. For cities located in poor countries (low-income and lower middle income), sustainable development depends mainly on their capacities to finance investment in green infrastructure and access to basic services. For cities located in richer countries (upper middle income and high-income), financing is needed for restructuring cities' design, infrastructure, transport and efficiency in the use of water and electricity.

Similarly, with a growing number of international migrants and rising inequalities among countries, global and medium cities in both developed and developing countries are challenged to provide adequate public services. On the other hand, immigration has often stimulated the economic and cultural revival of urban neighbourhoods and has been a source of labour vital for the growth and competitiveness of the cities. At the same time, many cities across the world need resources to finance the industrial processing of waste and the improvement of recycling systems.

A policy framework for sustainable financing

The creation of a policy framework for responding effectively to the challenge of financing the sustainability of cities requires multilayered cooperation among local national and global communities, including the development of partnerships to harness public and private resources for the purposes described above.

Financing investment in public infrastructure, including adaptation to and mitigation of climate change, is a daunting task, one that often demands large sums of upfront finance and an acceptance of the fact that returns will be seen mainly in the medium and long terms.

Regulatory measures, including market and non-market mechanisms, are important for determining pricing structures, taxes and subsidies for households and industry, e.g., for the development of compact neighbourhoods and the retrofitting of buildings. Various types of taxes—included, for example, in lower fares for public transportation—can be used to finance the gap between the financial outlay and the actual cost of services.

Thus, for cities in poor and rich countries alike, part of the financing would have to be directed towards limiting the damaging effects of climate change on the environment, biodiversity and the livelihoods of present and future generations. In this sense, the principle of common and differentiated responsibilities can guide the establishment of an international cooperation framework capable of supporting the development and resilience of poor countries.

Oil-exporting and emerging economies experiencing relatively high economic growth but with urban settlements vulnerable, for example, to sea-level rise, storms and droughts, should use part of the resources generated to finance cities' risk reduction strategies and improved infrastructure for adaptation, mitigation and provision of public services.

Examples of financing strategies

Bond banks and resource pooling can be useful instruments for reducing risk. In 1998, the Ahmedabad Municipal Corporation issued 1 billion rupees in bonds (without a State guarantee) to finance a water supply and sewerage project. The bond issue improved the city's finances (World Bank, 2013).

Public-private partnerships can also serve as viable instruments for raising funds for financing infrastructure projects, particularly in developing countries with limited access to long-term credit. Public-private partnerships can improve asset utilization and favour cost recovery through user fees. For example, improvement in the quality of public transportation services through engagement of the private sector can justify higher fees (see the annex for information on the public-private partnership established in Freiburg, Germany, to finance the production of renewable sources of energy).

Cities in poor countries may also leverage the value of land to finance infrastructure. In Cairo, for example, the auction of 3,100 hectares of desert land in 2007 generated $3.1 billion. This amount of resources was to be used to reimburse costs of internal infrastructure and build a connecting highway to the road surrounding Cairo. Leaseholds can also leverage the value of land. These instruments can generate the initial capital needed to cover the start-up costs of infrastructure investments. In the long run, other instruments, such as property taxes, can finance maintenance and upgrade of public investments. However, land-based financing instruments require relatively strong and effective institutions and well-articulated legal frameworks.

Viet Nam has been able to finance universal access to electricity and achieve high levels of access to water and sanitation. In the poorest provinces, equalization has enabled access to basic services. Cities also finance themselves through taxes, land leases, short-term debt, investment funds and cross-subsidies from provincial public utility companies. Land leases, for example, are becoming an increasingly important source of finance. Yet, financing infrastructure services is still a challenging task for many cities (World Bank, 2013).

Sources of finance can have different degrees of stability and predictability. Financing for Germany's cities is largely derived from tax income tied to business profits, which can fall during times of crisis. For example, since Berlin is liable for high interest payments on past borrowing, it has requested debt relief from the federal Government. In contrast, city budgets in France and Italy rely more on real estate taxes, partly because the revenues are more stable and easier to predict.

However, the situation of cities in many poor countries is more problematic. Financial support from national Governments and donor agencies is often minimal, and provided, typically, only for the initial construction of infrastructure and not for ongoing operations. Thus, cities rely mainly on fees, tariffs and property taxes. However, property valuations can be out of date or incomplete, while capacities to collect taxes remain weak. Sprawling, in particular, can weaken tax systems in dynamic cities since, frequently, suburban residents pay property taxes not in the city where they work but in a different—and smaller—community (PricewaterhouseCoopers, 2012).

In a context of policies of fiscal restraint, some national Governments are pressed to grant more autonomy to cities in generating resources and determining their destiny. For example, since 1988, the central Government of China has not financed local expenditure; hence, local governments have to provide and finance public services.

Annex
Examples of plans and policies for building sustainable cities

City	Population (thousands)	Disaster risk reduction	Education, training, research, and information programmes	Housing	Economic growth, green economy, jobs, training/retraining	Green infrastructure (buildings, public transportation)	Renewable energy and reduction of CO_2 emissions	Energy efficiency	Waste and recycling management	Water, sanitation and ecosystem management
Bogotá	9,000 (20 per cent of nation's population)	Focused on reducing seismic risks for schools; law No. 1523 of 2011 established a new National System for Disaster Risk Management with emphasis on engaging local communities	Yes (for water-use efficiency)		Green economy accounts for 28 per cent of city GDP	Green public transportation network; mass transit bus system (TransMilenio) modelled on that of Curitiba; park space; bicycle paths (Ciclovia programme); infrastructure for pedestrian safety	Air quality programme			Yes (efficiency)
Cape Town	2,480	Community action plan measures: clearing storm water drains (short-term); infrastructure (medium-term); transformation and integration of informal settlements (long-term). Emphasis on non-white areas and informal settlements		Poverty reduction based on the urban renewal programme, including housing (a Government programme launched in 2001)	High economic growth	MyCiti bus service and new cycle lanes; human-scale design of buildings and spaces	10 per cent of homes would use solar power by 2020; 10 per cent of energy consumption from renewable sources by 2020; possible mandatory solar panels in every building		14.5 per cent of households (the wealthy) produce half of the city's waste, which represents four times the waste per day produced by the poor	Since 1994, the goal has been to provide basic services to all (success with water and energy, not yet with sanitation)
Ilo	53	Yes	Yes				Yes, the Ilo Air Clean Project includes assessment of impact of air pollution on children and crops, and a contingency plan to limit impacts; plan to reduce health impact of CO_2 emissions		Yes	Yes
Kampala	1,660 (60 per cent live in slums)	Environmental protection measures such as tree planting and wetland conservation; relocation of residents in informal settlements along waterways; planting trees near schools to reduce wind damage and risks to children		Mapping; slum upgrading through the provision of clean water and better housing		EcoMobility includes cycling, wheeling, walking and public bus transportation (intermodality)			Improved waste and recycling management	

(cont'd)

City	Population (thousands)	Disaster risk reduction	Education, training, research, and information programmes	Housing	Economic growth, green economy, jobs, training/ retraining	Green infrastructure (buildings, public transportation)	Renewable energy and reduction of CO_2 emissions	Energy efficiency	Waste and recycling management	Water, sanitation and ecosystem management
Seoul	10,600	The Seoul metropolitan government has responded to disasters triggered by monsoons with the Storm and Flood Preparedness Plan, improving drainage systems and strengthening critical infrastructure	Dissemination of data to reinforce good habits, e.g. on the amount of carbon emissions by each transportation mode and route option		High economic growth, partly supported by green economy	Buildings; integrated transportation of bicycles, bus, trains and taxis; half of the bus fleet to become electric by 2020; bike paths and parking spaces; pedestrian areas	Wind, solar; during 2006–2010, air pollution was reduced by 20 per cent		Yes	
Copenhagen	509 (metro region: 1.7 million)	Climate Plan 2011 could deliver savings of €3 bill on over 100 years in losses from future extreme flooding from the sea and rain		Goal for 2015: 95 per cent of ome residents would be able to walk to a park, beach or swimming pool in less than 15 minutes (the proportion was 60 per cent in 2010)		Integrated transportation, including bicycle use; non-motorized transport or active transport; 1 out of 3 residents cycles to work; a network of 300 kilometres of bike lanes; green cycle routes for long-distance travelling; designed to minimize stops due to car traffic; the øresund bridge carries a highway and train line connecting Copenhagen and Malmö (Sweden) (ferry connection for goods transportation between these cities was closed)	Wind energy; rate of CO_2 emissions decreased by 15 per cent during 1992–2002; Climate Plan 2011 calls for 20 per cent cut in carbon emissions by 2001; goal: to become CO_2-neutral by 2025	In order to warm buildings in downtown areas, the city reuses excess heat from waste incinerators and power plants	Yes	The city's 2004 Parks Policy emphasizes enhanced recreation along the harbour and coast as well as improvement of water cleanliness; water consumption rate is 127 litres per resident per day (objective is to reach 110 litres)
Portland	568			Low-income housirg programme		Regional Transportation Plan 2000–2020; coordinated transportation by bus and light rail system; car-sharing programme; Portland Bicycle Plan for 2030: bicycle network of 510 kilometres, parking and integration with other transportation modes	Goal: 100 per cent green power and 50 per cent reduction in electricity use by 2020 relative to 2007; partnership between the city and Clean Energy Works to improve energy efficiency in 6,000 homes by 2013; goal: to achieve at least 10 megawatts of installed solar capacity by 2013; plan to reduce greenhouse gas emissions by 80 per cent by 2050		Residential Curbside Collection Service Programme has reduced 40 per cent of garbage in 2012; residents recycling 85 per cent of recyclable materials; goal to recover 90 per cent of city's waste by 2030; goal: fewer than 5,000 sheets of 100 per cent recycled paper used per department per year by 2015	Goal: by 2020, water used would equal amount of water that falls on city annually

(cont'd)

City	Population (thousands)	Disaster risk reduction	Education, training, research, and information programmes	Housing	Economic growth, green economy, jobs, training/retraining	Green infrastructure (buildings, public transportation)	Renewable energy and reduction of CO_2 emissions	Energy efficiency	Waste and recycling management	Water, sanitation and ecosystem management
Freiburg	220	Incentives for on-site management of storm water and landscape planning; use of green roofs and bioswales to promote creation of natural and permeable surfaces; metrics have been established for storm water fees by volume of impermeable property and estimated rainfall at residential and commercial sites; water retention reservoir built to reduce flood risks	The online CO_2 Diet calculator outlines a personal CO_2 footprint and information on how to offset personal emissions (www.freiburg.de/CO_2); centres of private and public research investigate renewable energy resources; Solar Training Centre for technicians and installers; protection of groundwater for safe drinking water supply through educational brochures (this intervention can be listed under the right-most column heading (Water, sanitation and ecosystem management)	Construction of "passive houses" with no need for an active system to maintain comfortable temperatures (they reduce energy loss by 90 per cent and require energy of only 15 kilowatt-hours per square metre per year); city promotes planned and dense environmental housing	The "environmental economy" employs nearly 10,000 people in 1,500 businesses, generating €500 million per year; economic benefits lie mainly in manufacturing, research and education, and tourism; companies produce solar cells and the machinery needed to manufacture them	Low-energy construction standard so that buildings have a maximum energy use of 65 kilowatt-hours per square metre per year; since the 1970s, building codes have been designed to enhance climate and "cool airflows"; integrated transportation: bus, tram, rail, bicycle and pedestrian; trips on public transit 18 per cent; walking 23 per cent; bicycling 27 per cent (on 420 kilometres of bicycle-friendly paths); inner city has over 5,000 bicycle parking bays available, plus 1,000 in the main train station; over 72 per cent of all commuters use the tram system; majority of the population is within half a kilometre of station	60 "plus energy" homes of the Solar Settlement create more energy than they consume, and earn €6,000 per year for residents; target of reducing CO_2 emissions by 40 per cent by 2030, from 1992 levels; city adopted speed limit of 30 kilometres per hour in main traffic axis; windmills, solar panels: the 450 renewable energy and solar companies employ more than 10,000 people; the regional public utility offers "solar investments subsidies" to residents and businesses that install solar panels; goal: to increase share of renewable energy in the electricity market from 5 per cent to 20 per cent by 2020	50 per cent of electricity produced by combined heat and power; support programme for home insulation and energy retrofits through municipal subsidies; clean air corridors in streets restrict fog from the Rhine River valley, limiting electricity used in lighting streets; linear time-variable electricity charges use meters to gauge by three different time zones, charging consumers accordingly; improved insulation of buildings; low-energy construction	City recycles more than the State and the figure is greater than the national average; waste is used as raw material and energy source; by 2009, 69 per cent of produced waste was recycled; number of landfills fell from 50,000 in the 1970s to 200 in 2010; each person produces 124 kilograms of house waste and bulk rubbish, lower than the national average of 143; heat produced during incineration of residual waste is used to generate electricity, which feeds the grid to supply 25,000 households	40 per cent of territory is communal forest; city adopted the 2010 Freiburg Forest Convention for sustainable forest management; 47 per cent green space/parks
Singapore (city State)	4,600	The Marina Barrage project acts as a tidal barrier to alleviate flooding in low-lying areas			High economic growth	Goal: greening 80 per cent of buildings by 2030; E- Symphony Card pays for road tolls, bus travel, taxis, metro and even shopping; goal: 70 per cent of all journeys by public transportation by 2030; Electronic Road Pricing system changes according to actual demand in a corridor (to reduce congestion)	Solar; goal: to reduce CO_2 emissions by 30 per cent by 2030; Vehicle Quota System policy: people bid for right to purchase a vehicle (which discourages car purchasing and generates revenue for repairing road infrastructure)	Goal: 35 per cent improvement in energy efficiency by 2030, from 2005 levels	Goal: recycling rate of 70 per cent by 2030; currently, 56 per cent of waste is recycled	Goal: to reduce water consumption to 140 litres per person per day by 2030, down from 156 litres in 2008; 30 per cent of city's water needs is covered by treated waste water (goal is to reach 50 per cent by 2060); goal: building 0.8 hectares of green space for every 1,000 residents

(cont'd)

City	Population (thousands)	Disaster risk reduction	Education, training, research, and information programmes	Housing	Economic growth, green economy, jobs, training/retraining	Green infrastructure (buildings, public transportation)	Renewable energy and reduction of CO_2 emissions	Energy efficiency	Waste and recycling management	Water, sanitation and ecosystem management
Shanghai	21,000	City's flood resistance standard can withstand once-in-200-years high-tide level and cope with gales of up to 133 kilometres per hour; levee of Huangpu River and urban flood control projects able to resist once-in-1,000-years high-tide level of the Huangpu	In 2006, city publicized the Shanghai Overall Preparedness Programme for Public Emergencies	Goal: to build 36 million affordable flats for low income people in cities between 2011 and 2015		Electronic ID Management System (smart ID and licence tag cards); public transport smart cards, bus smart information systems	Air quality programmes	Goal: to reduce energy usage per unit of GDP by 18 per cent and reduce carbon emissions per unit of GDP by 19 per cent in five years (2010–2015)	Domestic garbage treatment rate: 82 per cent; reduce per capita garbage to 0.8 kilogram per day in 2015, 20 per cent lower than in 2010	Tap-water access rate 100 per cent; waste-water treatment rate: 83.3 per cent; plan to reduce water usage per unit of output by more than 20 per cent by 2015, compared with 2010; 2015 target: to reach forest coverage of 15 per cent and green coverage of 38.5 per cent; management of green belt for forest conservation and reduction of groundwater pollution
London	7,400	Tidal waves are controlled by the Thames Barrier (1984), which can be raised to cut off advance of the North Sea tide; target: to reduce the impact of the urban heat island effect	Yes	Sustainable and affordable housing programme; experimental low-carbon housing development (BedZED) (2002), eco-development; Greenwich Millennium Village: includes an ecological park, use of environmentally sustainable materials, recycled and local materials, and mix of social needs-based rented housing and privately owned units	Green economy accounts for 19 per cent of United Kingdom GDP and 15 per cent of total employment (70 per cent of employment in London is private sector-based)	Public transport subsidized under a central authority (Transport for London), but services are franchised to various private firms (buses); city promotes smart travel, walking, cycling; reduce travel by car; target to achieve zero-carbon in residential buildings by 2016 and zero-carbon in non residential buildings by 2019; high priority given to bus travel ing, improved interchange between modes of transport; efficient distribution of freight; increase transport by water; sufficient cycle parking; improved sidewalks and small urban spaces; restricted car parking in new development	The Air Quality Strategy aims at reducing emissions from road transport and new development; results of urban congestion charges (2003): 21 per cent reduction of traffic, 30 per cent reduction of congestion, 43 per cent increase in cycling during first year; £125 million raised for public transport improvement; ecological footprint (land area for sustaining all activities) is 42 times its bio-capacity and 293 times its geographical area (estimation based on consumption of water, energy, food, production of waste, and so forth); Low Emission Zone standard (2008) enforced use of automatic licence plate recognition	Target of 60 per cent reduction of CO_2 emissions by 2025, below 1990 levels; target of 25 per cent of heat and power used must be generated by local decentralized systems by 2025; map tool assists identification of major energy consumers, CO_2 emissions, energy supply plants, community heating networks, and heat density; local authorities are developing energy master plans	Target of zero waste to landfill by minimizing waste by 2031; encouragement to reuse and increase recycling to 60 per cent by 2031	Trees and woodland are protected; local authorities are required to develop local tree strategies linked to their local open space strategies

(cont'd)

City	Population (thousands)	Disaster risk reduction	Education, training, research, and information programmes	Housing	Economic growth, green economy, jobs, training/ retraining	Green infrastructure (buildings, public transportation)	Renewable energy and reduction of CO_2 emissions	Energy efficiency	Waste and recycling management	Water, sanitation and ecosystem management
Paris	2,211 (population density: 25,200 residents per square kilometre)	Plan for heatwaves: isolated persons can register in Chalex database; during heatwaves, persons are contacted and visited; city supports insulation, shutters, sun-shading, ventilation and cooling systems by using district cooling and geothermal energy; maps of floodable areas are provided to all homebuyers	City sponsors public information campaigns to encourage solidarity between generations and neighbours		Paris and its surrounding region produce about 30 per cent of national GDP	Bike-sharing programme; new electric tramway lines replace overcrowded bus lines; the Paris transportation plan (2007) aims at reducing transportation-related greenhouse gas emissions by 25 per cent by 2013 and 60 per cent by 2020 (relative to 2004), mainly by reducing car use; the plan also supports low-emission vehicles with recharge stations and lower parking rates for small and electric vehicles; during 2001–2008, car traffic declined by 19 per cent; car-sharing programme adopted in 2011; plan to add 300 kilometres of bus lines, 120 kilometres of tramway lines, 105 kilometres of tram or train, 13 new multimodal nodes, and 80 kilometres of metro by 2020	Paris Climate Plan (2007) goal: to reduce greenhouse gas emissions by 25 per cent and use 25 per cent of city's energy from renewable sources by 2020, compared with 2004, and to reduce emissions by 75 per cent by 2050; renewable energy represents 2.5 per cent of city's total energy consumption	Paris Climate Plan (2007) goal: consumption of 25 per cent less energy by 2020, over 2004; development density bonuses in most energy-efficient buildings; since 2009, city offers free audits and decision support on insulation, and subsidizes insulation projects for condominium associations and owners; subsidies (grants) also used to fund efficient heating, water heating systems, ventilation, and renewable energies		Plan to clean water in Seine River to improve biodiversity; the Main Verte charter (2003) promotes organic gardening practices; there are 50 community gardens managed by neighbourhood non-profit organizations; drastic reduction of chemical fertilizers and pesticides in parks and gardens in the last 15 years; green roofs and walls; 400 beehives are dispersed throughout the city

Source: UN/DESA.

Note: The present annex does not provide an exhaustive description of all of the sustainability policies planned for and implemented in the cities listed. Blank cells may indicate that policy initiatives in a specific urban area are limited. Further research could provide additional relevant data and information on urban plans and policies.

Chapter IV

Ensuring food and nutrition security

Summary

- The persistence of malnutrition reflects deep inequalities in the distribution of and access to food at national and global levels. Ensuring that everyone in the world has access to enough nutritious food should be at the forefront of the post-2015 development discussions.

- Increasing food production in parallel with population growth, urbanization and a change in consumption patterns will require an integrated approach that takes into consideration the nexus of food, water, energy, environment and climate, while reorienting food production, distribution and consumption.

- Increasing agricultural productivity will be required, in particular in developing countries where the agriculture sector accounts for an important share of gross domestic product and where large productivity gaps still exist.

- Access of poor households to food and of isolated producers and smallholders to markets will need to be improved, in particular given that hunger can exist even in countries where there is enough food produced.

- Food consumption will need to be oriented towards diets that are less resource-intensive and more nutritious, which will be crucial for the sustainability of the food system and for better health outcomes.

- The transformation and development of the agricultural sector will require investments on a significant scale. The public sector should typically finance infrastructural needs as well as research and development, while introducing adequate incentives for private investments, such as risk protection and better access to credit markets. In addition, Governments need to design a regulatory framework that ensures inclusive and sustainable private investments.

Introduction

Ensuring that everyone in the world has access to enough nutritious food should be at the forefront of the post-2015 development discussions, as recently emphasized by the Secretary-General through the launch of the Zero Hunger Challenge.[1] The present chapter highlights the changes needed in the food system to ensure food and nutrition security by 2050 and the challenges involved, given that malnutrition is only partly an issue of food availability. The persistence of malnutrition reflects the deep inequalities in

---

1   Secretary-General Ban Ki-moon launched the Zero Hunger Challenge on June 20, 2012, at the Rio+20 United Nations Conference on Sustainable Development. For further information see http://www.un.org/en/zerohunger/challenge.shtml.

the distribution and access to food, knowing that one third of the food produced is not eaten—a missed opportunity to feed the growing world population (Food and Agriculture Organization of the United Nations, 2012b).

Recent studies have found that the challenge of malnutrition is broader than the issue of hunger or undernourishment, as highlighted by the United Nations Millennium Declaration.[2] Low quality and low diversity of food are other major sources of malnutrition. Individuals may have an intake of enough calories for daily subsistence, and still suffer from "hidden hunger", with low levels of micronutrients due to low diversification of diets. This is a problem in both developing and developed countries, affecting 30 per cent of the world's population. The excess intake of calories is another major global public-health concern, as overweight and obesity cause more than 2.8 million deaths per year among adults.

In addition to the multiple burdens of malnutrition, other problems are on the horizon. On the demand side, population growth, rapid urbanization and consequent changes in consumption patterns will require additional food. The Food and Agriculture Organization of the United Nations (FAO) estimates that food production will have to increase 70 per cent globally to feed an additional 2.3 billion people by 2050. At the same time, food demand has been shifting towards more resource-intensive agricultural products, such as livestock and dairy products, thereby exerting additional pressure on land, water and biodiversity resources.

An increase in food production will also require integrating sustainable practices, particularly regarding the use of natural resources. Many of the current agricultural practices have relied on cheap energy and abundant water and land, and are a leading source of greenhouse gas emissions (The Hague Conference, 2010). These practices are now proving unsustainable for the environment and health, due to contamination of air, land and water sources. At the same time, they have led to substantial productivity losses, thereby posing risks to food security.

Thus, increasing food production and improving distribution to respond to population growth, urbanization and a change in consumption patterns will require an integrated approach to addressing several challenges simultaneously along the entire food chain. Such an integrated approach to food security and environmental sustainability should also take into consideration the nexus of food, water, energy, environment and climate, while reorienting food production, distribution and consumption.

The first challenge is to increase food production, while minimizing the environmental impact and increasing natural resource efficiency. This will require increasing agricultural productivity, in particular in developing countries where the agricultural sector contributes an important share of gross domestic product (GDP) and where large productivity gaps still exist. The introduction of improved agronomical practices and advanced technologies will be central. Information and communications technologies (ICT), for instance, can be used to inform smallholders about new farming techniques and market prices (World Bank, 2008a), as well as to improve livestock traceability (Deloitte, 2012), maximizing output, while minimizing negative impacts on the environment. Additional investments in research and development (R&D) will be crucial in increasing productivity, but better dissemination and adaptation of existing technology in different agroecological regions will also need to be part of the solution. A broader rural development strategy is also required, including infrastructural investments to better connect producers and smallholders to output markets, including rural-urban linkages.

---

2   See General Assembly resolution 55/2.

The second major challenge will be to improve the access to food and markets, as hunger often occurs in countries where there is enough food produced. Income poverty is a major factor preventing access to food. Therefore, increasing the income level of poor households will help them obtain food that is adequate in quantity and quality, thereby reducing the prevalence of undernourishment. However, high inequality in the rural sector, in particular in the distribution of assets—such as land, water, capital, education and health—is an obstacle that needs to be addressed in order to enhance food security. The underlying issue of discrimination in the rural sector, including against women, also calls for concrete action. In addition, social protection mechanisms, including safety nets, must also be part of a broader strategy to facilitate access of lower-income groups to food, in particular during economic shocks.

The third challenge is to orient food consumption towards "sustainable diets", that is, diets that are less resource-intensive and more nutritious, which will be crucial for the sustainability of the food system. Such changes would also improve health conditions related to low diversification of diets, including obesity. Reducing food wastage will also contribute significantly to the sustainability of the food system. Currently, it is estimated that 32 per cent of the total food produced globally is wasted (Food and Agriculture Organization, 2012b). In order to substantially reduce the quantity of food lost and wasted, changes have to occur at different points along the food chain: production, storage, transportation and consumption. Strategies to reduce food waste will vary among countries according to their structural conditions.

Finally, in an increasingly interconnected world, improving agricultural productivity and the allocation of food within and across countries requires well-coordinated actions at local, national and global levels. At the local and national levels, in particular in food-insecure countries, institutions should promote transparency and accountability, as well as the participation of all individuals in the decisions that affect them. At the global level, the international community can help developing countries in their efforts to design and implement policies that increase resilience to food price volatility and to climatic shocks, as well as provide safety nets, especially for smallholders. Wealthier countries will also be required to change their production and consumption patterns through actions that should include reviewing trade policies to ensure that they are pro-food and pro-nutrition security, establishing regional and international strategic reserves, and addressing the issue of speculation in land, as well as enabling the adoption of sustainable diets.

Multiple dimensions of malnutrition: undernourishment, micronutrient deficiencies and over-nutrition

Malnutrition is a broad term encompassing conditions that hinder good health, including both under-nutrition and over-nutrition. Under-nutrition can be the result of undernourishment (energy deficiency) or micronutrient (vitamin and mineral) deficiencies. Undernourishment continues to affect the world's population (12.5 per cent), mainly in developing countries (Food and Agriculture Organization of the United Nations, 2012a), despite remarkable progress in reducing hunger during the last decade, while stunting and micronutrient deficiencies affect a significant number of people. Obesity, on the other hand, has been increasing rapidly in all countries, although its prevalence is still

The health risks associated with undernourishment and inadequate diets in many developing countries are running parallel to a rapid rise in non-communicable diseases in many developed and middle-income countries due to over-nutrition considerably higher in developed countries. Thus, today, the world as a whole is facing multiple burdens of malnutrition. The health risks associated with undernourishment and inadequate diets in many developing countries are running parallel to a rapid rise of non-communicable diseases in many developed and middle-income countries, owing to the rampant increase in over-nutrition.

Under-nutrition

Food insecurity[3] persists

Sub-Saharan Africa and Western Asia are facing the most serious challenges to reaching the Millennium Development Goal 1 hunger target by 2015

According to recent estimations, in 2010-2012, about 868 million people were chronically undernourished (Food and Agriculture Organization of the United Nations, 2012b). Despite the fact that this figure is still particularly high and represents, as noted above, 12.5 per cent of world population, it also indicates that there has clearly been progress in reducing hunger at the global level (figure IV.1).

In several regions, however, the food and financial crisis slowed down that progress, mainly owing to higher food prices, reflecting different levels of vulnerability to external shocks and different country capacities to increase food supply when needed. Sub-Saharan Africa and Western Asia are facing the most serious challenges to reaching the

Figure IV.1
Number of people undernourished and prevalence of undernourishment, 1990-2012

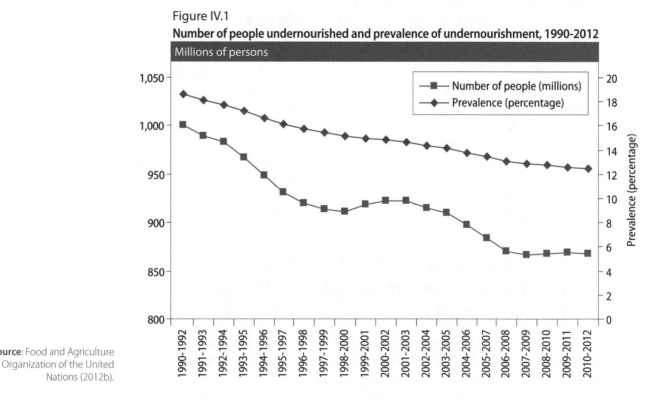

Source: Food and Agriculture Organization of the United Nations (2012b).

---

3   Food security has been defined as access by all people at all times to the food needed for a healthy life.

Millennium Development Goal 1 hunger target by 2015.[4] Western Asia, in particular, has experienced a significant increase in the number of people that are undernourished, from 8 million in 1990-1992 to 21 million in 2010-2012 (Food and Agriculture Organization of the United Nations, 2012b), increasing the prevalence of undernourishment over that period.

The distribution of undernourished people in the world has also been altered in line with different progression rates in hunger reduction during the past two decades (figure IV.2). In the past 20 years, the share of the world's undernourished people decreased in East Asia and the Pacific, from 41 per cent in 1990-1992 to 28 per cent in 2010-2012, whereas the proportion increased significantly in sub-Saharan Africa, from 17 per cent in 1990-1992 to 27 per cent in 2010-2012, as well as in Northern Africa and Western Asia, from 1 per cent in 1990-1992 to 3 per cent in 2010-2012.

Periods of high food prices in the past few years have affected countries and regions differently, according to their different levels of vulnerability to external shocks. For instance, many African countries, such as the Democratic Republic of the Congo, were fully exposed to price hikes and the global recession. Over the long run, the differences in hunger reduction across regions and countries are attributable to several factors. Inclusive economic growth, generating demand for the assets controlled by the extreme poor, has a much higher impact on hunger reduction. In addition, when poor households invest part of their increased income in health, sanitation and education, the impact of economic growth on hunger reduction is also stronger. In parallel, as seen in the case of Bangladesh, which is on track to reach the hunger target of Millennium Development Goal 1, higher public spending on health and education with targeted interventions increases nutritional success (Food and Agriculture Organization of the United Nations, 2012b).

Impacts of under-nutrition: undernourishment and micronutrient deficiencies

Undernourishment is the result of food intake that is inadequate as regards providing sufficient calories to meet people's physiological requirements on a continuing basis. Micronutrient deficiencies are also a result of under-nutrition, but in this case they are related to insufficient intake of vitamins and minerals.[5] An individual may take in enough or even too many calories for daily subsistence; however, if his or her diet is not diversified enough, the result may be low levels of micronutrients, a condition referred to as "hidden hunger". This is an issue in both developing and developed countries, affecting 30 per cent of the world's population (ibid.).

The relation between poor nutrition and poor health—including the existence of a vicious cycle of poor nutrition, poor health and low income—is well documented. For instance, iron deficiency anaemia impacts negatively on cognitive development and

An individual may take in enough or even too many calories for daily subsistence, but cases where diet is not diversified enough may lead to low levels of micronutrients

---

4   The impact of the food price and economic crises during the period 2007-2010 in undernourishment prevalence was less severe than previously estimated. According to FAO, there are two main reasons. First, the impact of economic shocks on developing economies was less severe than previously estimated. Many developing economies, in particular the largest ones, continued to grow at a relatively fast pace, albeit more slowly than in the pre-crisis period. Second, the methodology used by FAO estimates chronic undernourishment, which does not capture the effects of short-term shocks, such as price spikes. Therefore, the undernourishment indicator does not fully reflect the impact of price spikes and other short-term shocks.

5   Vitamin A, iron and iodine deficiencies are the most commonly measured micronutrient deficiencies because they are well known and have long been associated with specific health consequences (Food and Agriculture Organization of the United Nations, 2013).

Figure IV.2
Distribution of undernourished people in the world, by region, 1990-1992 and 2010-2012

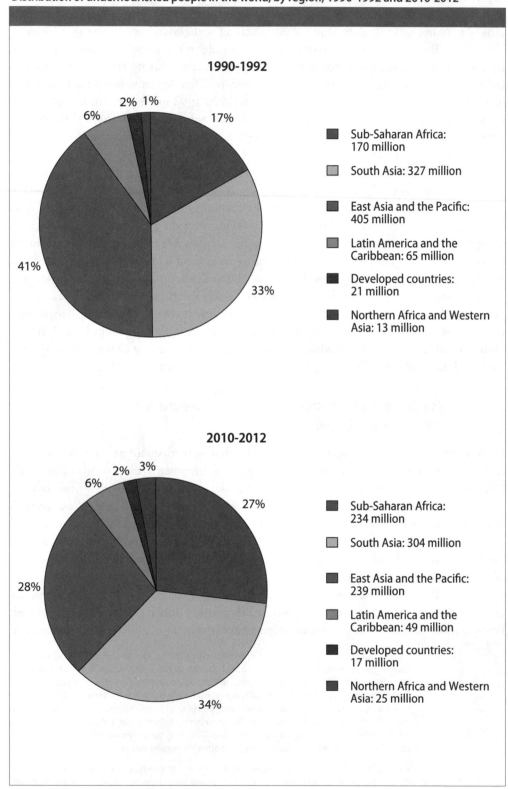

Source: Food and Agriculture Organization of the United Nations (2012b).

academic performance in school-age children (Food and Agriculture Organization of the United Nations, 2013). Short-term consequences in terms of learning disability, as well as long-term economic consequences, can be expected, since lower education levels lead to lower income opportunities.

Vitamin A deficiency, for instance, is a leading cause of blindness and corneal damage. In developing countries, 163 million children were estimated to be vitamin A-deficient, with a prevalence of more than 30 per cent in 2007, down from approximately 36 per cent in 1990 (United Nations System Standing Committee on Nutrition, 2010).

From a longer-term perspective, there is also the risk of intergenerational transmission of poor nutritional status. Women who suffer from undernourishment are more likely to give birth to underweight babies, whose development will then be affected throughout their life. Undernourishment may also lead to irreversible consequences, such as physical stunting, excluding individuals from better-rewarded tasks which demand greater physical strength. Ultimately, undernourishment affects individuals' freedom and well-being (Drèze and Sen, 1991).

Not only does undernourishment have microlevel negative consequences, but it affects the whole economy, reducing its rate of growth. For instance in India, stunting and iron and iodine deficiencies result in productivity losses equivalent to 2.95 per cent of GDP annually (World Bank, 2006). Despite the evidence of negative outcomes from poor nutrition in the short and long terms, nutritional health has not received sufficient priority in the development agenda (United Nations, 2012c). In particular, a good nutritional status for the whole population would have a positive impact on economic development.[6]

Over-nutrition

Obesity on the rise

Malnutrition has been traditionally associated with undernourishment; but in recent years, greater attention has been given to overweight (body mass index equal or superior to 25) and obesity (body mass index equal or superior to 30), as a major global public-health concern and a cause of death of at least 2.8 million adults per year (World Health Organization, 2012b). Overweight and obesity are often perceived as higher income economy issues, but in fact they have been on the rise, and at a fast pace, in low- and middle-income countries.

Globally, in 2008, the number of overweight adults reached more than 1.4 billion, surpassing the number of undernourished people worldwide.[7] Almost 13 per cent of the world's population are obese.

The prevalence of overweight and obese individuals varies across the world. Breaking down by World Health Organization (WHO) regions, in the Americas, overweight and obesity affect 62 per cent and 26 per cent of the population, respectively. On the opposite side of the spectrum, in South-East Asia, only 14 per cent of the population are overweight. In Organization for Economic Cooperation and Development (OECD)

Overweight and obesity are often perceived as higher income economy issues, but in fact they have been on the rise, and at a fast pace, in low- and middle-income countries

---

6　See FAO, "Incorporating nutrition considerations into development policies and programes: brief for policy-makers and programme planners in developing countries" (Rome, 2004). Available from http://www.fao.org/docrep/007/y5343e/y5343e04.htm.

7　WHO (2013).

countries for which data exist, the prevalence of obesity varies from 4 per cent in Japan and the Republic of Korea, to 30 per cent or more in the United States of America and Mexico.

Worldwide obesity almost doubled between 1980 and 2008 (figure IV.3). In OECD countries, until 1980, obesity affected less than 10 per cent of the population. Since then, that rate has doubled or tripled in many countries. In 2012, in 19 countries out of 34 OECD countries, the majority of the population was overweight. OECD projections suggest that more than 2 people out of 3 will be overweight or obese in some OECD countries by 2020.

Figure IV.3
Age-standardized prevalence of obesity[a] among adults aged 20 years or over, by WHO region, 1980 and 2008

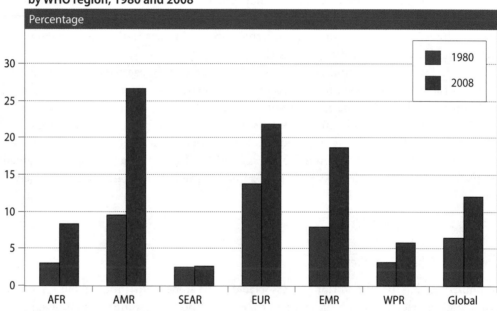

Source: UN/DESA, based on WHO (2012).

a Obesity is defined as a body mass index (BMI) greater than or equal to 30, where BMI is equal to a person's weight in kilograms (kg) divided by the square of his or her height in metres (m²).

Abbreviations: AFR, WHO African region; AMR, WHO Region of the Americas; SEAR, WHO South-East Asia Region; EUR, WHO European Region; EMR, WHO Eastern Mediterranean Region; WPR, WHO Western Pacific Region.

In low- and middle-income countries, the number of overweight children has been increasing. Out of 40 million overweight children worldwide, close to 35 million were living in developing countries in 2010 (Organization for Economic Cooperation and Development, 2012a). Thus, it is not surprising to see health challenges associated with over-nutrition in countries that are still facing the issue of undernourishment. These two dimensions of malnutrition are sometimes experienced within the same household. This is the result of the greater susceptibility to obesity of adults that have suffered from undernourishment during their childhood (Hoffman and others, 2000).

Impacts of over-nutrition

The health consequences of over-nutrition and obesity are quite different from those of hunger. There is an increase in non-communicable diseases instead of infectious and communicable diseases in those affected by over-nutrition and obesity. For instance, excessive consumption of meat (especially red meat), dairy products and eggs by older children and adults can have detrimental health effects and increase the risk of chronic non-communicable diseases such as heart disease, cancer, diabetes and obesity. Excessive consumption of refined sugars and carbohydrates has also been found to be associated with health issues such as diabetes, overweight and obesity.

According to WHO, overweight and obesity are the fifth leading risk factors for global deaths, posing a greater risk than underweight. At least 2.8 million adults die each year as a result of being overweight or obese. Compared with people of normal weight, severely obese people die 8-10 years sooner. Every 15 extra kilograms (kg) increase the risk of early death by approximately 30 per cent. In addition, 44 per cent of the diabetes burden, 23 per cent of the heart disease burden and 7-41 per cent of certain cancer burdens are attributable to overweight and obesity.

Obesity also represents an important source of health expenditure at the individual and macro levels. For instance, in any given year, an obese person incurs 25 per cent higher health expenditures than a person of normal weight. At the macrolevel, obesity accounts for 5-10 per cent of total health expenditures in the United States of America. At the same time, obesity negatively affects personal income. Obese people earn 18 per cent less than people who are not obese (Organization for Economic Cooperation and Development, 2012a).

> According to the World Health Organization, overweight and obesity are the fifth leading risk factors for global deaths, posing a greater risk than underweight

Increasing food availability

In developing countries, where the prevalence of undernourishment is higher and the population is growing faster, food production will need to almost double (Food and Agriculture Organization of the United Nations, 2009c). Therefore, the first concern will be increasing agricultural productivity, in particular in countries where the prevalence of hunger is higher and where large productivity gaps still exist. The main challenge, however, is to increase food production while minimizing the environmental impact and increasing natural resource use efficiency. Finally, food production requires additional investments in rural infrastructure, including in harvest technologies designed to reduce wastage at the production level.

> In order to improve food availability, the first concern will be increasing agricultural productivity, in particular in countries where the prevalence of hunger is higher and where large productivity gaps still exist

Increasing agricultural productivity

Low productivity and slow growth in the agricultural sector, including in small farms, raise specific concerns. Despite some improvements in total factor productivity in the agricultural sector (Fuglie, 2012), growth in yield, an indicator of land productivity, for most cereals has been declining since the 1980s (FAOSTAT). Today, important gaps between farmers' yields and technical potential yields still exist in many developing countries. In 2005, such gaps varied from 11 per cent in countries of East Asia to 76 per cent in sub-Saharan Africa (Food and Agriculture Organization of the United Nations, 2011b). Reducing these gaps would increase agricultural output, and consequently, food security, as well as nutrition outcomes, in many developing countries.

Extension services

The extensive menu of technologies and sustainable practices that are already available can, in part, reduce existing productivity gaps in agriculture. In sub-Saharan Africa for instance, where the prevalence of undernourishment is high, important productivity gains—on the order of a two- to threefold increase in average yields—can be achieved

> The extensive menu of technologies and sustainable practices that are already available can, in part, reduce existing productivity gaps in agriculture

through better use of existing knowledge and technology (Foresight, 2011). Dissemination of information and technical assistance will be an effective strategy for improving access to knowledge and technology. Further, agricultural extension services are a useful tool for helping farmers increase their productivity, and collaborate with a broader network of farmers and researchers. In the current context, a large number of actors (civil society organizations, the private sector, farmers and multilateral organizations) need to contribute towards this end.

A survey conducted by the Global Conference on Agricultural Research for Development (GCARD) 2010 points to the importance of official agricultural extension workers.[8] The general perception is that their number is inadequate, especially when measured against the needs of small-scale farm holders, who have limited access to the services they offer, services that represent an important vehicle for the transmission of knowledge, information and training (Lele and others, 2010).

Thus, a longer-term commitment to training and a new approach to technical education are required. Training and education have to be more practical in nature and oriented towards problem-solving and decision-making. At the same time, they must involve farmers and civil society organizations in finding interdisciplinary and creative solutions to new problems.

Focusing more on building capacity among farmers, in particular smallholders, is a better strategy than prescribing technological practices. The former approach, considered to embody the empowerment model, would help farmers to identify and take advantage of available opportunities (World Bank, 2008a). The exclusion of women from technical support also needs to be explicitly addressed. In Africa, women receive 7 per cent of agricultural extension services and less than 10 per cent of credit offered to small-scale farm holders. Gender analysis and targeted initiatives must be incorporated in agricultural education, research and extension services (Davis and others, 2007).

Increasing investment in R&D

In addition to existing technology and agricultural knowledge which already provide a range of alternatives for achieving better outcomes, continuous research and development in respect of new technologies are needed. In this regard, an important lesson from the previous green revolution is that the development of new technology requires long-term financial support for R&D, in parallel with wide and effective dissemination of information and know-how (United Nations, 2011b).

However, public expenditure for agricultural R&D remains low in many developing regions (figure IV.4), the main reason being that since the 1980s, international support for agriculture research has decreased and many national agricultural research centres have scaled back their programmes for the production and distribution of seeds (Dubin and Brennan, 2009). Thus, national initiatives must be designed to address the lack of investment in R&D, including through partnerships with the private sector.

---

8   While the main function of agricultural extension workers is to provide and transfer knowledge for increasing productivity, they are now increasingly being expected to fulfil a number of new functions, such as linking smallholder farmers to high-value and export markets, promoting environmental outcomes (involving, for example, watersheds, forests and irrigation water), supporting microcredit groups, and coping with the effects of HIV/AIDS and other health challenges (Lele and others, 2010).

Figure IV.4
Public research expenditure on food and agriculture, 1981-2008

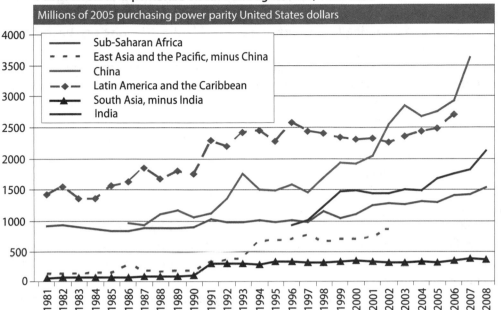

Source: Agricultural Science and Technology Indicators database (http://www.asti. cgiar.org/data/).

In developing countries, where agricultural R&D remains relatively weak, the main focus of the public research institutions should be the adaptation of technology to particular farming conditions and agroecological settings. However, the main challenge in developing countries is their national research institutions' lack of adequate resources. For instance, the development of a new variety of wheat, rice or corn, requires 7-10 years of breeding (Pardey and Beintema, 2001). The resulting discontinuity in funding compromises their independence and capacity to operate efficiently, while poor documentation of processes increases the risk of permanent loss of knowledge.

In addition to securing stable financial resources, national public research centres have to change their organizational culture. They need to improve their responsiveness to the needs of farmers, including through joint experimentation and learning. This requires that research institutions work more closely with farmers and other actors such as non-governmental organizations, farmers organizations and innovation brokers, which can make farmers' needs known to the research and government communities, using innovations made possible by ICT. In this field, participation of women, especially in sub-Saharan Africa where women constitute a large proportion of the agricultural labour force, will also be critical to enhancing their decision-making in agricultural research and extension services and to addressing their specific needs.

Research institutions also need to expand their traditional disciplinary approach to encompass an interdisciplinary focus in response to wide-ranging farmer demands. For instance, transformation of diverse agroecological rural economies requires the expertise of biologists, agronomists, water engineers, nutritionists, economists and social and political scientists (Lipton, 2010).

The private sector has become a more active player in agricultural R&D, but its involvement has not been sufficient to compensate for the reduction in public expenditure. In developing countries, public funding remains the main source of finance for agricultural

In developing countries, where agricultural research and development remains relatively weak, the main focus of the public research institutions should be the adaptation of technology to particular farming conditions and agroecological settings research. Moreover, the private sector tends to invest mainly in profitable research, including agricultural chemical inputs, machinery and biotechnology, targeting wealthier economies and larger farmers. The involvement of private research in managing natural resources and maintaining biodiversity also remains limited (Biodiversity International and others, 2012).

The private sector also can play an important role in promoting rapid technological innovation for achieving food security and tackling climate change. Biotechnology and innovative market access for smallholders constitute one of the areas where the private sector can play a major role in expanding research. Despite the fact that biotechnology remains a controversial issue, it nevertheless holds great potential for increasing agriculture productivity (United Nations, 2011b).

Today, one third of the rural population in developing countries lives in rain-fed regions, characterized by frequent moisture stress, which limits their agricultural output. Biotechnology could be an effective instrument for facilitating the transformation of agriculture in these agroecological regions affected by harsher conditions. It has a significant potential to increase yield gains by making crops herbicide-resistant, less dependent on chemical pesticides and more resilient to water stress, while conferring on them a greater nutritional value.

So far, private research in biotechnology has concentrated on the development of products that can be easily protected by patents and has focused mainly on the demand from large-scale farmers. The cost of seeds and inputs may discourage use of this technology by small farm holders, especially if the market continues to be dominated by a few large companies which exert influence over prices. The potential of genetically modified organisms to increase food production is limited not only by their excessive costs, but also by their unknown possible risks, including long-term environmental and health impacts. Independent assessments of the larger impacts of this technology are urgently needed.

Moving forward, the structure of incentives and the governance of innovation in this area require radical changes. New mechanisms for engaging the private sector need to be explored: results-based performance contracts granted on a competitive basis—for the development, for example, of improved seed or crop varieties with higher water-stress tolerance and greater responsiveness to fertilizers—may be one means of stimulating private research. Patent buyouts and prizes may be other means of doing so (Elliot, 2010; Bhagwati, 2005). Use of more traditional subsidies, co-financing arrangements and joint ventures, within a framework of appropriate protocols for maintaining the public-good nature of research products, could also be explored (Pardey and Beintema, 2001).

Many countries face serious challenges to addressing these complex technological changes. Overcoming these challenges will require the cooperation of the public, private and civil society organization sectors within countries, as well as between countries, towards adapting know-how to specific agricultural conditions (Biodiversity International and others, 2012). CGIAR (formerly the Consultative Group on International Agricultural Research) has a positive record in developing technology well suited for smallholders, although diffusion of these technologies has been a challenge. In 2008, CGIAR was reformed to refocus its research and develop partnerships with the capacity to increase the diffusion of results.

Yet, given the need to adapt technologies to different agroecological systems, CGIAR and other international research institutions must work more closely with national agricultural research centres so that they can adapt internationally developed technologies

Biotechnology could be an effective instrument for facilitating the transformation of agriculture in agroecological regions affected by harsher conditions to their various national contexts and "share back" their innovations with other countries. The growing capacity of large national agricultural systems in Brazil, China, India and South Africa, for instance, has generated South-South cooperation aimed at benefiting countries with limited resources, by allowing them to adopt or adapt the technologies of the countries with large agriculture systems, which are typically less capital-intensive and have less intellectual property rights protection.

Sustainable management of natural resources

An increase in food production will also require integrating sustainable practices, in particular in the use of natural resources. Many of the current agricultural practices have relied on cheap energy and abundant water and land, and are a leading source of greenhouse gas emissions. These practices are now proving unsustainable for the environment and health. At the same time, they have led to substantial productivity losses, thereby posing risks to food security. Thus, agricultural productivity and an efficient use of natural resources, as well as climate-related adaptation and resilience-building, should be part of an integrated policy approach.

Agricultural productivity and an efficient use of natural resources, as well as climate-related adaptation and resilience-building, should be part of an integrated policy approach

Current unsustainable practices

Even if 90 per cent of the growth in crops will come from higher yields, land availability will continue to be crucial for agriculture. Arable land would need to expand by 12 per cent in developing countries by 2050 (Food and Agriculture Organization of the United Nations, 2009a). However, available land for food cultivation has been shrinking, owing to land degradation and competition from other uses, such as urban development and production of non-food crops, like biofuels. In many regions, available agrarian land is constrained, especially when biodiversity and soil degradation are taken into account. Every year, about 12 million hectares of agricultural land are lost owing to land degradation, adding to the billions of hectares that are already degraded (Beddington and others, 2012). Soil degradation not only affects its fertility, reducing agricultural production opportunities, but also has negative effects on the hydrologic cycle, and climate, biodiversity, landscape and other ecosystem services.

Available land for food cultivation has been shrinking, owing to land degradation and competition from other uses, such as urban development and production of non-food crops

There are many factors leading to soil degradation which should be prevented. The excessive use of chemical fertilizers and pesticides is considered the major factor affecting the resilience of land. For instance, in the past 50 years, global fertilizer use increased by 500 per cent, causing widespread pollution (Earth Security Initiative, 2012). Managing the use of fertilizers will be crucial for long-term land development; for example, in the United States, it has been demonstrated that in the long term, organic agricultural methods can outperform conventional chemical farming in terms of crop yield, sustainability and profit (ibid.). While large-scale farming is, in general, identified as the main source of excessive use of fertilizers and soil degradation, land fragmentation and limited farm size can also be a source of soil degradation. In the *minifundias* of the Andean highlands of Latin America for instance, poor small-scale farm holders over-exploit natural resources, owing to population pressure and scarcity of suitable land (United Nations, 2011b).

The urbanization process is also increasing competition for arable land and wetlands. So far, urban areas occupy about 1 per cent of the total land surface (United Nations Environment Programme, 2012a), but urbanization is projected to continue at a fast pace in the next decades (see chap. III). Between 2012 and 2050, the world urban population is expected to increase by 69 per cent. At the same time, renewable energy strategies, such as use of biofuels, are increasing demand for land resources. Hence, developing the potential to create more sustainable land management systems, in order to reverse current trends in food insecurity and unsustainable land degradation, is desirable—and possible (United Nations Environment Programme, 2012a).

It is expected that the increasing and competing demands for water will aggravate the serious depletion of surface-water resources

More recently, the purchase (or long-term lease) of large extensions of land is subjecting use of land for cultivation and local food consumption to pressure (box IV.1). These transactions have raised concern about their implications for rural communities and for the food security of countries already vulnerable to insecure food supplies.[9] Improved national and international oversight mechanisms may be needed to prevent the unintended negative impacts of leasing arrangements for large extensions of land on the food and nutrition security of poor communities.

Box IV.1

Purchase of large extensions of land

The demand for agricultural land intensified at the peak of the food price crisis in 2007-2008. Estimates about the extension of land involved in large-scale acquisitions vary wildly, from 120 million acres, as reported by the World Bank in 2010, to 560 million acres, as reported by Oxfam in 2012.[a] There are many factors explaining the accelerated interest in foreign land. Reportedly, over 60 per cent of foreign investment in land is for food exports and around two thirds of land deals in the last 10 years were made with a view to producing crops for biofuels (Oxfam, 2012, p. 6). In addition, land is also becoming an asset that offers portfolio diversification for international investors, such as large pension funds and financial institutions (Earth Security Initiative, 2012).

There is a large controversy about the recent interest of foreigners in purchasing or leasing large landholdings: some see an opportunity to leverage foreign investment for agriculture and rural development, while others warn against the risk of displacing traditional rural communities and pastoralists from their land, thereby increasing food insecurity in countries already at risk. In countries like Ethiopia, Mali, Mozambique and the Sudan, this development has raised widespread concerns over forced evictions, social vulnerability and dwindling water resources (Earth Security Initiative, 2012). Pearce (2012) found that in countries selling (or leasing) large extensions of land, in the largest majority of cases, local communities lose access to forests, pastures and water resources, with no major gains in employment, owing to the use of capital-intensive technology in large farms.

In the absence of policies and institutions that provide secure tenure and adequate safeguards to domestic smallholders and their communities, large-scale purchases of land may have unintended negative consequences for rural communities and small-scale farmers. Countries such as Argentina and Brazil have already erected legal barriers in relation to the amount of farmland that can be owned by foreigners (Earth Security Initiative, 2012). More recently, United Nations entities (such as the United Nations Conference on Trade and Development, the Food and Agriculture Organization of the United Nations, the International Fund for Agricultural Development and the World Bank) adopted the Principles for Responsible Agricultural Investment with the intention of providing some form of protection to rural dwellers. Globally agreed safeguards to protect the rights of traditional communities, often lacking legal recognition of their rights to land, water and forests, are particularly relevant for countries in sub-Saharan Africa and Latin America where, according to the World Bank, most of the 450 million hectares of "available land"[b] are located.

a Oxfam (2012) recently reported an area of 203 million hectares under consideration or negotiation in 2001-2010 (Oxfam, 2012).

b "Available land" in the World Bank estimates is defined as land that is uncultivated, unforested and productive (World Bank, 2011).

---

9   By some accounts, two thirds of land purchases occur in countries already facing hunger (Oxfam, 2012).

Water is another essential natural resource for agriculture, whose limit of sustainability may have already been reached in many regions. Global water withdrawals have tripled over the last 50 years and water withdrawals for irrigation are expected to increase by almost 11 per cent by 2050 (Food and Agriculture Organization of the United Nations, 2009d). Yet, today, 80 per cent of the world's population lives in areas with high levels of threat to water security, particularly in developing countries (United Nations Environment Programme, 2012b). In addition, it is expected that the increasing and competing demands for water will aggravate the serious depletion of surface-water resources. Water scarcity represents an important challenge for agriculture, which uses 70 per cent of global freshwater.[10]

There are several causes of water scarcity. Intensive agriculture, including livestock production, has become a major factor in water quality degradation (United Nations, 2011b). Excessive use of agrochemicals (pesticides and fertilizers) contaminates waterways. Energy production and climate change are also main causes of water scarcity. For instance, use of traditional sources for energy production results in increased greenhouse gas emissions and climate change, increasing the frequency and intensity of extreme climatic events such as flood and droughts, sea-level rise, and the loss of glacial and polar sea ice, all of which contribute to water scarcity. Alternative solutions, such as utilization of energy sources with lower carbon footprints, can also have implications for the water environment. Hydropower production can contribute to fragmentation of river systems, while the construction of some solar-energy infrastructure consumes significant quantities of water (United Nations Environment Programme, 2012a).

Finally, climate has been changing, mainly owing to the levels of greenhouse gases in the atmosphere, presenting a serious threat to agriculture. Extreme weather events such as droughts and floods, have been affecting food production, with dramatic consequences for various agroecosystems. In the coming decades, it is expected that climate change will continue to have adverse effects on agricultural production. Even a modest climate change of about 2° Celsius can change rainfall patterns, resulting in a shorter growing season and lower agricultural production, particularly in areas that are already hot and dry, for example, in Africa and South Asia (Beddington and others, 2012). Communities already plagued with high levels of food insecurity and environmental degradation are disproportionally affected. In particular, smallholders relying on rain-fed agriculture are more vulnerable to climate change.

There are several factors contributing to the problem of climate change. Current agriculture practices, including land clearing for cultivation and inefficient use of fertilizers and organic residues, constitute one such factor, being responsible for 25-33 per cent of greenhouse gas emissions (Beddington and others, 2012). While agriculture is a major contributor to global greenhouse gas emissions, it can also be part of the solution to the problem of climate change. There is ample room for lowering emissions throughout the food system, through more efficient productive techniques and better demand management. On the production side, climate change can be mitigated through carbon sequestration in both vegetation (forests, for example) and soil. On the demand side, reducing wastage, for instance, will be important (see the sect., entitled "Diets and consumption patterns", below), as well as increasing demand for organic and eco-certified products, which should encourage producers to pay more attention to sustainable practices. Despite international and national awareness of the risks related to climate change, there has so far been limited financial and political support for implementing more sustainable practices.

> Extreme weather events such as droughts and floods have been affecting food production, with dramatic consequences for various agroecosystems

> Adaptation measures involving organic soil nutrient enhancement and other ecologically sound methods—an approach popularly known as climate-smart agriculture—can contribute to reducing greenhouse gas emissions

---

10   See Food and Agriculture Organization of the United Nations (2009b).

Improving management of natural resources

Improving agricultural outcomes will therefore require an integrated approach which promotes the resource efficiency of the whole agriculture and food system, while mitigating its environmental impacts. In this regard, government policies can foster an agricultural innovation system approach to developing a comprehensive policy framework for innovation, which can respond to the double challenge of increasing agricultural productivity and achieving environmental sustainability (United Nations, 2011b).

The Southern Agricultural Growth Corridor of the United Republic of Tanzania (SAGCOT) exemplifies such an integrated approach. The Growth Corridor brings together the capabilities and resources of businesses, government and civil society within a common platform in order to overcome the country's various ecosystems barriers to achieving the triple objective of agricultural productivity, food security and livelihoods creation in a sustainable manner. By encompassing the entire agricultural value chain, the SAGCOT approach attempts not just to raise agricultural productivity but to ensure the necessary infrastructure, policy environment and access to knowledge required to create an efficient, well-functioning agricultural value chain.

Traditional practices have recently also gained in importance within the context of adaptation to climate change. For instance, local farmers and communities have shown a great capacity to innovate in response to weather and other shocks. There are thousands of successful experiences of localized enhanced pest and weed management, water efficiency and biodiversity, including stories of highly successful innovation in the most challenging circumstances characterized by a poor natural resource base and widespread poverty.[11] Traditional practices, such as low-tillage farming, crop rotation and interplanting, water harvesting and recycling, water-efficient cropping, and integrated pest management, have also proved their relevance to increasing productivity and ensuring environmental sustainability.

Agricultural research should also consider the climatic, soil and water conditions of the relevant agroecological region. Adaptation measures involving organic soil nutrient enhancement and other ecologically sound methods—an approach popularly known as climate-smart agriculture—can contribute to reducing greenhouse gas emissions. As noted above, there is much interest in the climate change mitigation potential of carbon sequestration, in both vegetation (forests in particular) and soil (United Nations, 2011b). The use of ICT and better access to information facilitate the transition to precision agriculture adapted to different agroecological regions. For instance, using satellite-based remote monitoring and in-field sensing technologies is of great help in the global and regional monitoring of crop productivity and weather-related impacts.

Investments in rural infrastructures

Addressing the structural constraints on food production and distribution within a wider framework of sustainable natural resource management will require investments in infrastructure in rural areas

In respect of addressing the structural constraints on food production and distribution within a wider framework of sustainable natural resource management, investments in infrastructure in rural areas will also be determinant. In particular, small farm holders in developing countries face limited access to output markets, which affects the efficiency of their farming. As a result of the existence of such inefficiencies, an opportunity is missed to increase agricultural output. This is especially regrettable since most of the findings

---

11   See United Nations (2011b) for a more elaborate discussion of this topic.

presented in the literature dealing with agricultural development in low-income countries indicate that small farm units tend to show higher productivity than large-scale farms.[12]

In agriculture-based countries, in sub-Saharan Africa and South Asia in particular, the priority should be expansions of basic infrastructure such as roads, electricity supply and potable water. In many African countries, for instance, transportation can account for 50-60 per cent of total marketing costs. Improving road connections is thus crucial for bringing marketing costs down and stimulating local economies (World Bank, 2008a).

By addressing long-term structural constraints on food production, investments in physical infrastructure can be a catalyst of productivity growth. In poor agriculture-based countries, public investment will also play an important role in leveraging private investment, which will otherwise not flow in sufficient amounts to meet needs, owing to the perception that agricultural production is high-risk. Larger public investment in infrastructure will provide greater incentives to increase private investment within a wider framework of sustainable natural resource management.

The case of Uganda (box IV.2) not only provides a good illustration of the potentially large impact that public infrastructure can have in increasing productivity, but also raises important questions about the larger macroeconomic impacts of increasing government expenditures and the need to take into account the trade-offs involved in this decision. Carefully crafted strategies for achieving food security will require national consensus and the political will to prioritize investments, as well as greater government capacities to stimulate large productivity gains through sustainable finance. Development cooperation would have an important role in at least two areas: (a) support for development of capacity, especially within least developed countries, to conduct policy assessments, and (b) provision of additional resources for infrastructure development. Enhancing the outreach and volume of resources in the Aid for Trade initiative for infrastructure development would make an outstanding contribution to achieving the objective of sustainable food security.

In some countries, the focus should also be on crop harvesting technologies, as significant wastage occurs at the producer end and before reaching the market, owing to inadequate harvesting techniques (Institution of Mechanical Engineers, 2013). The amount of food wasted represents not only an economic cost but, more importantly, a waste of energy and natural resources. As mechanized harvested systems are implemented, food distribution and storage systems will need to be improved in parallel. Access to affordable energy and cooling systems, for instance, could provide storage options and also facilitate their installation by smaller scale farmers, isolated from markets, which would ultimately increase food availability throughout the whole year.

> In some countries, the focus should also be on crop harvesting technologies, as significant wastage occurs at the producer end and before reaching the market

Many developing countries, especially those with an agriculture-based economy, will need external support to increase their investments in infrastructure. In 2010, the international community launched the Global Agriculture and Food Security Programme (GAFSP), which, among several activities, has been channelling long-term investments in food and nutrition security. However, this Programme is costly and has required a high level of funding that has not become available. Of the $1.2 billion pledged, $752 million have already been received, of which $658 million have been allocated to country-led programmes in 18 countries. More funds should be provided, however, to help implement these strategies and support the development of new ones so as to reinforce the resilience of the food production system.

---

12 These advantages may disappear for certain crops whose cultivation benefits from significant economies of scale and input-intensive technologies.

Box IV.2

Infrastructure's potential to drive productivity and sustainable food production: the case of Uganda

Uganda is a low-income country with severe deficits in physical infrastructure, where agriculture still generates about 23 per cent of GDP, which is relatively high compared with an average of 12 per cent in sub-Saharan Africa. Several policy scenarios illustrate the potential of Government investments in physical infrastructure to drive productivity growth and enhance food production capacity. These scenarios are compared with a baseline that delineates a continuation of currently expected economic growth and public spending interventions up to 2030.[a]

Public spending in agriculture infrastructure, mostly for irrigation projects, represents only 0.7 per cent of Uganda's GDP under the baseline. The first scenario assumes an increase of public investment in agriculture by the Government equivalent to 2 percentage points of GDP over the period 2016-2030. As a result, factor productivity growth in agriculture—of about 2.4 per cent per year under the baseline—is pushed up by an additional 1.3 percentage points per year during the period 2016-2030. Consequently, agricultural output growth increases by about 1.5 percentage points per year. In a second round of effects, public spending spurs export growth and a higher level of household consumption, especially of agricultural goods, but the results are also favourable at the national level (see table).

These results support the idea that public investment in agriculture infrastructure contributes to productivity gains. While investments in other public infrastructure, mainly roads and electricity supply, also yield positive results, they are relatively less significant in magnitude, particularly for agriculture, compared with the results under the first three scenarios.

The main concern for policymakers is how to finance the new investments in infrastructure. The financing requirements could create undesirable macroeconomic hardships and may be politically unattainable. In the case of Uganda, for example, the scenarios show that financing new infrastructures through higher direct-tax revenues spurs GDP growth and household consumption relatively less than does, for example, financing them through foreign resources. However, the use of foreign resources affects export growth negatively, owing to real exchange rate appreciation. In addition to these macroeconomic hardships, other factors, like debt sustainability, (declining) support from foreign donors and the issue of the real feasibility of raising tax burdens, need to be taken into consideration as well when defining a financing strategy.

According to these simulations, the ideal scenario entails the creation of fiscal space by reducing other government expenditures, which avoids the said macroeconomic trade-offs. The feasibility of this scenario will depend, however, on the political conditions for improving the efficiency of government spending and/or reallocating resources towards the agricultural sector.

a The scenarios have been generated using a dynamic economy-wide modelling framework known as the Maquette for MDG Simulations (MAMS) (Lofgren, Cicowiez and Díaz-Bonilla, 2013), which involves, inter alia, a microeconomic analysis of determinants of productivity growth where the stock of public infrastructure is one of the key drivers at underlying country-specific elasticity values. Uganda's baseline scenario was first generated for the period 2007-2015 by national researchers and Government experts, with technical support from UN/DESA and the World Bank (Matovu and others, 2013). UN/DESA extended this scenario up to 2030 for the analysis presented here.

Improving access to food

Investments in food production systems need to be complemented by programmes designed to increase the incomes of the poor, as well as by social protection and safety nets

Although crucial to improving nutrition outcomes, improving food availability is not sufficient to ensure access to food. Food insecurity is more often the result of limited access to food. As explained by A. Sen (1981), "starvation is a matter of some people not having enough food to eat, and not a matter of there being not enough food to eat". Thus, investments in food production systems need to be complemented by programmes designed to increase the incomes of the poor, as well as social protection and safety nets. At the international level, measures also have to be taken to prevent excessive food price volatility and to ensure that a pro-food security trade system is in place.

Box IV.2 (cont'd)

Uganda: selected real macro indicators under simulation scenarios, 2016-2030

Annual average growth rate				
	Baseline	Direct-tax revenue	Foreign transfers	Allocative efficiency
Irrigation systems				
Agriculture				
GDP	5.3	6.6	6.5	6.7
Exports of agricultural goods	3.5	7.3	6.2	7.0
Household consumption of agricultural goods	5.0	5.4	5.8	5.8
National				
GDP	7.0	7.2	7.6	7.4
Exports of goods and services	7.0	7.8	7.0	8.0
Household consumption	6.5	6.2	7.0	6.9
Roads and electricity supply				
Agriculture				
GDP	5.3	5.5	5.5	5.6
Exports of agricultural goods	3.5	4.1	3.6	3.7
Household consumption of agricultural goods	5.0	5.0	5.2	5.2
National				
GDP	7.0	7.1	7.4	7.2
Exports of goods and services	7.0	7.3	6.9	7.6
Household consumption	6.5	6.2	6.8	6.7

Source: UN/DESA, based on an updated version of MAMS for Uganda, presented initially in Matovu and others (2013).

Note: In non-baseline scenarios, the Government generates the fiscal space needed to expand investments in infrastructure by 2 percentage points of GDP above the baseline in 2016-2030. The new investments are financed through higher direct-tax revenues, foreign transfers or allocative efficiency of government spending achieved by reducing "wasteful" spending or "overlapping" government functions.

Limited access to food

Income poverty is obviously a main underlying factor preventing access to food. For instance, when comparing the highest and the lowest income quintiles of the population in developing countries, the poorer children are almost 3 times more likely to be underweight than children in the wealthiest 20 per cent of households (United Nations, 2012c). Hence, increasing the income level of poor households will help ensure adequate food quantity and quality, and reduce the prevalence of undernourishment. However, in many regions and countries, economic growth has not been inclusive enough to provide employment and income-earning opportunities for the poor.

Increasing the income level of poor households will help ensure adequate food quantity and quality, and reduce the prevalence of undernourishment

As many poor people live in rural areas, it is not surprising that it is in those areas that the prevalence of undernourishment is also higher. For instance, in developing regions, children living in rural areas are almost twice as likely to be underweight than children in urban households (ibid.). Therefore, economic growth should generate demand for the assets controlled by the poor (Food and Agriculture Organization of the United Nations, 2012b), in particular the rural poor.

Among the rural poor, the situation of small farm holders is at the heart of the food security challenge. Small farmers face limited resources and assets, either for purchasing or for producing the quantity of food that is adequate to their needs. Empirically, it has been observed that the majority of the extremely poor and about half of the undernourished people in the world, which includes 1.5 billion people in least developed countries, live on small farms of less than two hectares, representing 90 per cent of farms worldwide (United Nations, 2011b). Further, according to the most recent data, average farm sizes are still declining in many countries, for example, in Africa, and in India (World Bank, 2008a).

Thus, addressing the issue of food availability and undernourishment in rural areas necessarily implies responding to the challenges faced by smallholders. In particular, high inequality in distribution of assets—such as land, water, capital, education and health care—is a main obstacle which needs to be addressed so as to enhance food security. This is particularly evident in countries where large farms have been controlling a larger proportion of the land, while exacerbating the asset squeeze on smallholders (ibid.).

Discrimination against women in the rural sector also has a negative impact on the outcomes of efforts to secure access to food and nutrition. Women make up over 40 per cent of the agricultural workforce in Africa and East and South Asia, but they constitute only 5 per cent of landholders in Northern and West Africa, 15 per cent in sub-Saharan Africa and 25 per cent in several countries in Latin America. Women have restricted access not only to land but also to credit and technology, which increases their economic vulnerability and the instability of their situation with respect to nutrition. These restrictions imposed on women exacerbate gender discrepancies with regard to nutrition, with serious intergenerational effects, as nutrition in children under age 5 depends critically on the nutrition of their mothers during pregnancy and lactation (Horton, 2008; Copenhagen Consensus, 2008).

> High inequality in the distribution of assets—such as land, water, capital, education and healthcare—is a main obstacle which needs to be addressed so as to enhance food security

Generating income in rural areas

The ability to generate income for the rural poor will be a main determinant of food security. Generating an increase in agricultural productivity is an important strategy for increasing food availability, but it may not improve access to food of a large portion of the population, including vulnerable social groups.

Improving agricultural income

A successful strategy for increasing rural households' income entails promoting the diversification of their farming activities. When comparing households relying on more diversified farming activities with those that remain engaged in more traditional farming, it is evident that the former are more successful in moving out of poverty. In Uganda, for instance, the combination of higher productivity of land and diversification of crops, in particular cash crops, has led to lower rural poverty (World Bank, 2008a).

> A successful strategy for increasing rural households' income entails promoting the diversification of their farming activities

In addition, a diversified farming system, integrating, for instance, horticulture and livestock, can enhance nutritional outcomes, as it improves rural households' access to foods from animal sources, fruits and vegetables. In Viet Nam, for example, the vegetation, aquaculture, and cages for animal Husbandry (VAC) system, which includes a diversified farming system at the household level, has contributed to improvements in both incomes and nutritional outcomes, in terms of consumption of foods from animal sources and fruits and vegetables (Food and Agriculture Organization of the United Nations, 2013). This experience shows that integrated farming projects can be particularly successful in raising micronutrient intake, in addition to improving income stability.

However, a main challenge is the unequal access to rural assets, which prevent many households from adopting market-oriented strategies and moving out of poverty. There are gaps in the institutional structure required for the operation of land markets, financial services, input markets and producer organizations. An appropriate institutional setting is also crucial for supporting small-scale farming, so as to increase agricultural investment and productivity, while preserving natural resources. Improving women's access, for instance, to several assets, such as land, input markets and technology, could increase agricultural production by as much as 2.5-4.0 per cent, thereby reducing the number of undernourished people by 12-17 per cent, equivalent to freeing 100 million-150 million people from hunger (Food and Agriculture Organization of the United Nations, 2011b).

Moreover, flexible land management and the capacity to innovate in production, storage and marketing practices and techniques require the appropriate use of information and technology, as part of a continuous learning process (Davis and others, 2007). Therefore, rapid expansion of quality education in rural areas, including adult literacy and training, should receive the highest priority in any strategy aimed at strengthening farmers' capacity for response to rapidly changing market conditions. Innovative mechanisms for the transmission of knowledge and training also need to be strengthened. The experience of the Farmer Field Schools—operating in 87 countries—shows that innovation and flexible natural resource management can be advanced through farmer-to-farmer learning, including participation in formal and informal research institutions. In-service and on-the-job training and distance education have also proved effective and are increasingly complementing extension services (United Nations, 2011b).

> Adult literacy and training should be a priority in any strategy aimed at strengthening farmers' capacity for response to rapidly changing market conditions

Non-farm economy

As has been extensively documented, many rural households complement their own agricultural activity with non-farm sources of income. In agriculture-based economies, the share of rural income derived from non-agricultural sources may be only 20-30 per cent, but in urbanizing economies, it can be as high as 60-70 per cent (Food and Agriculture Organization of the United Nations, 2012b). That is to say, many rural households diversify their source of income by dividing their time and labour units between farming and non-farm activities.

Thus, in agriculture-based countries, growth in the agriculture sector can be complemented by non-farm activities, creating a virtuous cycle of rural growth and employment generation (ibid.). However, as noted above (see the previous sect. on increasing food availability), developing rural infrastructure and improving rural-urban linkages will also be important for promoting additional sources of revenue. For instance, stimulating rural-urban migration will help in diversifying the income sources of the household and reducing poverty, particularly in urbanizing economies. In China, for instance, the existence of areas of high population density combined with lower transport costs has stimulated labour-intensive manufacturing for export markets using the labour force from rural areas (ibid.).

Rural development strategies should enhance opportunities for smallholders to diversify their agricultural as well as non-farm activities

Moving forward, rural development strategies should enhance opportunities for smallholders to diversify their agricultural as well as non-farm activities. These strategies can at the same time reduce rural poverty and under-nutrition. First, they can enable households to both diversify their sources of income, by incorporating more cash crops in their agricultural production, and secure higher-productivity jobs outside the agricultural sector. Second, they can lead to direct improvement of nutritional conditions through enhanced access to a more diversified source of nutrients.

However, access to assets, individuals' skills and migration opportunities will all be determining factors in the process of moving out of rural poverty. Infrastructural as well as institutional changes will be necessary to ensure access to rural assets, such as land and water. Access to education will also be crucial to ensuring that the rural poor and specific social groups, such as women, can take advantage of new income opportunities.

Social security and safety nets

As discussed above, one of the main obstacles to achieving food security is the lack of access to food, in particular among lower-income groups which lack the necessary purchasing power. The 2007-2008 food price crisis exacerbated the problem of food accessibility and nutrition outcomes, in particular for poor people, who spend 50-70 per cent of their income on food. A social protection system, including safety nets, can protect the most vulnerable against short-term economic and food price shocks. Several large countries were able to protect consumers by insulating their markets from international price shocks with additional safety net programmes. Social protection can also contribute to long-term resilience by facilitating access to food and by strengthening the ability of smallholders to manage risks and adopt new technologies with higher productivity (Food and Agriculture Organization of the United Nations, 2012a). The types of social protection instruments will vary depending on national social needs, development objectives and fiscal space.

Safety nets in the short term

In the short term, emergency food assistance and safety nets are effective tools for meeting urgent food needs and protecting the most vulnerable against price and climatic shocks

As regards short-term relevance, emergency food assistance and safety nets are effective tools for meeting urgent food needs and protecting the poor and the most vulnerable against price or climatic shocks. Safety nets include community support systems, transfers (direct and indirect), subsidies, public works and microcredit. For instance, in the aftermath of the 2007-2008 food price crisis, 23 countries introduced or expanded cash transfer programmes, 19 countries introduced food assistance programmes and 16 countries increased disposable income measures (Food and Agriculture Organization of the United Nations, 2009c). Multiple solutions are possible, but, in general, scaling up existing social protection interventions has proved to be the best strategy for facing urgent challenges.

An adequate safety net can also ensure a basic level of consumption, which enables poorer farmers to assume the higher risks associated with higher-return strategies, which, potentially, could break the vicious circle of poverty and hunger. Public works (or cash for work) programmes, such as India's National Employment Guarantee Scheme, represent typical employment-based safety nets which entitle individuals to a minimal amount of work and income, while they contribute to labour-intensive infrastructure development projects (Food and Agriculture Organization of the United Nations, 2009c). These employment programmes can also incorporate training components, thereby enhancing human capital at the local level.

Social security in the long term

Long-term resilience and food security will require a more comprehensive social security system. The main goal should be to establish systematic and predictable programmes, targeting specific social groups, including the poor and smallholders, which can enhance human capital and stimulate the adoption of new technologies. For instance, nutrition intervention in early childhood, especially in the first thousand days, can lead to higher adult economic productivity. In Guatemala, a study showed that children who had received nutritional supplements before reaching the age of 3 earned hourly wages as adults that were 46 per cent higher (Food and Agriculture Organization of the United Nations, 2012b).

> Long-term resilience and food security will require a more comprehensive social security system

Much has been learned about how best to design social protection floors, how to determine which combinations of plans work and where, and how to target them. The international community can provide assistance to developing countries in designing such plans in a cost-effective time-bound manner so as to realize the right to food, as well as stimulate rural development, agricultural production and poverty alleviation. Support should also be offered to help integrate the social protection floor plan within the national agricultural strategies. The leaders of the G20, at their 2012 Summit, recognized the importance of establishing nationally determined social protection floors. They are being endorsed within International Labour Organization conference processes, which could support national efforts. The international community may also need to help the least developed countries finance their own social protection programmes.

A pro-food security international trade system

In today's interdependent world, the implementation of national strategies to improve access to food also requires concrete actions at the global level. As observed during the 2007-2008 food price crisis, higher food prices deeply affected nutrition and macroeconomic conditions of net food importing countries, especially in sub-Saharan Africa (Food and Agriculture Organization of the United Nations, 2011d), in part owing to a shortage of the foreign currency required to increase food imports. Conditions promoting trade and food market transparency needed to reduce price distortions and volatility will be crucial to stimulating staple food production at the local level and ensuring access to food at the same time.

> Conditions promoting trade and food market transparency needed to reduce price distortions and volatility will be crucial to stimulating staple food production at the local level and ensuring access to food at the same time

The trade system

Agricultural trade is potentially a pathway for GDP growth, lower rural poverty and food security. However, global markets have been working in favour of major production companies and some food exporting countries, often to the detriment of small landholders. The main challenge for the international trade system is to become more food security-oriented, in particular as regards food importing countries. For instance, the export subsidies and import protection granted by developed countries continue to create price distortions in global food markets, with large negative consequences for developing countries. As a result, several countries have reduced investment in their agriculture sector. In this regard, as suggested in the specific proposals for the review of World Trade Organization rules, the trade system should be flexible in order to protect non-traded agricultural sectors that are vital to food security.

In food exporting countries, export restrictions must be disciplined, as agreed at the G20 Cannes Summit in 2011 within the context of food crisis situations. Export restrictions provide a disincentive to farmers to invest in food production and undermine progress towards multilateral trade reforms and freer trade in the agriculture sector. At the same time, in food importing countries, import and domestic taxes on food must be temporarily reduced, especially when taxes constitute a significant proportion of the final price. For instance, tax reductions could be a better option than a subsidy programme, despite some of the negative effects on public revenue.

In the longer run, a fairer international trading system, taking into account the food security, livelihood security and rural development needs of developing countries, will be crucial. For instance, in higher-income countries, agricultural trade distortions need to be eliminated, in particular subsidies and market restrictions, which have devastating consequences for farmers in lower-income countries. In this regard, the Doha Round of World Trade Organization negotiations should be completed, with the Marrakesh Ministerial Decision on Measures Concerning the Possible Negative Effects of the Reform Programme on Least Developed and Net Food-importing Developing Countries[13] assisting countries in the implementation process.

Food security stocks and information transparency

Maintaining food stocks at the global and regional levels is an additional useful mechanism not only for improving emergency access to food, but also for stabilizing food prices. A certain level of world stock could be a sufficient condition for price stability (Committee on World Food Security, High-level Panel of Experts on Food Security and Nutrition, 2011). Supporting and improving access to these stocks can enhance food security and prevent humanitarian crises in countries under emergency conditions. These stocks should, however, target lower-income countries and be released strategically to support programmes that facilitate food access to the most vulnerable populations. In this regard, the High-level Panel of Experts on Food Security and Nutrition of the Committee on World Food Security made two important recommendations on how to maintain a minimum level of world stocks and ultimately reduce food insecurity.

Pursuant to those recommendations, first, there is need for better information, with the creation of a transparent and coordinated food market information system. The elimination of most public stocks in OECD countries and the privatization of most State-trading enterprises have concentrated knowledge concerning agricultural commodity availability in the hands of a small number of companies which maintain this information as proprietary. One of the most important elements of the Action Plan on Food Price Volatility, agreed by the G20 Agriculture Ministers at their meeting held in Paris on 22 and 23 June 2011, was the launching of the Agricultural Market Information System (AMIS) to improve market information and transparency of data on current stocks, and promote coordination of policy responses (see Ministerial declaration, para. 26). The High-level Panel of Experts at the same time recommended that given the importance of

> Maintaining food stocks at the global and regional levels is an additional useful mechanism for improving emergency access to food and stabilizing food prices

> There is need for better information, with the creation of a transparent and coordinated food market information system

---

13   See *Legal Instruments Embodying the Results of the Uruguay Round of Multilateral Trade Negotiations, done at Marrakesh on 15 April 1994* (GATT secretariat publication, Sales No. GATT/1994-7).

food insecurity, trading firms should be mandated to report on stocks instead of being allowed to do so voluntarily. AMIS market information should also be extended to include food crops other than the usual global cereals, including livestock and fish. Second, assuming the role traditionally played by the United States of America and China as stock holders, the international community should maintain a minimum level of world food stock. The objective would not be to defend a price band but rather to avert price spikes through the release of stock when prices started to boom.

In addition, increasing food reserves managed by the World Food Programme (WFP) could reduce delivery time and costs when a situation reaches crisis level. Since WFP usually relies on cash to purchase food for its work, upward price spikes limit the quantity of food it can purchase and its ability to respond to human needs. In order to fill these gaps, including delivery time, WFP initiated a regional stocking programme in 2008—the Forward Purchase Facility—in Eastern and Southern Africa. This system offered several advantages, such as more accurate provision due to reduced time lags between requests and provision, and could be expanded to other regions. However, the lack of funding, and of available advance financing in particular, constitutes a major constraint on expanding this pilot project.

Diets and consumption patterns

Nutrition outcomes are largely determined not only by food production and accessibility but also by food quality and diversity. A considerable potential for increasing the nutritional status of people and the efficiency of the whole food chain lies in encouraging changes in diet and consumption patterns, as well as designing pro-nutrition policies in other sectors, such as health and education. In addition, reducing food losses is a cost-effective means of increasing the availability of safe and nutritious food for all. Preventing food wastage would also reduce the challenge of how to increase production in a world with limited natural resources.

Sustainable diets

The challenge of feeding a rising and increasingly affluent population also requires behavioural changes in terms of consumption, including dietary patterns. In particular, the livestock sector, which has grown rapidly to meet the increasing demand for meat, is a prime contribution to water scarcity, pollution, land degradation and greenhouse gas emissions. This has prompted calls for support of more sustainable diets with a more balanced content of calories derived from animal food. While the caloric content of meat is, on average, not substantially higher than that of cereals, meat production is much more demanding in terms of natural resources. On average, grain-meat conversion ratios, i.e., the number of kilograms of cereals needed to produce one kilogram of poultry or beef ranges from 2 to 1 for poultry all the way up to 7 to 1 for beef (United Nations Convention to Combat Desertification, 2012).

Consumption by an increasingly affluent population in 2050 will exacerbate pressures on the use of land and water and increase greenhouse gas emissions from agriculture (see previous sect. on increasing food availability). A decrease in the consumption of meat through adoption of more sustainable diets can lead to a substantial reduction in the use of land and other natural resources, thus improving the prospects of sustainable development, as illustrated in box IV.3.

A decrease in the consumption of meat can lead to a substantial reduction in the use of land and other natural resources, thus improving the prospects for sustainable development

Health and education policies to enhance nutrition security

There is a strong consensus that better nutrition will also require pro-nutrition policies in other, related sectors. Public policies and programmes designed to improve health, water and sanitation services will be particularly important. Increasing individuals' awareness of the benefits of healthier diets, through information campaigns and educational programmes, is also relevant. A multifaceted approach to improving the nutritional status of people,

---

Box IV.3

Sustainable diets and reduced food waste

The Food and Agriculture Organization of the United Nations (FAO) has estimated that meat consumption in 2050 will amount approximately to 4.65 billion tons. Poultry meat consumption level is expected to be 2.3 times higher than in 2010, while consumption of other livestock products is expected to be between 1.4 and 1.8 times higher (Food and Agriculture Organization of the United Nations, 2009d). The world's average daily calorie availability is projected to rise from an average of 2,789 kilocalories per person in 2000 to 3,130 kilocalories per person in 2050, a 12 per cent increase. Further, current food waste is around 30-50 per cent of total production (Food and Agriculture Organization of the United Nations, 2011d; Institution of Mechanical Engineers, 2013).

Using the T21 model,[a] the Millennium Institute simulated the impact of reducing meat consumption and food waste on the demand for land.[b] The simulation assumes an overall reduction in the consumption of meat to provide 500 calories per capita per day in 2050 (down from the 620 projected by FAO). In addition, food waste and loss are assumed to decrease slightly from the current 32 per cent of total production to 30 per cent. These two assumptions result in a substantial reduction in harvested area, from an estimated 1.31 billion hectares required in 2050 to 1.065 billion hectares, a savings of almost 20 per cent in respect of the demand for harvested land.

While the changes projected do not seem ambitious, much larger changes will have to occur in each country, according to their starting point. For meat consumption, it is assumed that there is a global convergence towards the current world average of 500 calories per capita per day from animal food, which would require an increase in the consumption of animal food in low-income countries in Africa, the Caribbean and Asia and a reduction in the consumption of animal food in high-income countries in Europe, North America and Oceania of 30-35 per cent.

Similarly, the projected decrease of food waste and loss, from the current 32 per cent to approximately 30 per cent by 2050 is based on the assumption of a global convergence towards a level of about 200 kilograms per capita per year. This allows for some slight increase in food waste and loss in low-income countries (mainly driven by an expected substantial increase in production), a gradual decrease of food waste and loss in middle-income countries, and a more drastic reduction in high-income countries.

While these results demonstrate that even a conservative change in global consumption patterns will yield significant reductions in the demand for harvested land, with consequent lower pressure on the use of water, soil nutrients and energy, they also indicate that even small steps towards improving the use of available resources require major changes at country level, in the way that food is produced, transported and consumed.

The available policy options for inducing these changes are largely country-specific and require a large degree of coordination and consistency across multiple policy areas, with agriculture, health and education being the most obvious. Achieving an understanding of the policy instruments available to countries for inducing a change in diets within different contexts requires further research and policy experimentation. Policy instruments such as taxing meat products or refined sugars and carbohydrates to discourage unhealthy diets, educational programmes, mandating corporate social responsibility and labelling standards, production disincentives for meats and production incentives for whole grain cereals, vegetables and fruits, etc., need to be tested against the overall objective of promoting (and enabling) the adoption of sustainable diets.

Source: UN/DESA, based on Millennium Institute, "Global food and nutrition scenarios", background paper prepared for the *World Economic and Social Survey 2013* (2013).

a The T21 model is a dynamic simulation tool designed to support comprehensive, integrated long-term national development planning.

b In addition to the simulation presented in this box, the Millennium Institute designed three more simulation scenarios with different assumptions on changes in consumption and waste patterns. For a full discussion of the results, see Millennium Institute, "Global food and nutrition scenarios", background paper prepared for the *World Economic and Social Survey 2013* (2013).

including in preventing overconsumption and obesity, is essential. Hence, health and educational policies need to incorporate nutrition-related considerations in their programmes.

Health

Nutrition and health are inextricable, as a good nutritional status can be achieved only within the context of overall conditions of good health. For instance, in developing countries, access to basic health services is often inadequate owing to an insufficient number of health centres and qualified personnel. The resulting poor health conditions and illnesses, such as measles and gastroenteritis, will then have a negative impact on nutritional status. Similarly, the lack of safe water and of adequate sanitation leads to many diseases and illnesses, while compromising the nutritional status of people.

A multisectoral approach to improving the nutritional status of people, including in preventing overconsumption and obesity, is essential

Thus, health policies should include preventive health and hygiene measures, which are essential for good nutrition, as well as ensure that nutrition components are part of their programme. In developing countries, access to health-care facilities and services for the poor, particularly women and children, has positive impacts on the nutritional status of individuals (Food and Agriculture Organization of the United Nations, 2004). In particular, as has been emphasized on many occasions, the first thousand days of life are crucial for children's survival, as well as being a determinant for their nutrition and health status as adults. For instance, infants and small children should be breastfed exclusively up to the age of six months. After those first six months and for up to two years, breastfeeding should be complemented with safe and nutritious foods for infants (Food and Agriculture Organization of the United Nations, 2013).

Considering the negative effects of both under- and over-nutrition on health throughout life stages (see previous sect. on the multiple dimensions of malnutrition), health and nutrition must be part of a life-course approach, in particular for the prevention of chronic diseases. First, healthier diets and physical activity should be part of preventive measures to reduce negative health consequences in the long term. Second, national health policies need to strengthen health systems, enabling them to respond more effectively and equitably to health-care needs (World Health Organization, 2008).

Health systems need to be strengthened to respond more effectively and equitably to the health-care needs of people throughout the life course and prevent negative health consequences

Information campaigns and educational programmes

In the case of lower-income groups in developing countries, the income elasticity of demand for dietary energy is positive and greater than for other income groups (Food and Agriculture Organization of the United Nations, 2012a). However, as income increases, there is a tendency to purchase more expensive foods, based on taste preferences, which may not improve nutrition outcomes. In many cases, individuals are unaware of the health problems associated with consuming certain types of foods, as well as of the importance of certain micronutrients. In developed countries, people may be unaware of the health problems associated with a less diversified diet and consumption of specific foods. In countries where overweight and obesity have increased, diets have typically shifted towards higher intake of energy-dense foods which are high in fat, salt and sugars but low in vitamins, minerals and other micronutrients.

Thus, education programmes can improve the health and nutritional status of the population in general, and of women and children in particular. Women with better education are more aware of the importance of adequate diets and can secure access to better-paying jobs. Several studies have shown that women with higher income

In developed countries, it has been observed that poorly educated women are 2-3 times more likely to be overweight than those with high levels of education and greater bargaining power within the family exert a more positive influence on child nutrition, health and education outcomes (Food and Agriculture Organization of the United Nations, 2013). In developed countries, it has been observed that poorly educated women are 2-3 times more likely to be overweight than those with high levels of education (Organization for Economic Cooperation and Development, 2012a). Although the link between education, knowledge and dietary intake is not clear, the impact of education and knowledge is most evident when those at highest risk are considered (Food and Agriculture Organization of the United Nations, 2013).

Inculcating basic knowledge of good nutrition, including family nutrition practices, in primary and secondary schools, can help individuals make informed dietary choices. Nutrition education could be included in the school curriculum and offered in community centres targeting adults. Recent evaluations of various school-based nutrition education programmes in Italy and Portugal showed that those programmes had positive impacts in terms of both attitudes and consumption and health outcomes (ibid.). In particular, nutritional education for women has a positive impact in terms of dietary intake and malnutrition (ibid.). Yet, in many developing countries, gender discrimination preventing school enrolment of girls is still a challenge, which ultimately has negative impacts on nutrition outcomes.

Dietary guidelines constitute one example of the public information tools used in many countries which should be encouraged

In addition to education, information and nutrition advocacy can also have positive impacts on population conditions related to nutrition. Strategies aimed at influencing consumer choice based on enhanced consumer awareness and knowledge should also be considered, as they may lead to a change in consumption habits. Dietary guidelines constitute one example of the public information tools used in many countries which should be encouraged. Information and communications measures are particularly relevant to preventing obesity. However, nutrition-related messages must be appropriate in order to be effective. They should be delivered by health professionals, among others, through a variety of channels and over an extended period of time.

Consumption patterns: reducing waste

Globally, approximately one third of the total food produced for consumption, amounting to 1.3 billion tons per year, is lost or wasted (Food and Agriculture Organization of the United Nations, 2012c). Because of food waste, an opportunity is lost to reduce malnutrition and significant unnecessary pressure is imposed on natural resources, including through greenhouse gas emissions caused by production of food. There are several sources of food wastage throughout the supply chain, from initial agricultural production down to final household consumption (figure IV.5). This section examines food wastage occurring at the consumption end is examined, along with the underlying factors associated with different socioeconomic and agricultural development conditions.

The amount of food wasted in developed countries is higher than that in developing countries. Recent estimations show that the weight of food wasted per capita by consumers in Europe and North America amounts to 95-115 kg/year, compared with the figure for sub-Saharan Africa and South and South-East Asia, which is only 6-11 kg/year (Food and Agriculture Organization of the United Nations, 2012c).

In developed countries, food wastage occurs more frequently at the retail and consumer end, owing, in part, to management practices and consumption habits

In developed countries, food wastage occurs more frequently at the retail and consumer end, owing, in part, to management practices and consumption habits. In wealthier countries, sales agreements between producers and distributors may contribute

Figure IV.5
Lost and wasted food, by type of product

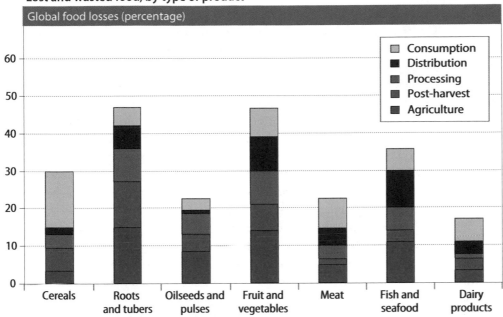

Source: Food and Agriculture Organization of the United Nations (2012c).

to the wastage of quantities of food due to the application of quality standards. As much as 30 per cent of total harvested food does not reach the marketplace as a result of quality selection and cosmetic considerations (Institution of Mechanical Engineers, 2013). Also, food production tends to exceed demand in developed countries as a precautionary measure, in order to ensure delivery of agreed quantities. This situation entails a financial loss for producers and additional pressure on natural resources.

In industrialized countries, once food production reaches the market, perishable products are displayed for a minimum period of time in supermarkets, reducing in-store wastage. However, of the 70 per cent of harvested food that reaches the marketplace, 30-50 per cent is wasted at home by the final consumer (Institution of Mechanical Engineers, 2013). Insufficient purchase planning and conservative expiration dates on labelling, as well as significant discounts when food is purchased in higher quantities, are the main factors explaining the large degree of waste at the consumer level.

In developing countries, the situation is relatively different, as waste may occur primarily at the producer level, owing to inadequate harvesting methods and at the marketplace, owing to inappropriate storage, rather than at home. At the producer level, premature harvesting of crops usually causes a loss in nutritional value and, as a result, a significant portion is wasted as it is not suitable for consumption. At the marketplace, waste also occurs when vendors keep food displayed in stalls for a long period of time, using unhealthy preservation methods. However, urban households keep wastage at minimum levels by buying small portions each time they purchase food.

In developing countries, the situation is relatively different, as waste may occur primarily at the producer level, owing to inadequate harvesting methods, and at the marketplace, owing to inappropriate storage

In developed countries, retail and consumption patterns will require profound cultural changes, particularly regarding preferences and rejection of food based on cosmetic characteristics. As surveys show, consumers are willing to buy such food as long as the taste is not affected (Food and Agriculture Organization of the United Nations, 2011e). Raising awareness in food industries, and among retailers and consumers, is a key

In developed countries, retail and consumption patterns will require profound cultural changes

element in ensuring that consumers are offered a broader range of quality products in retail stores. Further, a significant proportion of the food that is currently discarded but still suitable for consumption could be sold or donated to commercial or charity organizations.

Governments may have to implement policies designed to stimulate different marketing and food management practices which can modify retailer and consumer decisions, and ultimately reduce the amount of food wasted at the marketplace and at home. Such policies are particularly applicable to consumable fresh food products that do not reach the market owing to cosmetic considerations. Publicity, advocacy, education and even legislation can also be used to bring about ideological, cultural and behavioural changes so as to reduce high levels of retail and domestic food waste in the developed world. In addition, in wealthier countries, price incentives in retail spaces lead to overconsumption, which ultimately increases food waste and health issues linked to excessive caloric intake. As long as food market prices remain relatively low, there will be no incentives to alter behavioural practices.

In developing countries, investments in infrastructure will be crucial to reducing food wastage

In developing countries, as discussed previously (see sect. on increasing food availability), investments in infrastructure will be crucial to reducing food wastage. Public investments should focus on main infrastructures, such as roads and energy production. In parallel, private sector investments could concentrate efforts on storage and cooling systems. At the same time, it is important that food chain operators be trained to improve production, handling and storage methods, in line with food safety standards.

Increasing financing for the agricultural sector

The transformation and development of the agricultural sector discussed in previous sections will require investments on a significant scale. There have been several studies on and estimations of the financing requirements for agricultural development. Considered within a long-term perspective, investment needs for primary agriculture and its downstream industries in developing countries were estimated at US$ 9.2 trillion (2009 dollars) over the 44-year period from 2005-2007 to 2050 (Food and Agriculture Organization of the United Nations, 2009a). This level of investments will have to be sourced from both the public and the private sector. The public sector should typically finance infrastructural needs as well as research and development. These investments would improve productivity in the agricultural sector and attract private investment, which will benefit from positive externalities. Yet, the policy environment must provide the right incentives for private investments. Risk protection and better access to credit markets, for example, can stimulate private investments, from smallholders in particular.

The importance of increasing public investment in agriculture

The public sector needs to take the lead in those areas that offer little incentive for private investments—such as rural infrastructure, and research and development, as well as extension services—to increase agricultural productivity

In many developing countries, the share of agriculture in public expenditure has to increase in order to improve the agricultural system, as emphasized by the Secretary-General's High-level Task Force on the Global Food Security Crisis (United Nations, 2008). The public sector needs to take the lead in those areas that offer little incentive for private investments—such as rural infrastructure, and research and development, as well as extension services—to increase agricultural productivity. Scaling up investment in these agricultural public goods and services has the potential not only to improve agricultural productivity, but also to crowd in private investment. In addition, greater public investment in community capacity development and social infrastructure has been considered indispensable to improving the management of natural resources and the livelihoods of small-scale farms (Food and Agriculture Organization of the United Nations, 2012a).

The main challenge, however, lies in the fact that public resources allocated to the agricultural sector have been falling short of the required levels, including in developing countries where food insecurity is higher and where smallholders need more support in order to engage with the market. Government spending on agriculture has decreased from the 1980s to the mid-2000s, representing only 6 per cent of total public expenditures (United Nations, Department of Economic and Social Affairs, 2008). In Africa, for instance, despite the landmark decision of Heads of State and Government of the African Union, at the second ordinary session of the Union Assembly, held in July 2003, to adopt the Maputo Declaration on Agriculture and Food Security,[14] Governments have not increased their allocation of resources to the agricultural sector as expected. Heads of State and Government had committed to the allocation of at least 10 per cent of budgetary resources to agriculture and rural development within five years. The commitment to allocate the same percentage by 2015 to coincide with the deadline for reaching the Millennium Development Goal 1 target of halving hunger was renewed in 2009. However, in 2008, only 8 countries out of 45 allocated 10 per cent or more of their total budgetary resources to agriculture and rural development (figure IV.6). These countries were Burkina Faso, Ethiopia, Ghana, Guinea, Malawi, Mali, the Niger and Senegal (Omilola and others, 2010). Six of these countries are least developed countries, and were at the same time the larger beneficiaries of official development assistance (ODA) and characterized by less favourable agriculture conditions (Benin and others, 2010).

Major national emergencies, lack of peace and stability, HIV/AIDS and natural disasters were among the major challenges faced by Governments during the last decade, leading to fewer resources for agriculture. However, there are also several governance issues preventing more and better allocation of public resources to agriculture which need to be addressed. The lack of transparency and political will is an underlying factor leading to low levels of public spending in agriculture. Contrary to the common perception, low economic growth and low aggregate wealth in a country are not necessarily an impediment to allocating higher public spending to agriculture. For instance, in Africa, a small economy such as Malawi had already complied with the Maputo Declaration, allocating more than 13 per cent of the total public budget to agriculture (te Lintelo and others, 2013).

> Contrary to the common perception, low economic growth and low aggregate wealth in a country are not necessarily an impediment to higher public spending on agriculture

Another major challenge is the inadequacy of agricultural sector policy strategies, including diversion of public spending from long-term investment to agricultural subsidies. While subsidies, such as for energy, or fertilizer subsidies for agriculture, can help overcoming short-term market failures, they tend to remain in effect much beyond the original planned time frame, leading to inefficient use of resources. For instance, in Zambia more than half of the agriculture budget during fiscal year 2005 was spent on subsidies for fertilizers and crop marketing, while investment in infrastructure represented only 3 per cent of the budget. Moreover, only 29 per cent of farmers were buying fertilizers, namely, those who were wealthier and closer to roads (World Bank, 2008a).

---

14   See document A/58/626, annex I.

Figure IV.6

Agricultural expenditures and the Comprehensive Africa Agriculture Development Programme (CAADP) 10 per cent target, 2008 (unless otherwise noted)

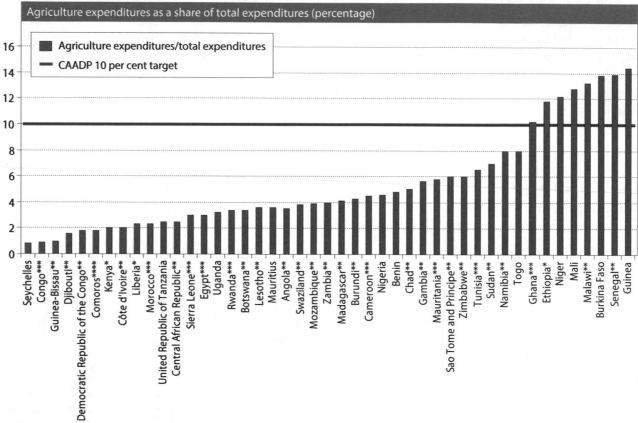

Sources: Based on Regional Strategic Analysis and Knowledge Support System (ReSAKSS) data collected from various national Government sources; and International Monetary Fund (2009).

* = 2009
** = 2007
*** = 2006
**** = 2005

Incentives for private investment

Creating the right incentives and regulations is a major influence in encouraging both large- and small-scale private investments, while improving smallholders' livelihoods

Insufficient public investment in agriculture is an important barrier to improving and ensuring food and nutrition security. At the same time, low private investment, including from smallholders in their own farming activities, constitutes another major constraint on improving food production. Creating the right incentives and regulations is a main determinant for encouraging both large- and small-scale private investments, while improving smallholders' livelihoods.

There is scope for increasing production, food security and rural incomes with greater investments in small farms. In particular, if investment focuses on the production of food staples, rather than high-value products or export-oriented crops, there will be better opportunities to increase food security in highly food insecure countries. In Africa, for instance, it is estimated that the value of domestic and regional markets can amount to more than 50 billion dollars annually, more than the value of total international agricultural exports from the region (World Bank, 2008a; Sahan and Mikhail, 2012). Furthermore, diversifying small farms' food production is the best strategy for improving rural households' income and nutrition conditions.

There are numerous obstacles preventing higher investment in small farms. The above-mentioned insufficiency of public goods and services limits potential returns to farmers' investments. The second issue is related to the lack of price incentives for small-scale producers, in particular when there are price controls on food products which reduce their potential net revenue. A third issue is the lack of access by smallholders to formal insurance protection against risks, which, typically, include natural disasters, pest infestations and price volatility, leading to lower investments in small farms, as a safeguarding measure.

An additional obstacle—and, arguably, the most important—is the lack of access to credit markets. In many developing countries, agricultural financial services remain underdeveloped, in particular the supply of seasonal credit for small farms, preventing farm-level investments. In many cases, when credit is available, banks increase risk premiums and interest rates to prohibitive levels, as they perceive small-scale production as particularly risky. Thus, expanding rural financial institutions and creating specific financial products for small-scale farms will be a key determinant as regards boosting productivity in the agricultural sector. The public sector can not only supply specific insurance and financing products to farmers, but also stimulate the development of insurance and credit markets for smallholders (Organization for Economic Cooperation and Development, 2010). Specific products could include leasing, matching grants, warehouse receipt systems, commodity-based financial products, and overdraft facilities for input dealers (United Nations, 2008).

Private investments in agriculture, particularly international private investments, are needed and can play an important role in boosting productivity and ensuring food security, when directed towards strategic needs (Hallam, 2009). However, in order to increase the positive impact of these investments, Governments need to design policies and legislation that can create a more conducive climate for inclusive and sustainable investments. Direct incentives, for instance, such as tax incentives, can encourage investments that directly support local smallholders. Contract farming can also lead to positive investment, when small-scale farmers are assisted in contract negotiation and dispute resolution (Sahan and Mikhail, 2012).

The onus of increasing the positive impact of private investment is on recipient countries, even if a regulatory framework is often missing in developing countries. While international standards and voluntary actions can partly bridge the gap, it is still essential that national Governments create regulations and incentives to ensure a positive impact. For instance, as observed above, large-scale land acquisitions from foreign private investors must be regulated in order to maximize benefits for local communities. In relation to land, several mechanisms can be used, such as legal protection of all land rights and the inclusion of local communities in political decision-making processes (Sahan and Mikhail, 2012). Similarly, sustainable farming investments can also be encouraged with adequate incentives and regulations for protecting the environment.

International support for agriculture

The support of the international community—bilateral and multilateral organizations, international non-governmental organizations and other development partners—will be crucial for the allocation of more resources to long-term investments in agriculture. In the last few decades, agriculture has been considerably neglected by donors and development partners. In the 1980s and 1990s, total ODA to agriculture exhibited a declining trend, as a consequence of structural adjustment programmes that favoured industrial sectors

Expanding rural financial institutions and creating specific financial products for small-scale farms will be a key determinant in boosting productivity in the agricultural sector

It is still essential that national Governments create regulations and incentives to ensure the positive impact of private investments, particularly international private investments

Developing countries will need additional financial support from the international community in order to increase the allocation of resources to long-term investments in agriculture in developing countries. From the 1980s to 2008, aid to agriculture fell by 43 per cent (figure IV.7). In terms of total aid programmes, the share of aid to agriculture declined even more sharply, from 17 per cent in the 1980s to 6 per cent in 2008.

Despite the long-term decline, bilateral aid to agriculture showed an upward trend in recent years, during the period 2003-2008. This recent trend coincided with the onset of the new millennium and commitments made by the donor community, in particular to Africa. In addition, in 2007-2008, the total annual average aid commitments to agriculture amounted to US$ 7.2 billion (Organization for Economic Cooperation and Development, 2010), which represented a positive step towards increasing financing for agriculture in developing countries. Still, in 2008, the High-level Task Force on the Global Food Security Crisis urged donor countries to double ODA for food assistance, other types of nutritional support and safety net programmes, and to increase the proportion of ODA to be invested in food security and agricultural development from the current 3 to 10 per cent within five years (and beyond if needed) so as to reverse the historic underinvestment in agriculture (United Nations, 2008). Further, global support of US$ 20 billion for agriculture over a three-year period was promised at the Group of Eight (G8) Summit, held in L'Aquila, Italy, from 8 to 10 July 2009 (see L'Aquila joint statement on global food security, para. 12). By the time of the 2012 Camp David G8 meeting, 48 per cent of the L'Aquila pledge had been disbursed. Some countries such as Canada, Italy, the Netherlandas and the UK had already fully disbursed their pledges (Organization for Economic Cooperation and Development, 2012b).

Figure IV.7

Trends in aid to agriculture: commitments, 1973-2008
(Five-year moving averages and annual figures, constant 2007 prices)

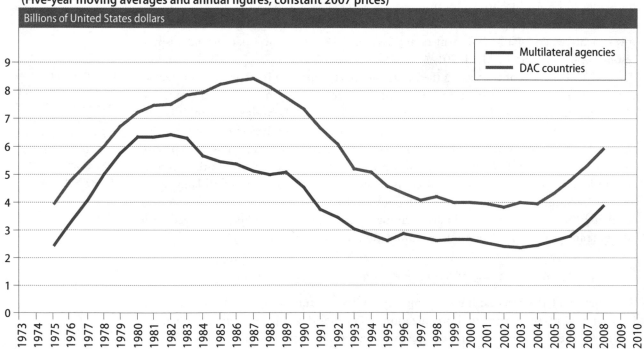

Source: Organization for Economic Cooperation and Development (2012b).

In order to maximize the positive impact of external aid on agriculture, countries that face food insecurity and small-scale farms should be prioritized. In line with this perspective, sub-Saharan Africa and South and Central Asia have received, respectively, 31 per cent and 22 per cent of the total aid flows to agriculture in 2007-2008 (Organization for Economic Cooperation and Development, 2010). However, continuity and coherence of ODA for agriculture are also crucial for its effectiveness.

In addition, new mechanisms in global governance of agriculture are needed to provide political support, coordinate across sectors and, in particular, ensure continuous and appropriate funding (World Bank, 2008a). Concerted action is needed by the international community in addressing the issues of trade and global public goods (research and technology), as well as helping developing countries confront climate change challenges. In the case of climate change, for instance, it is accepted that wealthier countries bear the major responsibility for its emergence, while vulnerable farmers in developing countries suffer most of its consequences. Thus, within the context of the United Nations Framework Convention on Climate Change, several funds were created to finance adaptation in vulnerable developing countries. In 2010, aid for climate change mitigation was estimated at US$ 17.6 billion, and climate change adaptation at US$8.9 billion (Organization for Economic Cooperation and Development, 2012b). However, as observed earlier, the international community is underinvesting in global public goods for food and agriculture, as these have only long-term pay-offs. Nevertheless, greater and better allocation of financial resources is possible, once the international community acknowledges that investing in sustainable agriculture is a means of ensuring global equity and stability.

New mechanisms in global governance of agriculture will also be important for better coordination across sectors and for ensuring continuous and appropriate funding

Chapter V
The energy transformation challenge

Summary

- The latest estimates confirm that trends in emissions are likely to lead to increases in world temperature which could have catastrophic consequences. Even after accounting for recent mitigation policies—including expanded use of renewable energy sources and improvements in energy efficiency—the accumulated concentrations of emissions will be well above the safety mark of 450 parts per million of carbon dioxide equivalent by 2050.

- Pathways to an energy transformation for sustainable development are multiple: there is flexibility in the energy technologies that need to be available and in the sectors in which energy efficiency should improve, and there are options with respect to the economic, social and cultural envelopes that could contain the increase in emissions, while still allowing for a rise in welfare.

- Despite their variety, sustainable pathways share some common ground. First, the sooner policies scale up, the greater the technological flexibility will be and the less costly mitigation will become. Second, policies increasing efficiency in the delivery of energy services can go a long way. Indeed, if it chooses to, the world can avoid the use of controversial technologies with high risks and high costs, including nuclear power and carbon capture and storage.

- This Survey finds a certain degree of technological over-optimism in the assessment of sustainable pathways. While technology per se might not be the main limiting factor, its implementation faces challenges. In this regard, our analysis is less sanguine about the economic, social and cultural hurdles to be overcome in implementing the decisive and coherent national policies that are called for, as well as in securing the commensurate level of international cooperation. The world needs a public investment-led big push, capable of catalysing private sector investment and innovation so as to sustainably transform the energy system.

- The sustainable energy transformation is consistent with economic and social inclusion; moreover, policies promoting economic and social inclusion can, in some cases, also result in reduced emissions. Universal access to clean cooking fuels and electricity can be consistent with measures to contain the increase of emissions and, pertinently, this can be achieved at a comparatively modest investment cost:

- The investment necessary to render the energy system sustainable is, in principle, affordable. However, the full costing of investment needs calls for resource allocations several times larger than the direct energy investments that are needed to keep the world on a sustainable pathway. Additional investments needed to achieve universal access to modern energy by 2030 are, in comparison quite affordable.

Introduction

The world economic system is in need of deep transformation as a means of re-establishing a balanced relationship with the Earth's boundaries while accommodating the legitimate development aspirations of the billions of people who would like to have access to quality and nutritious food, decent clothing and shelter, health, good-quality education, water and sanitation, and modern amenities. At the heart of this transformation lies the revamping of the world "energy system," as it is energy that underpins the production of the goods and services that sustain human life. The energy system harnesses natural resources and transforms them into energy carriers, to be used by the appliances and machinery that provide energy services, such as heat, refrigeration and transport. Providing energy services to current and future generations requires energy systems that are sustainable, in terms of both the use of natural resources and the disposal and absorption of the pollutants associated with the generation and use of energy. To the extent that an energy system is engaged in multiple interactions with the economy, society and the environment (including interrelations with other physical resource and commodity systems), the only way to build sustainability in the energy system is to introduce sustainable management of those economic, social and environmental interactions.

The transformation of the energy system should be a core element in any agenda for sustainable development that aims at improving the living standards of people within a framework of equity and environmental sustainability. In the context of the Secretary-General's Sustainable Energy for All Initiative and at other occasions, explicit energy goals (or targets) are needed to eradicate dependence on traditional use of biomass as a source of thermal energy; to improve access to reliable and adequate quality electricity; and to ensure that unreliable or low-quality energy sources do not compromise the opportunities of those among the working poor who are self-employed or run household enterprises.

Achieving these objectives entails confronting the challenge of formulating policies that adequately resolve the issue of potential trade-offs and take advantage of potential synergies. Policies need to explore possible synergies with other development goals, by promoting, for example, health, education, training and employment creation through improvement of workers' skills in the areas of design, deployment and maintenance of sustainable energy systems.

The evidence for climate change and human-activity generated emissions

A large number of studies have examined current energy trends and found them to be outright unsustainable. They do, however, offer alternatives and have proposed a variety of paths that have the potential to re-establish a balance between human activity and Earth's carrying capacity. Presented below are some of the major institutional exercises focused on energy trends and alternative sustainable pathways.[1]

---

[1]   The release by the Intergovernmental Panel on Climate Change of its Fifth Assessment Report (to be finalized in 2014) will further enrich our understanding of sustainable paths.

The room for effective action is shrinking

The growing body of analytical evidence provided by the scientific community unmistakably confirms that current incremental policies will not suffice to keep human impact within the Earth's boundaries. If current trends continue, the further infringement of those boundaries will lead to a dangerous increase in the risk of devastating consequences. If one looks at the rise in the use of renewable energy, the advances made in reducing pollution in many cities, the increase in the number of protected areas, the implementation of policies to improve sustainable use of natural resources, and the adoption of international agreements to improve environmental sustainability, the world is probably greener today than it would have been if no actions had been taken. Certainly, the world is, increasingly, using energy more efficiently and there has been a 25 per cent improvement over 1980 efficiency indicators. Some countries, notably China, and some regions have achieved large improvements. However, even after taking into account all of these actions, the likely outlook does not meet desired emissions reduction targets. Simulations incorporating current economic and demographic trends, energy policies, emissions levels and current commitments indicate that present efforts do not suffice to maintain accumulated emissions within acceptable boundaries and safe temperature limits. Introducing policies and regulations that can effectively bring about a shift to a sustainable energy path is becoming evermore urgent.

World Energy Outlook 2012 (International Energy Agency, 2012) considers two baseline scenarios and presents estimates extending to 2035. The "current policies scenario" includes the implementation only of policies that had been adopted by mid-2012. The "new policies scenario" includes all policies in the current policies scenario plus a cautious implementation of recently announced policy commitments and the expected impact of adopting new technologies (ibid.). In a sense, then, the second baseline scenario takes an optimistic view of recent policies and technology development, mainly because it assumes that they will be fully implemented. A comparison of these baseline scenarios highlights two important points. First, new policy and technology developments are important steps in the right direction, for they imply a noticeable lessening in the increase in emissions between 2010 and 2035 (figure V.1). Second, even after optimistically accounting for recent green developments, the world is still a long way from a sustainable pathway, as emissions will still be well above the sustainable prescribed level. While the current policies scenario implies a long-term average increase in global temperature of 5.3° C, the updated new policies baseline scenario softens the impact on world temperature by 1.7° C, yet still leads to a risky increase of 3.6° C. Based on scientific assessments, it has been established that world temperature should not increase by more than 2° C.

A comprehensive review by the Intergovernmental Panel on Climate Change (2012c) of 16 global energy-economy and integrated assessment models found a remarkable increase in the use of renewable energy in many baseline scenarios. Based on the increases in the use of renewable sources of energy foreseen by such baseline scenarios, by 2030 the level of use of renewables will have doubled. Under other scenarios, the use of renewable energy will be 3 or even 4 times the current level. Yet, again, these baseline scenarios result in emissions implying dangerous increases in world temperature.

The baseline scenario presented in *OECD Outlook 2050* (Organization for Economic Cooperation and Development, 2012c) implies that concentrations of

The latest assessments of energy trends confirm the urgency of transformative action to prevent undue accumulation of CO_2 and risky increases in temperature

Figure V.1
Global energy-related CO$_2$ emissions by scenario, OECD and non-OECD, 2010, 2020 and 2035

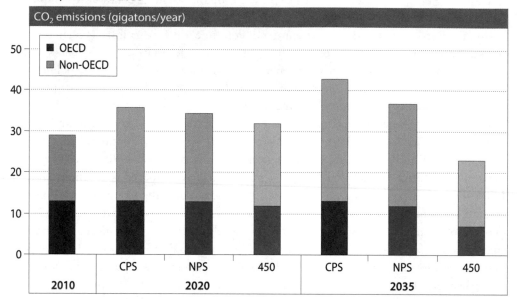

Source: International Energy Agency (2012), p. 52, Figure 2.2.

Note: NPS = new policies scenario; CPS = current policies scenario; 450 = 450 scenario.

greenhouse gas emissions will rise to 685 parts per million (ppm) of carbon dioxide equivalent (ppm CO$_2$e) by 2050 and to over 1,000 ppm of CO$_2$e by 2100, well above the internationally agreed target of cumulative concentrations of required 450 ppm of CO$_2$e by 2050 required to stabilize world temperature (Intergovernmental Panel on Climate Change, 2007b). These increases in greenhouse gas emissions will lead to temperature hikes ranging between 2.0° C and 2.8° C by 2050 and between 3.7° C and 5.6° C by 2100. The predicted business-as-usual emissions are thus likely to trigger increases in world temperature with potentially disastrous consequences for the environment and people's well-being: aggravated losses of biodiversity, increased pollution in cities, heightened competition for water and a doubling of the number of premature deaths.

The projections and reviews of scenarios undertaken by the United Nations Environment Programme (UNEP) (2012b) also suggest that current policies and underlying trends fall short of what is required to prevent risky increases in world temperature. UNEP scenarios are presented in conformity with countries' emissions reduction pledges under the United Nations Framework Convention on Climate Change,[2] i.e., from the time commitments were made to the year 2020. According to UNEP estimates, current commitments are insufficient and will likely lead to a rise in temperature of more than 4° C. To stay within the safe temperature range, the world needs to reduce emissions by another 14 gigatons (Gt) of CO$_2$e (GtCO$_2$e)/year by 2020, beyond current commitments to reductions in emissions.

The many paths to a sustainable energy transformation

There are a large number of pathways towards transforming the energy system so that the world can achieve sustainable development

There has been progress in the understanding of the changes that will be required to achieve a sustainable energy transformation that keeps the Earth within safe boundaries. One overriding message from the hundreds of scenarios that have been produced by scientists is that the world can follow a large number of paths to achieving sustainability.

---

2   United Nations, Treaty Series, vol. 1771. No. 30822.

The IPCC special report on renewables (2012)

The IPCC special report on renewables (2012c) looks at 164 scenarios presenting the results of policies aimed at increasing the role of renewables in the energy system. Under more than half of these policy scenarios, there is a significant increase in the use of renewables with figures ranging from 64 exajoules (EJ)/year to more than 173 EJ/year and in some instances to 400 EJ/year over current levels (figure V.2). The share of renewables in the energy mix will increase in these scenarios from 13 per cent in 2008 to more than 17 per cent and 27 per cent in 2030 and 2050, respectively. The most ambitious scenarios project renewables sources accounting for about 43 per cent and 77 per cent of total energy in 2030 and 2050, respectively.

The IPCC review suggests that scenarios aimed at controlling emissions more strictly require an energy mix with a higher share of renewables. To what extent renewables can contribute to the control of emissions is still somewhat uncertain, however. For any single level of emissions, there is a wide range of renewable energy combinations that are compatible with that level of emissions; such large variation reflects the difficulty in modelling the environmental impact of renewables, which in part stems from uncertainties surrounding the deployment of renewable technologies (see legend in figure V.2). While there is a need to increase our understanding of the interactions between renewable energy and emissions, the IPCC review suggests a large potential for increasing the use of renewables.[3]

United Nations Environment Programme emissions gap report

Noting the slow progress in international negotiations on reducing emissions, the UNEP report (2012b) looks at scenarios where some important actions to curb emissions occur only after 2020.[4] Comparing these scenarios with scenarios under which most of the significant environmental policy actions occur before 2020 helps highlight important trade-offs. The first observation is that under scenarios assuming strong mitigation only after 2020, there is obviously more flexibility given to the type of changes in the energy system that need to take place in the short term. The trade-off is that under these scenarios, there is greater pressure to accelerate progress after 2020, with the world becoming more dependent on technological breakthroughs to be able to achieve the required reduction in emissions. For example, the UNEP report concludes that not a single later action scenario published up to 2012 can meet the target of controlling the rise in world temperature without bio-carbon capture and storage (United Nations Environmental Programme, 2012b, p. 29). A similar trade-off applies to policy options and societal choices: the widening of options in the short term narrows the room for future policy action (because higher emissions increase the risk of rising temperature and climate changes).

OECD Environmental Outlook to 2050

OECD Environmental Outlook to 2050 (2012c) analyses the costs and benefits of an array of policies aimed at transforming the energy system and avoiding high climate change risks. The OECD core scenario makes several assumptions: (a) that mitigation options are

---

3   See also the discussion in IEA (2012b), chap. 7 entitled "Renewable energy outlook".

4   There are only a handful of studies that have examine this type of scenarios, including Vuuren and others (2013), Organization for Economic Cooperation and Development (2012c), and Rogelj, McCollum and Riahi (2013).

Figure V.2
Global renewable primary energy supply (direct equivalent) versus fossil fuel and industrial CO$_2$ emissions, 2030 and 2050

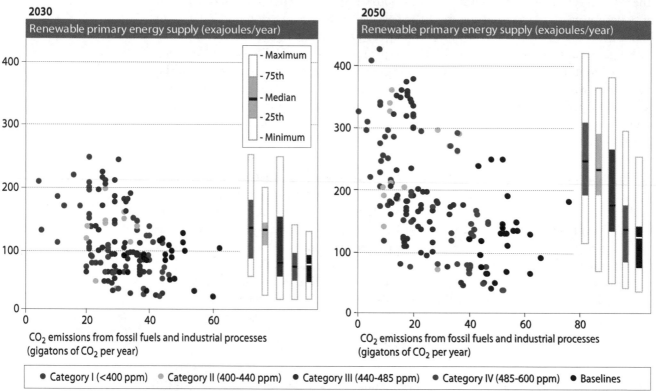

Category I (<400 ppm)   Category II (400-440 ppm)   Category III (440-485 ppm)   Category IV (485-600 ppm)   Baselines

Source: Intergovernmental
Panel on Climate Change,
2012c, p. 21,
figure SPM.9.

fully flexible, (b) that all the necessary cooperation exists to implement an all-encompassing and harmonized global carbon market and (c) that least-cost mitigation options are adopted. The core scenario is set to achieve the target of keeping the CO$_2$e concentration at 450 ppm. To achieve the target, this scenario simulates a set of policies that could achieve such a target, including actions to establish a global carbon price, followed by immediate use of least-cost mitigation options in all sectors and regions, and gradual progress in the decarbonization of the energy sector—stimulated by higher carbon prices, extensive use of low-cost advanced technologies, including biomass energy with carbon capture and storage. While the cost to the economy of keeping emissions in check under these assumptions would not be large, it would vary significantly across regions. Costs would entail reductions of 2050 gross domestic product (GDP) ranging from -2.1 percent for OECD countries to -8 per cent for Brazil, India, Indochina and China eliminated, with other regions facing reductions of -4.4 per cent.[5]

OECD explicitly probes the effects of policies designed to curb emissions and the impact that such policies would have on biodiversity, whose boundaries are among the Earth's most severely infringed. Under the OECD baseline scenario, by 2050 the world will have lost 10 per cent of biodiversity, over and above the already reduced level for the year 2010. The set of policies and technologies that lead to limiting emissions to 450 ppm of CO$_2$e in the OECD core scenario are unfortunately incapable of addressing the loss

---

5   Reductions in the Russian Federation are of the order of -6.5 per cent (see Organization for Economic Cooperation and Development (2012c), p. 115, figure 3.18, panel B).

in biodiversity. The OECD core scenario reduces the loss of biodiversity by 9.9 per cent relative to the biodiversity in baseline 2010, that is, there is a net gain of 0.1 percentage points over the baseline projection to year 2050. A more detailed look at the simulation helps reveal potential trade-offs. Most policies and positive climate change effects under this scenario reduce the loss of biodiversity by 1.5 percentage points with respect to the 2050 baseline projection, but more intensive use of bioenergy under this scenario effectively adds 1.4 percentage points to the loss of biodiversity. Combining these two figures yields the above-mentioned 0.1 percentage point net gain. Thus, the use of bio-energy to help reduce emissions involves a trade-off of increasing biodiversity loss. Simulations using technology combinations that rely less importantly on bio-energy result in larger net gains. On the other hand, complementary policies can be of great assistance. When the core 450 scenario is reinforced with increases in land productivity, ranging between 3 and 18 per cent depending on type of land and region, the net loss in biodiversity is reduced by 1.2 percentage points.

Global Energy Assessment

The *Global Energy Assessment* (International Institute for Applied Systems Analysis, 2012) builds 60 scenarios that include fundamental changes in energy and development policies, e.g., policies related to the energy sector, changes in the user-end point demand for energy, and changes in the transport sector, as well as policies broadening access to modern energy, enhancing energy security and keeping emissions within safe levels (Riahi and others, 2012). The 60 scenarios are organized around three sets of options. The first set of options includes different combinations of changes in the course of the evolution of the supply of and demand for energy. At one extreme, the world relies mainly on improvements in the supply of energy to meet the needs of a growing and increasingly more affluent world population: the supply path. At the other extreme, the world population is still growing and is becoming more affluent but in this case, measures are taken to improve efficiency in the use of energy: the efficiency path. Between the two extremes, there is a mix of improvements in supply and demand: the mix path. Of particular relevance to an increasingly urbanized world (see chap. III), each of these three configurations of demand- and supply-side changes can be deployed along with two different transport sectors systems: one that continues to rely on conventional technologies and fuels (liquid) and one that uses advanced technologies and fuels (hydrogen and electricity).

The set of three supply and demand possibilities and the set of two transport options, as described, define six technological paths. For each of these six paths, the exercise considers 10 possible variations in the portfolio of technologies, e.g., one where all technologies are available, one comprising all but nuclear, one comprising all but carbon capture and storage (CCS), etc. In total, 60 alternative paths are considered. The results of running these 60 scenarios are measured with a checklist to determine whether or not they meet sustainability goals. Four sustainability goals are defined: (a) to attain almost universal access to electricity and clean cooking fuels by 2030; (b) to ensure that the majority of the world's population live in areas that meet the air quality guidelines of the World Health Organization (WHO); (c) to limit global average temperature increase to 2° C (with a likelihood greater than 50 per cent); and (d) to limit energy trade and increase the diversity and resilience of the energy supply. Scenario results are subject to the test of meeting all four defined sustainability goals. A total of 41 out of the 60 scenarios successfully meet the test, underscoring the view that there are a variety of paths towards keeping emissions and the rise in temperature within safe limits.

The most important insight provided by this ensemble of scenarios is that the world can go a long way towards controlling emissions if there are adequate investments in energy efficiency. The 60 scenarios can be divided into 20 scenarios within the supply path, 20 scenarios within the efficiency path and 20 within the mix path. While all 20 scenarios that emphasize measures for efficiency in demand meet all four sustainability goals, 13 out of the 20 scenarios that assume a mix of supply and demand changes meet the goals and only 8 of the scenarios emphasizing the supply side pass the sustainability test.

The explanation for these results is that the increase in energy efficiency provides enough room for all combinations of the two transportation paths and all five technology portfolios to meet the sustainability goals. If gains in efficiency are small, however, the world becomes more dependent on the capacity to increase the supply of clean energy, which depends in turn on the ability to innovate and adopt new technologies. If substantial efficiency improvements are ruled out, the number of scenarios that meet all four sustainability goals are reduced to only two, regardless of whether or not it is possible to migrate from conventional to modern transport systems.

Another important insight that can be derived from this exercise is that the technologies with greater technological, economic and social uncertainties—nuclear energy, carbon capture storage (CCS), and bio-energy with carbon capture storage (BECCS)—are not indispensable for achieving the four sustainability goals adopted in the Global Energy Assessment exercise. That is, even if the world phases out nuclear energy and/or discards the option of carbon capture storage and bio-energy with carbon capture storage, the four Global Energy Assessment sustainability goals can still be achieved as long as it keeps the demand for energy low and renewable technologies are implemented as assumed in scenarios. The main lesson is that if the world cannot control the demand for energy with efficiency measures, then nuclear, carbon capture storage and bio-energy with carbon capture storage technologies will have to be accepted.[6]

Sustainable energy with economic and social inclusion

Since the IPCC Fourth Assessment Report review (2007b), many energy and climate scenarios have included the assumption that countries' GDP will converge towards the top. Take, for example, the Global Energy Assessment and OECD modelling. The Global Energy Assessment scenarios assume that the country or region with the lowest income will have a GDP per capita of 8,000 purchasing power parity (PPP) United States dollars by 2050 and US$ 26,000 in ppp prices by 2100. This means that regional income disparity, measured as the ratio of the top to the lowest income per capita, will drop from 17 in 2010 to 6 in 2050 and to 3 in 2100. The OECD modelling assumes that by 2050, the lowest country or region GDP per capita will be US$ 13,000 ppp and the ratio of the top to the lowest income per capita will have decreased, in ppp terms, from 12 in 2010 to 6 in 2050. The OECD modelling, explicitly builds changes in GDP based on the effects of a set of growth drivers, including the age structure of the population, the labour-force participation and unemployment rates, and education attainment, among others. The procedure explicitly discusses the role of important interactions determining growth, such as the slowing-down effect that ageing has on growth and the upward effect that education

---

6   Consistent with the known economic, social and cultural difficulties associated with the use of some of the proposed technologies substituting fossil fuels, the IEA (2012b) sustainable scenarios do not include nuclear energy and carbon capture and storage.

attainment has on labour productivity and thereby on growth. The assumption of GDP convergence is driven by the assumption of convergence in education.

The fact that these models include numerous scenarios where emissions meet the 450 ppm target and income convergence is still allowed for, implicitly demonstrates that environmental goals are consistent with inclusive economic growth. IPCC (2007b) found that models assuming GDP convergence tend to yield lower emissions mainly because the increase in income is allowed to occur in countries where emissions per capita (emissions/population) and the intensity of emissions (emissions/GDP) are lower because resources and technologies are allowed to flow to countries and regions where availability is more restricted.[7] Hence, convergence of GDP per capita not only is consistent with, but might also actively contribute to, environmental sustainability.

The relevance of GDP convergence to environmental sustainability goes beyond the reduction of between-country inequalities. Within each country, appropriate and coherent policies promoting upward income convergence can result in great progress towards implementation of an inclusive development agenda. To the extent that social and economic inclusion indicators correlate with GDP per capita, reaching a GDP per capita floor of say 10,000 PPP dollars by 2050 might also mean that the incidence of one dollar-per-day income poverty would be about 5 per cent (figure V.3; see also World Bank (2012b), p. 5, figure 0.2). Similar patterns would apply to other indicators such as child mortality, female literacy, education attainment, health outcomes and access to water and sanitation, among others. All of this suggests that economic and social inclusion, including upward convergence of GDP, is consistent with—and can even be a net contributor to—the curbing of greenhouse gas emissions. Consistency, however, is not equivalent to sufficiency. Economic and social inclusion politices will have to be designed and implemented as the world transforms its energy system.

Income convergence allows for convergence in human development but does not assure it, particularly under conditions of persistent and, at times, aggravating inequalities (see chap. I). Climate change/energy/economy models have also looked at issues of energy and environment-related poverty.

We begin by recalling that the Global Energy Assessment exercise specifically included elimination of energy poverty among its four goals and found that 41 of its 60 scenarios fulfilled all four goals, i.e., universal access to electricity and clean cooking fuels by 2030; compliance of cities with WHO air quality guidelines; limiting the global average temperature increase to 2° C; and limiting energy trade and increasing the diversity and resilience of the energy supply.[8] Although the 60 scenarios incorporate the economic and social inclusion dimensions of sustainable development and establish whether or not they are compatible with the 450 ppm target, the exercise does not indicate what specifically would be required to achieve economic and social inclusion in an environmentally sustainable path. To address this question, the Global Energy Assessment compared two scenarios, one including policies to achieve universal access to clean fuels and stoves for cooking and access to electricity with another incorporating none of these policies. The

> Not only is economic and social inclusion, including upward convergence of GDP, consistent with the curbing of greenhouse gas emissions, but it can also be an active contributor in this regard

---

[7]   In general, scenarios featuring between-regions/between-countries income per capita convergences result in lower emissions because slower growth rates in lower-income countries tend to be associated with slower adoption of low-emissions technologies (Intergovernmental Panel on Climate Change, 2007b, chap. 3, p.177). Accordingly, the more inclusive the income paths underlying energy transformation scenarios are, the larger the gains in the stabilizing of emissions.

[8]   Rogelj, McCollum and Riahi (2013) also find that access to modern energy, as reflected in the United Nations Sustainable Energy for All Initiative (United Nations, 2012d), is consistent with environmental sustainability.

analysis was carried out for three key regions—sub-Saharan Africa, South Asia and Pacific Asia—where access to modern energy is a critical issue.

The results of the comparison indicate that with the absence of energy poverty policies, 2.4 billion people will still rely on solid fuels for cooking by 2030 (figure V.4), that is, 300 million more people than the 2.1 billion so reliant in 2005. The implementation of the most ambitious package providing clean energy fuel, which combines microfinancing and fuel subsidies to cover the upfront costs of enabling access to modern energy and the purchase of appliances (assuming a 50 per cent fuel subsidy in relation to market prices), has the potential to ensure access to modern energy services for 1.9 billion people who

Figure V.3
Income per capita, and social and economic inclusion

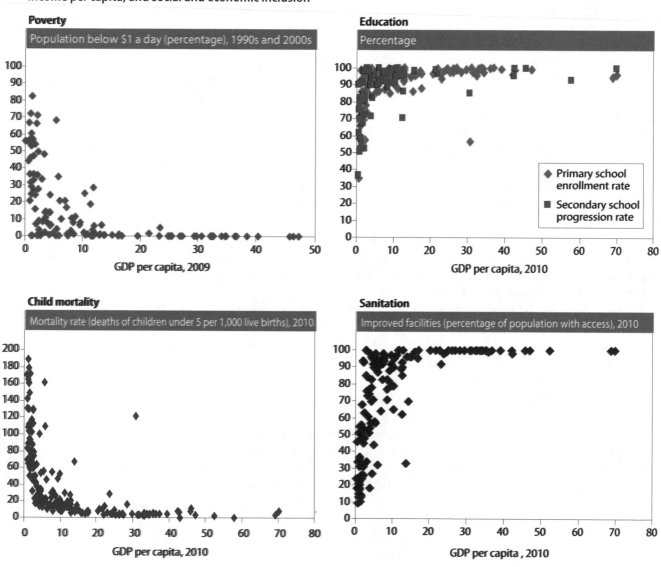

Sources: World Bank, "Global poverty and inequality: a review of the evidence," *World Bank Policy Working paper*, No. 4623 (2008); and World Bank, World Development Indicators.

would otherwise still rely on solid fuels for cooking.[9] This set of policies, however, will still leave 500 million people without access to clean cooking fuels.

Separately, the Global Energy Assessment looks at access to grid-electricity in the rural areas of three regions: sub-Saharan Africa, Pacific Asia and South Asia.[10] The baseline scenario indicates that in the absence of access to electricity policies, between 70-85 per cent of the rural population of sub-Saharan Africa and 18-23 per cent of the rural population of Pacific and South Asia will still be deprived of electricity by 2030. Implementing policies aimed at providing universal access to clean cooking fuels and electricity in these three regions will have no visible impact on emissions. Actually, greenhouse gas emissions will be slightly lower than the emissions under the baseline scenario.

The International Energy Agency (IEA) *World Energy Outlook 2012* provides an interesting perspective on access to modern energy and the climate change implications thereof. The IEA core new policies baseline scenario predicts that by 2030, 1 billion people will still be without electricity and 2.6 billion people will lack clean cooking facilities. The simulation of a scenario with granting universal access to clean cooking fuel and electricity indicates that these policies can be implemented without significantly increasing emissions.

OECD Environment Outlook to 2050 examines the benefits of combining environmental policies and policies aimed at reaching the Millennium Development Goal of access to water and sanitation. The report presents a scenario where the number of people

> Providing the world's poor with access to clean cooking fuel and electricity is possible without significantly changing global emissions

Figure V.4
Impact of access policies on cleaner cooking in three developing regions

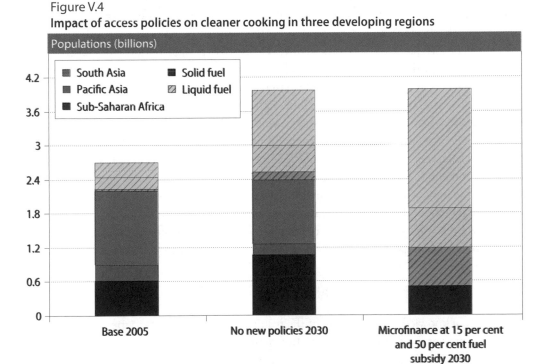

Source: Riahi and others (2012), p. 1,263, figure 17.31.

---

9   The Global Energy Assessment acknowledges that fuel subsidies are controversial (see, for example, International Monetary Fund (2013)), but subsidies in this simulation are used to make access to modern fuels affordable. Other policies specifically designed to address poverty and environmental sustainability, such as tailored cash transfers, might be more appropriate.

10   Owing to lack of reliable data, the analysis leaves out the provision of off-grid electricity, which could be a more appropriate and lower-cost alternative.

without access to improved water in 2005 will have been reduced to half by 2030, followed by universal access to an improved water source and basic sanitation by 2050. The benefits of such a scenario include prevention of premature deaths, better health conditions and economic rewards to such sectors as fisheries and tourism (Organization for Economic Cooperation and Development, 2012c, p. 247).[11]

The brief and selective review of sustainable pathways towards transforming the energy system has yielded the following insights: (a) long-term trends are not sustainable even if the effects of recent mitigation policies are taken into account; (b) transformative changes can follow multiple paths; (c) transforming the energy system is consistent with increasing economic and social inclusion; (d) a closer look at available scenarios warrants the conclusion that not only is mitigation consistent with economic and social inclusion but, in some instances, it also benefits from economic and social inclusion; (e) all feasible paths require policies, resources and international cooperation well beyond current standards and trends. In sum, full sustainable development is possible, but it needs strong policy interventions at global and country levels.

The challenge of transforming the energy system

Successful mitigation and sustainable development face multiple challenges. To begin with, there is the challenge of ensuring that people and policymakers learn from scientific and factual evidence and modify their views and current consumption patterns accordingly. Yet, even if the world is fully convinced of the environmental risks of continuing current trends, the task is daunting. The task involves the timely transformation of the energy system. The accomplishment of this task involves a complex and potentially lengthy process. The "energy system" harnesses natural resources and transforms them into energy carriers to be used by the appliances and machinery that provide energy services, such as heat, refrigeration and transport, among others (see box V.1 on the energy system). Providing energy services to current and future generations requires sustainable energy systems. To the extent that energy systems have multiple interactions with the economy, society and the environment (including interrelations with other physical resource and commodity systems), the only way to build sustainability in the energy system is to introduce sustainable management of those economic, social and environmental interactions. In the present section, we discuss issues regarding two challenges to the transformation of the energy system: the technological challenge and the economic, social and political challenge.

The technology challenge

Technology per se is not the limiting factor. The most difficult obstacles to the implementation of sustainable technologies lie in the economic, social and cultural domains

It is widely acknowledged that many of the technologies necessary for supporting sustainable development are already available. The challenge is how to improve these technologies, how to accelerate cost reductions and achieve meaningful changes, how to integrate them along coherent development paths that respond to specific local and sectoral needs, and how to provide incentives and mechanisms for rapid innovation, diffusions and knowledge-sharing (United Nations, 2011b, p. ix).

[11]   It should be noted that if instead of access to improved water, the focus shifts to access to safe water, the reduction in mortality rates would be stronger (Organization for Economic Cooperation and Development, 2012c, p. 303).

Climate change-energy models, which look carefully at available and foreseeable technologies, confirm the view that technology is not the main obstacle. For example, the Intergovernmental Panel on Climate Change Special Report on Renewables (2012c), looked at four illustrative scenarios in which emissions were controlled and the use of renewables increased significantly, and noted that in these cases only 2.5 per cent of the globally available technological potential was used (Intergovernmental Panel on Climate Change, 2012c, p. 23 and 796). The UNEP 2012 emissions gap report estimates that the technological potential for reducing emissions between now and 2020 to be anywhere between 14 and 20 $GtCO_2e$, which is enough to accomplish the emissions reductions of 8-13 $GtCO_2e$ that still need to be achieved beyond current reduction commitments. These two examples confirm that current or foreseeable availability of technologies is not the obstacle to achieving environmental sustainability, but also suggest that a significant degree of uncertainty still pervades the assessment of technical possibilities.

Climate change-energy models coincide in pointing out that implementing in the real world the modelled assumptions represents a daunting task. There are technical and engineering obstacles that need to be overcome in order to implement the new technologies (see United Nations, 2011b, pp. 54-58 and United Nations, 2012b). Still more challenging are the unavoidable economic, social and cultural obstacles that will need to be overcome in order to implement new technologies that are to replace the currently dominant fuel-based technology envelope. Obstacles include not only the entrenched interests of the energy industry but also challenges associated with shifts in land use and changes in the economic structure and its associated consumption patterns. Finally, one should not forget that implementation challenges are exacerbated by the fact that changes need to take place in a short period of time (United Nations, 2011b).

The kinds of economic, social and cultural changes that might be involved in switching energy sources are suggested by the following illustration. A technically feasible large-scale plan intended to supply energy from solar sources to 1 billion people in Europe and North Africa and half a billion in North America will require an expanse of solar farms in the Sahara desert and North America equivalent in size to the State of Arizona. The economic, social and political challenges associated with changing land-use patterns so that such large extensions of land can be allocated to the generation of solar energy attest to the magnitude of the obstacles that need to be overcome when scaling up renewable energy alternatives (United Nations, 2011b, pp. 55-56; MacKay, 2009). Another illustration is provided by the seemingly simple substitution of fossil fuel-driven automobiles with electricity-propelled cars. Even if technically feasible and environmentally sound (see MacKay, 2009, pp. 126-132), such a change will not occur unless the retail network that supplies gasoline is altered and the auto repair sector revamped, changes that would require significant investments and might be strongly resisted by vested interests. However, such large investments might be made attractive if the full cost to the environment is properly internalized in the price of buying and using fossil fuel-driven cars.

This simple example also helps to illustrate the role of cultural factors. It is often suggested that a shift to electric automobiles would be out of the question until electric cars could perform at par with fossil fuel-driven cars, as if cultural norms were static and unchangeable. This claim ignores the fact that preferences could (and probably should) change in favour of clean transportation and that it might be possible to change behaviours, tastes and social views if consumers were confronted with prices for fossil-fuelled cars that fully reflected emissions and other environmental costs. If this was the case,

Box V.1

The energy system[a]

The energy system constitutes the ensemble of production, conversion and use of energy and is thus closely linked to the Earth's carrying capacity and to the economic, social and cultural organization of human life (figures A and B). The energy system comprises primary energy resources (e.g., coal, oil and gas) which are converted to energy carriers (e.g., electricity, gasoline and liquefied gas). These carriers then serve in end-use applications for the provision of various energy forms (e.g., heat, transport and light), required to deliver final energy services (e.g., thermal comfort, transportation and illumination).

Energy conversion technologies are the critical component defining the energy system: the energy systems can be characterized by the dominant set of technologies used to convert primary energy resources into useful energy (secondary energy). Energy systems can be further differentiated into the energy supply sector and the end-use energy sector. The energy supply sector encompasses the extraction of energy resources (involving so-called upstream activities), their conversion into suitable forms of secondary energy and their delivery to the locus of demand (involving so-called downstream activities). The end-use energy sector, in turn, handles with the provision of services such as cooking, illumination, heating, refrigerated storage and transportation. The ultimate goal of the energy system is to meet the demand for energy services required to satisfy human needs.

Figure A
Global energy flows of primary to useful energy, including conversion losses (waste and rejected energy), in exajoules (EJ) for 2005

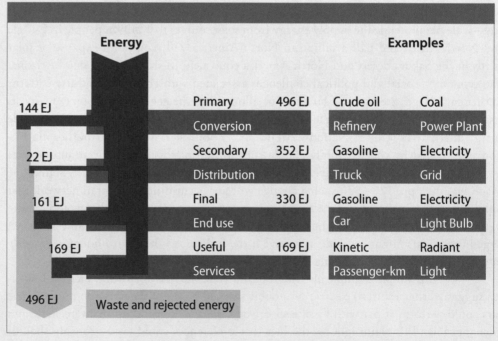

Source: Grübler and others (2012a), figure 1.2, p. 104.

a This box draws heavily on Grübler and others (2012a).

Box V.1 (cont'd)

Figure B

Schematic diagram of the energy system: illustrative examples of the energy sector and energy end use and services

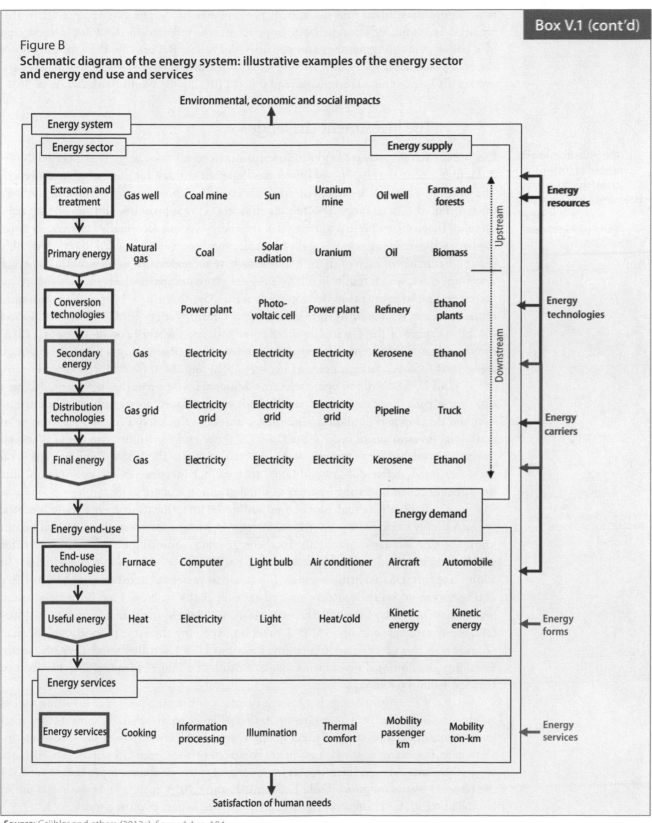

Source: Grübler and others (2012a), figure 1.1, p. 104.

many consumers might find the current performance of electric cars acceptable. In this regard, an example of a rapid change in preferences is reflected in the 2008 introduction of a policy combining bonuses and penalties in France. Reportedly, the introduction of the policy coincided with a sudden 5 per cent drop and subsequent reductions in new cars' average CO_2 emissions (Durremayer and others (2011), p. 8; World Bank 2012b, p. 56).

The investment challenge

The initial investment needed to sustainably transform the energy system implies a significant increase in energy-related investments

Despite the sixfold increase in global investments in renewable energy in the period 2004-2011, investments leading to sustainable development still fall far short of what is needed. The range of estimates is large, reflecting uncertainties about costs that are still not well known; but the large range also reflects differences in approaches and modelling techniques.[12] Investments needed to transform the energy system are usually classified as ranging between energy investments and additional other investments needed to transform this system. Estimates of each of these investments have to deal with a number of unknown or uncertain costs, which results in a large range of estimates, particularly on non-energy investments and investments in developing countries. Synthesizing the investment estimates of the Food and Agriculture Organization of the United Nations (FAO), IEA, OECD, and UNEP, a report of the Green Growth Action Alliance (World Economic Forum, 2013) indicates that the additional investments needed to put the world on a sustainable path are at least US$ 0.7 trillion per year between 2010 and 2030 (World Economic Forum, 2013). This US$ 0.7 trillion figure refers to additional investments that will be needed on a sustainable path in six sectors with readily available estimates (power generation, transmission and development, buildings, industry, transport vehicles and forestry). Estimates of additional investments in other sectors, such as water and agriculture, are not well known or not yet available, e.g., for roads, rail, airports and ports. The US$ 0.7 trillion figure, on the other hand, refers only to additional incremental investments—it does not include investment needed under the business-as-usual greening scenario.

To obtain a rough idea of total additional investments in energy-related sectors, one can simply impute the proportional increase in known sectors to those we still do not know and give a range for variation. Total energy-related annual investments in sectors for which there is an estimate amount to US$ 2.1 trillion in a business-as-usual scenario. In addition to this, US$ 0.7 trillion annual investments are needed in these sectors, an increase of 33 per cent, to set the economy on a sustainable pathway. Now, total business-as-usual investments in sectors for which the report does not include an estimate of additional sustainable investments add up to US$ 2.9 trillion. Applying the same proportional increase of known sectors gives an additional investment of US$ 1.6 trillion; and given the sector variability in additional investments, one can think of a range of from US$ 1.1 trillion to US$ 2.4 trillion (table V.1).

It is worth noting that these estimates confirm the view that investing makes good economic sense. The Green Growth Action Alliance reports that, for some sectors, total investments under a sustainable scenario might actually be lower than business-as-usual investments. For example, the IEA estimates compiled by the Green Growth Action Alliance suggest that annual green investments in power and transmission are 8 per cent lower than the business-as-usual figure (World Economic Forum, 2013, table 1.1). Investments might also be lower in, for example, infrastructure for the transport of oil and gas.

---

[12]   See, for example, the discussions of needed investments in United Nations (2011b), pp. 174-175.

Table V.1
Additional investments for sustainable development, 2010-2050

Billions of US dollars				
Sector	Business-as-usual scenario	Additional investments on a 2°C scenario	Percentage change	Source
Known additional energy investments for sustainability, 2010-2030				
Power generation	347	160	46.1	IEA
Power transmission and development	272	-21	-7.7	IEA
Energy total	**619**	**139**	**22.5**	-
Buildings	358	296	82.7	IEA
Industry	255	35	13.7	IEA
Building and Industrial	**613**	**331**	**54.0**	-
Transport: vehicles	845	187	22.1	IEA
Forestry	64	40	62.5	UNEP
Transport and Forestry total	**909**	**227**	**25.0**	-
Total known additional investment estimates	**2141**	**697**	**32.6**	-
Unknown additional energy investments for sustainability, 2010-2030				
Road	400	-	-	OECD
Rail	250	-	-	OECD
Airports	115	-	-	OECD
Ports	40	-	-	OECD
Transport	**805**	**-**	**-**	-
Water	1320	-	-	OECD
Agriculture	125	-	-	FAO
Telecommunications	600	-	-	OECD
Other sectors	**2045**	**-**	**-**	-
Total unknown green investment estimates	**2850**	**-**	**-**	-
Additional energy investments for sustainability, 2010-2030				
Needed at least*	4,991	697	14	-
Needed lower	4,991	1,148	23	-
Needed mid	4,991	1,625	33	-
Needed higher	4,991	2,361	47	-
Additional inclusion investments for sustainability goals, 2010-2050				
*Lower**	*Business as usual*	*2°C*	*Percentage*	
Clean cooking and electricity:				
Low a	15	34	125	IEA
Low b	n.a.	36	-	GEA
High	n.a.	41	-	GEA
Sanitation and water	n.a.	5	-	OECD

Source: Data from World Economic Forum (2013), p. 13, table I.1, compiling data from IEA, OECD and UNEP; inclusion investment estimates are from International Institute of Applied Systems Analysis (2012), p. 1258, table 17.13; data on sanitation and water from the Organization for Economic Cooperation and Development (2012c), p. 248.

* Only known investment estimates.

** Lower is calculated as the percentage of the first quartile, and higher as the third quartile of the six sector percentage changes.

Green Growth Action Alliance estimates, like any others, are contingent on the policy and technology assumptions of simulated scenarios. The Global Energy Assessment exercise provides useful insights on how assumptions about policies and availability of technologies can affect estimates of needed investments. The Global Energy Assessment estimates total energy supply-related investments at US$ 960 billion in 2010 (Riahi and others, 2012); a figure consistent with the Green Growth Action Alliance compilations. The annual average total energy investments in the baseline scenario is equal to US$ 1.8 trillion, while the mean of the annual total energy investments needed in sustainable pathways is US$ 2.4 trillion. This means the mean additional annual investment in the 41 scenarios is US$ 0.6 trillion (very close to the Green Growth Action Alliance at-least figure of US$ 0.7 trillion). Now, additional sustainable investments vary significantly depending on the assumptions about efficiency demand, mode of transport and portfolio of technologies: the range of additional annual investments in the 41 scenarios starts at the low figure of US$ 0.14 trillion but rises up to US$ 1.16 trillion.

> Focusing on efficiency and investing sooner rather than later reduces the size of the total investment needed

The main driver determining the magnitude of additional investments in the 41 scenarios is efficiency. Pathways stressing energy supply policies have investment tags ranging from US$ 0.72 trillion to US$ 1.16 trillion (figure V.5a). In contrast, pathways emphasizing efficiency tend to necessitate lower additional investments, ranging from US$ 0.14 trillion to US$ 0.65 trillion. Varying technology portfolios reveals interesting investment patterns. Confirming the importance of maintaining flexibility in technology choices, full portfolio pathways tend to have low additional investments (figure V.5b). Portfolios that discard carbon capture and storage technologies tend to have low additional investments, as these are expensive options. Running in the opposite direction, technology portfolios featuring restrictions in the capacity to use renewables or bio-energy raise the range of needed investments. The sharpest upward shift in the range of needed investment is associated with portfolios excluding carbon sink technologies. More restricted portfolios tend to result in some of the highest investment tags, particularly portfolios with no bio-energy, no sink or limited bio-energy. One extreme case illustrates well the importance of maintaining flexibility in technology portfolios. A high-efficiency technology pathway featuring technology restrictions, no bio-carbon storage, no carbon sink technologies and restricted use of bio-energy, turns out to carry an additional investment ticket of US$ 1.08 trillion, way above the US$ 0.32 trillion median investment of efficiency pathways (figure V.5a).[13]

> The proportional size of sustainable energy investments is larger for developing than for developed countries

Energy investments differ, of course, by region (figure V.5c). To explore regional investments needs, we should focus on proportional changes, for both baseline and additional sustainable investments might vary significant across regions. While total energy investment in 2010 represents about 2 per cent of global GDP, energy investments in developing countries represent about 3.5 per cent of GDP, but only 1.3 per cent of GDP in developed countries (Riahi and others, 2012, p. 1253). In the Western European Union region, for example, rates are below 1 per cent of GDP, but in the sub-Saharan African region rates are above 3.5 per cent; oil producing regions are characterized by high investment rates, above 5 per cent of GDP (own estimates based on the Global Energy Assessment online database). Additional investments needed to achieve sustainability, relative to the baseline, across the

---

13   The largest investment tickets in Global Energy Assessment scenarios correspond to efficiency (US$ 0.29 trillion-US$ 0.80 trillion), renewables (US$ 0.26 trillion-US$ 1.01 trillion), and infrastructure (US$ 0.31 trillion-US$ 0.50 trillion) (Riahi and others, 2012, Table 17.13, p. 1258). Nuclear energy and carbon capture and storage imply investments ranging from no investment to US$ 0.21 trillion.

Figure V.5a
Additional investments in sustainable pathways, by supply, mix and efficiency policies

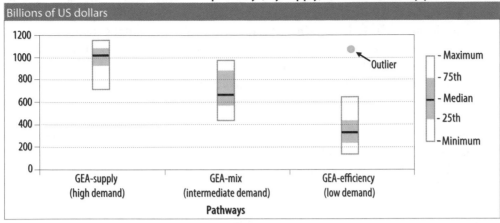

Source: See Global Energy Assessment 2012 online database http://www. iiasa.ac.at/web-apps/ ene/geadb/dsd?Action= htmlpage&page=about.

Figure V.5b
Additional investments in sustainable pathways, by technology portfolio

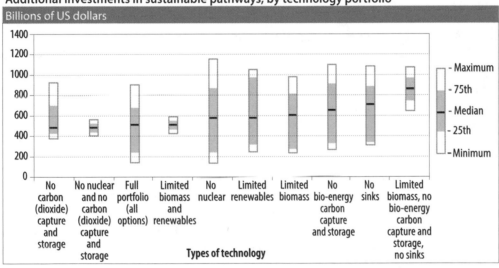

Source: See Global Energy Assessment 2012 online database http://www. iiasa.ac.at/web-apps/ ene/geadb/dsd?Action= htmlpage&page=about.

Figure V.5c
Additional investments in sustainable pathways, by region

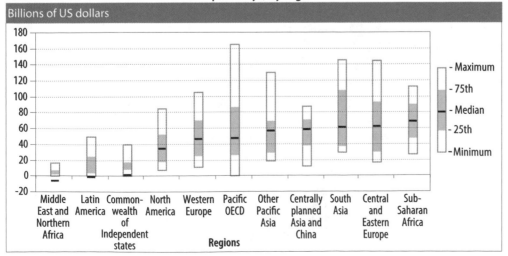

Source: See Global Energy Assessment 2012 online database http://www. iiasa.ac.at/web-apps/ ene/geadb/dsd?Action= htmlpage&page=about.

11 regions and 41 scenarios vary between -18 and 156 per cent.[14] Additional investments cluster in three regional groups: the first group, showing high relative investments, comprises sub-Saharan Africa, Central and Eastern Europe and South Asia; the second group showing medium relative investments, includes economies of centrally planned Asia and China, Pacific OECD, other Pacific Asia, Western Europe and North America, and; the third group showing low relative investments, includes the Commonwealth of Independent States, Latin America and the Middle East and Northern Africa. Minimum and maximum investments by region also tend to cluster in these three groups, albeit imperfectly (figure V.6a). Caution should be exercised when interpreting these estimates. For example, negative regional investments tend to be associated with regions that currently engage heavily in the production and export of fossil fuels, which suggests that the global shift to non-fossil fuel sources of energy implies disinvestment in current production capacity. More generally, caution should also be exercised when interpreting the investment tags for developing regions, as there is a tendency to underestimate required investments in energy infrastructure and shelter in developing countries (O'Connor, 2009).

The size of additional investments also varies with other factors, among which, timing is crucial. According to UNEP, the total cost of mitigation policies that begin only after 2020 is 10-15 per cent higher than the cost of policies that start mitigation promptly in 2013 (United Nations Environment Programme, 2012b, p. 28).[15]

A thorough accounting of energy-related investments and energy services-related investments might multiply by 10 the size of initial needed investments

Investments needed to transform the energy system include investments beyond sectors, namely, investments in rendering sustainable the demand for energy. Investments needed to change the demand for energy are likely to be significantly higher than investments in the supply of energy, but the size of the needed investments is also more difficult to estimate. The Global Energy Assessment report estimates that there are additional needed investments in the demand side of energy ranging from US$ 0.1 trillion to US$ 0.7 trillion (Riahi and others, 2012, p. 1254). These investments include those related to services on engines in cars, boilers in building heating systems, and compressors, fans and heating appliances in households, among others. Accounting for the full cost of demand-side energy technologies increases the investment figure by one order of magnitude, to a range between US$ 1 trillion and US$ 3.5 trillion (ibid.). These include investments in innovation, market formation and diffusion (Grübler and others 2012b, pp. 1691-1695 and 1713-1724).

In contrast, the cost of targeted investments to achieve economic and social inclusion is small. The Global Energy Assessment estimates that policies aimed at providing universal access to clean fuel cooking and electricity will require annual investments ranging between US$ 0.036 trillion and US$ 0.041 trillion (see table V.1 and the above discussion on inclusion). Similarly, IEA estimates at US$ 0.34 trillion the additional investments needed to achieve universal access to clean cooking fuel and electricity.[16] The OECD scenarios simulating policies designed to achieve universal access to an improved water source and sanitation by 2050 find that those policies will require additional annual

---

14   The range of additional needed global investments across the 41 scenarios varies between 8 and 64 per cent, with a mean increase of 33 per cent.

15   See also OECD (2012c) estimates of significant negative competitiveness and income impacts of delayed action (table 3.8, p. 127, and p. 129, figure 3.24).

16   Energy access is defined here as reliable and affordable access by a household to clean cooking facilities and a first electricity supply connection, with a minimum level of consumption (250 kilowatt-hours (kWh) per year for a rural household and 500 kWh per year for an urban household), which increases over time to reach the regional average.

investments of about US$ 0.005 trillion. One main message stemming from the reviewed scenarios simulating policies designed to achieve energy inclusion is that the investment needed to implement them is well within reach at the global scale.

Implementing sustainable development

There is an emerging consensus that the world needs to urgently undertake to achieve transformative changes so as to avert increases in greenhouse gas emissions which have potentially catastrophic consequences. Climate change-energy models have made invaluable contributions to our understanding of the range of possible means of transforming the energy system. Less is known about how to proceed in countries and how best to organize international cooperation so as to effectively transform energy systems in developed and developing countries. Based on analytical contributions, a good number of policy proposals addressing the challenges of sustainable development were put forward in anticipation of the United Nations Conference on Sustainable Development. In the present section, we selectively look at three of those proposals and revisit the proposals broached in *World Economic and Social Survey, 2009* (United Nations, 2009) and *World Economic and Social Survey, 2011* (United Nations, 2011b). The three proposals selected encompass the green energy strategies of Organization for Economic Cooperation and Development (2011a; 2011b), United Nations Environment Programme (2011) and World Bank (2012c). These strategies, which are comprehensive in their coverage of issues, aim at rationalizing the transition from the current state to an alternative path on which the environment is taken fully into account. These exercises offer insights on alternative means of moving towards sustainable development strategies. The emphasis is on the short term: "green growth should focus on what needs to be done in the next 5 to 10 years." (World Bank, 2012b, p. 1). The *World Economic and Social Survey (2009 and 2011)* takes a more ambitious approach. It argues that the world needs a big-push investment-driven transformation of the energy system. We briefly highlight some of the arguments underlying these proposals.

Sustainable development pathways

OECD proposes to tackle the challenges with "an operational policy agenda that can help achieve concrete, measurable progress at the interface between the economy and the environment"; a green growth agenda (OECD, 2011b, p. 11). Policymakers seeking to harmonize the economic and the environmental goals in a green policy agenda face three obstacles, namely, (a) low returns to green investment, which leads to (b) lack of investment and (c) slow innovation. To overcome these obstacles, OECD proposes that use be made of a green growth diagnostic tool which classifies the main obstacles to green growth into those causing low economic returns and those causing low capacity to appropriate generated returns, or low appropriability of returns (figure V.6). The first obstacle (low returns) is further categorized as a problem related to: (a) inertia, as reflected in, e.g., low returns to research and development and the presence of barriers to competition; or (b) low social returns, as reflected in, e.g., infrastructure deficiencies and low human capital. The second obstacle, low appropriability of returns, is further specified as: (a) government failure, as reflected in, e.g., policy unpredictability and perverse subsidies; or (b) market failure, as reflected in, e.g., the existence of negative externalities and informational imperfections.

Figure V.6
Green growth diagnostic

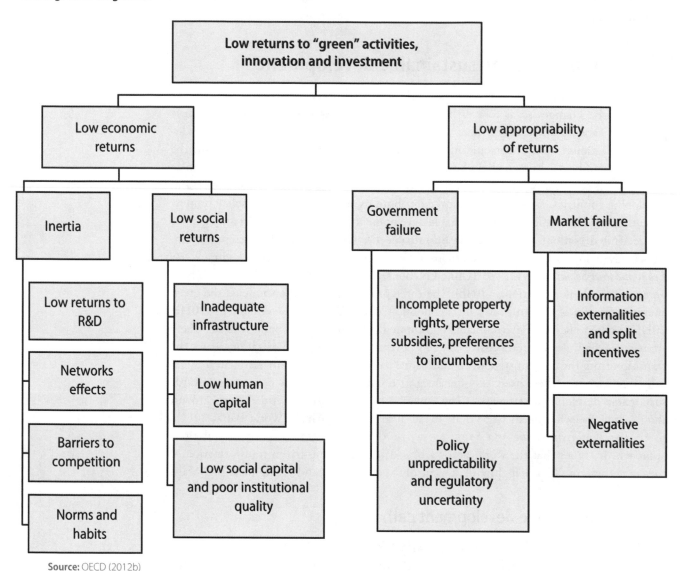

Source: OECD (2012b)
p. 128, figure 5.1.

Once the main obstacles have been identified, OECD proposes that effective institutional arrangements and policy packages be built for the transition towards green growth.

This policy package generates useful guidelines for building green-growth strategies for countries at different levels of development (table V.2). For example, developed countries may consider enhancing the link between R&D and technological innovation, investing in low-carbon infrastructures and using market-based pricing of externalities. Developing countries, for their part, could focus on policies designed to enable a shift away from carbon-intensive infrastructure, the promotion of energy efficiency, strengthening government capacities and providing incentives for the development, diffusion and transfer of technology. Least developed countries might consider discouraging open-access to natural resources, increasing productivity in the use of natural resources, designing adaptation strategies and investing in infrastructure to support market access (OECD, 2011a, pp. 1-15; see also OECD, 2011b).

The World Bank sees green growth as "the pathway to sustainable development" and "a vital tool for achieving sustainable development" (World Bank, 2012b, p. xi). It proposes a green growth strategy that rests on three pillars:

(a) Maximizing local and immediate economic or social benefits and avoidance of the lock-in of economies in fossil fuel technologies for several decades (this pillar seeks to prevent irreversibility in the adoption of energy systems and reduce inertia);

(b) Providing incentives to engage in smart decision-making. Examples of the measures covered in this pillar are green accounting (see box II.2), getting prices right so as to overcome behavioural biases, providing incentives and regulations to engage firms in green growth, and using regulations, innovation strategies and industrial policies;

(c) Addressing the problem of financing green growth through the adoption of innovative financing tools designed to tackle high upfront financing needs. The overall strategy allocates different priorities to developed and developing countries (World Bank, 2012b, pp.15-22; see also World Bank, 2012c).

One example of the priority-setting that could emerge from this policy framework, mainly under the second pillar, would entail a focus by developing countries, particularly low–income ones, on two actions: actions that create synergies across the environmental, social and economic dimensions of development; and actions that have high welfare benefits or do not carry large costs (table V.2). This policy framework would recommend developing countries to focus on, for example, measures to reduce local

Table V.2
Some guiding principles for establishing green growth strategies

		Local and immediate benefits	
		LOWER	HIGHER
		Trade-offs exist between short-and-long-term or local and global benefits	*Policies provide local and immediate benefits*
Inertia and/or risk of lock-in and irreversibility	LOWER (action is less urgent)	• Lower-carbon, higher-cost energy supply • Carbon pricing • Stricter wastewater regulation	• Drinking water and sanitation, solid waste management • Lower-carbon, lower-cost energy supply • Loss reduction in electricity supply • Energy demand management • Small-scale multipurpose water reservoirs
	HIGHER (action is urgent)	• Reduced deforestation • Coastal zone and natural area protectiion • Fisheries catch management	• Land use planning • Public urban transport • Family planning • Sustainable intensification in agriculture • Large-scale multipurpose water reservoirs

Source: World Bank (2012b), table O.1, page 17.

pollution, which could provide significant welfare benefits to poor families, by leading to improved health and hence improved labour productivity. As regards developed countries, the strategy suggests a concentration on policies that could exert a long-term impact on emissions.

UNEP closely associates green growth with a process "that results in improved human well-being and social equity, while significantly reducing environmental risks and ecological scarcities" (United Nations Environment Programme, 2010b as quoted in United Nations Environment Programme, 2011, p. 102) and characterizes sustainable development as "improving the quality of human life within the carrying capacity of supporting ecosystems" (IUCN/UNEP/WWF (1991), as quoted in United Nations Environment Programme, 2011). UNEP further identifies a series of enabling conditions for a green economy, including reducing subsidies that are harmful to the environment, targeting public investments to green sectors, implementing government policies to encourage innovation and growth and establishing aggressive environmental regulation, among others (United Nations Environment Programme, 2011, pp. 22-23).

World Economic and Social Survey 2009 and 2011 emphasize that prompt, integrated and decisive policies are needed to achieve sustainable development (see the discussion in United Nations, Department of Economic and Social Affairs, 2012). *World Economic and Social Survey 2011* specifically views the green economy approach as being fully compatible with sustainable development. Consistent with the magnitude of the investments needed, their urgency, and the broad implications for the rest of the economy and society, the view is that only a strong jump-start can effectively and in a timely manner extract the economy away from the inertia of business as usual and move it towards the transformation of the energy system. Transformative changes would be initiated through a public investment-led big push and decisive public interventions to promote technological innovation and implementation. This approach is not intended to substitute markets—on the contrary, it rests on the assumption that only clearly defined sustainable development policies can unleash the power of markets to bring about the needed energy transformation *on time*. As the *World Economic and Social Survey* acknowledges that a realistic and desirable path towards sustainable development must allow for rapid economic growth in the developing world, it argues that the transformation of the energy system must include policies crafted to allow developing countries to simultaneously build low-carbon energy systems and accelerate economic growth. It further argues that a carefully crafted public investment-led approach will not disrupt economic balances and could actually crowd in private investment. *World Economic and Social Survey* macroeconomic simulations of the big-push approach confirm the assumption implicit in climate-energy models that a low-carbon and converging sustainable development pathway is feasible (United Nations, 2009, particularly box IV.4).

The big-push approach is a realistic, well-grounded proposal which incorporates, inter alia, the historical lessons of the New Deal initiative (see United Nations, 2011b and United Nations, 2012b). The challenge, however, is much bigger now. When compared with that of the mid-twentieth century, the world economy is currently not only larger, but also more affluent, interconnected and natural-resource thirsty (see chap. I of this publication). Public-led investment has proved capable of accomplishing large socioeconomic transformations which would not have been feasible through implementation of incremental policies. A high degree of realism will be needed to properly gauge the dimension and complexity of the obstacles that the world needs to overcome.

> Transformative changes can be initiated through a public investment-led big push and decisive public interventions to promote technological innovation and implementation

The enabling conditions for the transformation of the energy system

Making low-carbon inclusive growth a reality requires putting in place the set of conditions needed to create an "enabling environment". Schematically, these enablers can be organized into four groups: policy space and coherence; international financing; international cooperation; and enabling international institutions: rules and norms. First, the transformation of the energy system will require a policy-setting framework within which developing countries can design and implement industrial policies to accelerate growth, foster green sectors and diversify the industrial and service sectors. Industrial policies have been and continue to be used across a wide range of countries, but many developing countries are constrained by international regulations and practices, notably in the trade and property rights domains. Second, there is a need to make adequate international financing available to developing—and, particularly least developed—countries; while domestic sources should be tapped to the extent possible, the size of investments required to promote sustainable development makes international finance indispensable. Third, designing national sustainable strategies demands the integration of complex processes across the macroeconomy, the energy sector, the deployment of technology, labour-market regulations, policies for social and economic inclusion, and the environment. Building national capacities and international cooperation in these areas will be important catalysts for the formulation of coherent sustainable national development strategies. Fourth, of particular importance is strengthening international cooperation to ensure that technological innovation and its adaptation occur where they are most needed and at the lowest possible cost. An important enabler will be a fluid process of technological innovation and adaptation facilitated by efficient technology transfer and cooperation at the regional and international levels.

    The magnitude of the endeavour is such that neither Governments nor markets alone can tackle the desired energy transformation with success. While Governments and markets have been successful in increasing the world's aggregate affluence, they now need to ensure that the entire world population enjoys equitable well-being while re-establishing a balance with respect to the Earth's boundaries. This change in priorities will require a new institutional set-up to enable markets to carry out the required sustainable energy transformation. As the global trade system is an important component of the institutional framework within which markets operate, the world trade system should adopt sustainability as one of its fundamental guiding principles. Meeting the challenge of building policy coherent rules and interventions at global, regional and national levels will be critical to accelerating the required transformation of energy systems.

Coherent national policies for sustainable development

While global models have contributed significantly to the debate by laying out a number of recommendations on policies and measures for a sustainable energy transformation, there is a need to gain a better understanding of the design and implementation of energy transformation strategies at country level and how to best forge and harness international cooperation. A number of country experiences can shed light on policy alternatives. In the present section, we review some concrete experiences that illustrate the complexity of policy challenges and provide further guidelines for policy design.

The experience in using carbon taxes to pursue green-economy objectives has by now a record spanning more than two decades, mainly involving developed countries. More recently, a number of studies on carbon taxes in developing countries also started to emerge, most of them sponsored by Governments, international organizations and academia. China and South Africa, for example, have been considering the implementation of carbon taxes, but concerns about negative social and economic impacts in different areas have delayed their introduction (see, for example, "Mitigating circumstances", 2013; and Birdsall and MacDonald, 2013). Studies suggest that, while taxing carbon can contribute to curbing emissions, this seems to work better in combination with well-defined regulatory measures and complementary policies designed to offset (or compensate) the often regressive income distribution effects of carbon taxes.

There are opportunities to coherently combine low-carbon growth policies with strategies for economic and social inclusion

Furthermore, carbon or carbon-related taxes might represent an important source of revenue, which raises the issue of how to make best use of them. A simulation exercise probing the effects of raising the price of oil through a tax on domestic consumption in Bolivia (Plurinational State of) (a gas exporting country), Costa Rica (a country where 90 per cent of electricity is hydro-generated) and Uganda (a country dependent on oil imports to satisfy its energy demand) demonstrates the possibility of using carbon-related public revenues to finance economic and social inclusion programmes (see box V.2 entitled Taxing oil to invest in education). Under the simulation, taxes are increased up to the point where countries collect 2 additional percentage points of GDP in tax revenue. Simulations show that the introduction of this tax reduces oil consumption in productive sectors and among households, which has the effect of reducing emissions, but at the cost of decreasing GDP. Allocating additional revenues to investment helps to slow down the fall in GDP and, in some instances, even results in a net increase in GDP (figure V.7). Most importantly, the use of additional revenues to finance investments in education significantly improves education outcomes. Even though these simulations do not include the impact of higher education on labour productivity, it should be expected

Figure V.7
Impact on real GDP growth of a tax on oil and investment in education

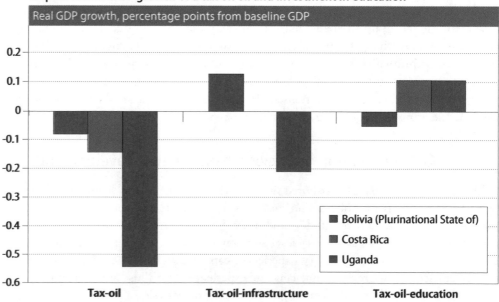

Source: Box. V.2, table.

Box V.2

Tax oil to invest in education

Coherent policies to curb carbon emissions, promote economic growth and pursue human development: examples for oil-importing developing countries

The experience in using carbon taxes to pursue green-economy objectives has an interesting record spanning more than two decades of experience, mainly in developed countries. More recently, a number of studies on carbon taxes in developing countries have also started to emerge, most of them sponsored by Governments, international organizations and academia.[a] China and South Africa, for example, have been considering the implementation of carbon taxes, but concerns about negative social and economic impacts in different areas have delayed their introduction (see "Mitigating circumstances", 2013).

Fiscal policy can be instrumental for enabling developing countries to curb carbon emissions while such markets develop. Not only could fiscal policy contribute to reducing carbon emissions but it could also, if combined with a set of coherent policies, promote human development, and offset some of its potential economic costs. Three policy scenarios are simulated to illustrate that this may be the case, using an economy-wide modelling framework applied with data sets for three oil-importing developing countries (Bolivia (Plurinational State of), Costa Rica and Uganda).[b] These scenarios are compared with a baseline which delineates a continuation of currently expected economic growth and public spending interventions up to 2030.

In the first scenario (**Tax-oil**), the domestic price of fuel oil is increased by steadily raising (baseline) tax rates on domestic consumption and imports of oil in order to generate new revenue averaging 2.0 per cent of GDP per year during 2016-2030.[c] The new revenue is used to reduce the budget deficit. The second scenario is identical to the first except that new revenue, instead of financing the budget deficit, is used for financing investments in public infrastructure such as roads, bridges and electricity networks (**Tax-oil-infrastructure**). The third scenario is identical to the second except that the revenue is used to increase spending in education (**Tax-oil-education**). Public infrastructure and a larger pool of better-educated workers are drivers of productivity growth in the scenarios. Moreover, new public infrastructure—which facilitates access to and functioning of education centres—and increased service delivery in education favourably impact attendance and promotion in all school cycles.

The results show that, keeping all other things equal, unilateral fiscal policy restrictions on the domestic price of fuel oil would depress intermediate and especially final consumption of fuel oil in the three countries (figure A). Carbon emissions would consequently likely be curbed—by a margin not estimated here—but, on the other hand, industries that supply oil-intensive goods for the domestic market and exports would be penalized. In fact, GDP growth is 0.54 percentage points per year less in Uganda, and it also slows down in the other two countries, though by much less, as they also produce and rely on alternative sources of energy, i.e., fuel gas in the Plurinational State of Bolivia and hydroelectric power in Costa Rica (table).

The simulated price shock has been smoothed by spreading it out over a period of 15 years to make it more realistic. It is conservative in comparison with shocks that oil importing countries have endured owing to world oil price hikes. Using a similar economy-wide modelling framework, Sánchez (2011) shows that the negative impact on real GDP of the most recent oil price boom (2002-2008) has been substantial in six oil-importing developing countries, and as high as 2.0 to 3.0 per cent of GDP per year in some cases. In the first policy scenario presented here, however, real GDP is only 0.3-0.4 per cent per year below the baseline levels. The simulated fiscal policy will also be feasible should it not be used for protectionist purposes.

a See, for example, Alton and others (2012); Devarajan and others (2011); Gonzalez (2012); Jaafar Al-Amin and Siwar (2008); van der Ploeg and Withagen (2011), Resnick, Tarp and Thurlow (2012); Sumner, Bird and Smith (2009); and Yusuf and Ramayandii (2008).

b A dynamic economy-wide modelling framework called Maquette for MDG Simulations (MAMS) is used to generate the scenarios (Lofgren, Cicowiez and Díaz-Bonilla, 2013). Its application involves, inter alia, detailed (country-specific) microeconomic analyses of determinants of a set of human development indicators and productivity growth drivers such as the stocks of public infrastructure and highly educated workers. The application of this modelling framework with data for the three countries and extensions made to it are described in Sánchez and Cicowiez (2013).

c The domestic price shift directly affects domestic consumption of refined oil in all three countries, imports of refined oil in Bolivia (Plurinational State of) and Uganda and imports of crude oil in Costa Rica.

Box V.2 (cont'd)

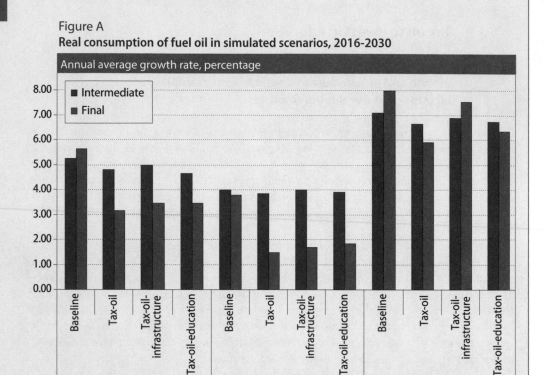

Figure A
Real consumption of fuel oil in simulated scenarios, 2016-2030

Annual average growth rate, percentage

Source: Box V.2, table.

If, alternatively, the new revenue were allocated to investing in public infrastructure, on one hand, or to expanding service delivery in education, on the other, instead of using it to finance the budget deficit, the output loss would be offset partially or fully. This is mainly because such investments would spur productivity growth, but industries would also start employing more capital (table). Oil-intensive industries would also be favourably impacted by increased availability of public infrastructure or better-educated workers. Interestingly, consumption of fuel oil would continue to be unambiguously lower compared with the baseline (figure A). Increased public infrastructure or service delivery in education would also trigger a positive synergy with human development. Promotion in all cycles of education, for example, would increase remarkably owing mainly to more service delivery, but also to a lesser extent inasmuch as new roads facilitate access to and functioning of education centres (see figure B, for primary education).**d** Without these coherent policy interventions, taxing fuel oil consumption alone would actually reduce promotion rates in primary education, as household demand for education shrinks in tandem with the contraction of economic activity, as seen under the first simulated scenario.

The new revenue from taxing consumption of fuel oil more could alternatively have been invested in other social sectors (health, water and sanitation, and so on) or used to enhance sectoral production capacity. For example, a scenario analysis similar to that presented here shows that investing 2 additional percentage points of GDP in Uganda's agriculture infrastructure would bring about productivity gains that contributed to agricultural output without expanding land use, while enhancing food security and even spurring export capacity (see box IV.2).

d There are additional gains—not shown here—in terms of human development when investments in public infrastructure are stepped up. Child and maternal mortality rates, for example, exhibit a reduction, as the increased stock of public roads, bridges and electricity networks facilitates access to and functioning of health centres and hospitals. The reduction in child mortality, a proxy for the health status of the student population, in turn, triggers a positive synergy for promotion rates and other educational attainment indicators.

Box V.2 (cont'd)

Figure B
Promotion rates in primary education in simulated scenarios, 2016-2030

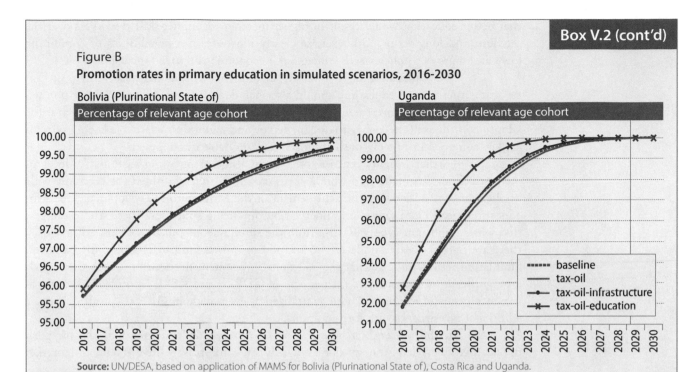

Source: UN/DESA, based on application of MAMS for Bolivia (Plurinational State of), Costa Rica and Uganda.

Real GDP growth and its supply driving factors in simulated scenarios, 2016-2030

Period annual averages, per cent				
	baseline	*tax-oil*	*tax-oil-infrastructure*	*tax-oil-education*
Bolivia (Plurinational State of)				
GDP at factor cost	5.00	4.92	5.13	4.95
Total factor productivity	2.61	2.61	2.78	2.63
Total factor employment	2.39	2.31	2.36	2.32
Costa Rica				
GDP at factor cost	4.25	4.11	4.25	4.36
Total factor productivity	2.22	2.18	2.29	2.25
Total factor employment	2.03	1.93	1.96	2.11
Uganda				
GDP at factor cost	7.00	6.46	6.79	7.11
Total factor productivity	3.71	3.42	3.67	3.74
Total factor employment	3.29	3.05	3.12	3.38

Source: UN/DESA, based on application of MAMS for Bolivia (Plurinational State of), Costa Rica and Uganda.

In the long run, the feasibility of the simulated policies will depend on countries' ability to shift towards alternative sources of energy. In a country like the Plurinational State of Bolivia, for example, taxing fuel oil more may eventually lead to an increase in the demand for gas, another fossil fuel. Thus, the shift to be pursued should be towards more environmentally friendly sources of energy. The case of Costa Rica is interesting in this respect, as over the years, nearly 90 per cent of this country's growing demand for electricity has been met through hydropower plants, the construction of which has taken into consideration their environmental and social implications. Thus, taxing fuel oil in this country may eventually incentivize further developments of environmentally friendly hydropower generation and energy efficiency.

that better education would result in higher incomes for higher-skilled workers over the medium and long terms. This exercise clearly illustrates the possibilities of combining low-carbon growth policies with strategies for economic and social inclusion.

The reallocation of resources to investments with a long-term return, such as for infrastructure and education, should also include policies to enhance labour productivity. In addition to investments in formal education, investments in training and the adoption of the skills necessary to design, deploy and maintain sustainable energy systems are key components of a big-push approach to sustainable development.

Further insights centring on the challenge of pursuing sustainable development strategies can be derived from a series of studies that examined the economy-wide implications of accelerating the achievement of the Millennium Development Goals for education, health and sanitation under various financing strategies. These studies suggest that while important synergies arise from the simultaneous pursuit of these three goals, there are also noticeable trade-offs in relation to growth and macroeconomic balances. Simulation results indicate that the additional investment necessary to reach these goals are significant, in the order of 1-4 per cent of GDP (figure V.8).[17] In these studies, negative macroeconomic effects can be neutralized or even made positive, if countries finance additional investments with foreign grants.

In the *World Economic and Social Survey 2011* presentation, the big-push public investment-led strategy does not substitute for private investment and market

Figure V.8
Growth impact of policies aimed towards achieving the Millennium Development Goals, selected countries

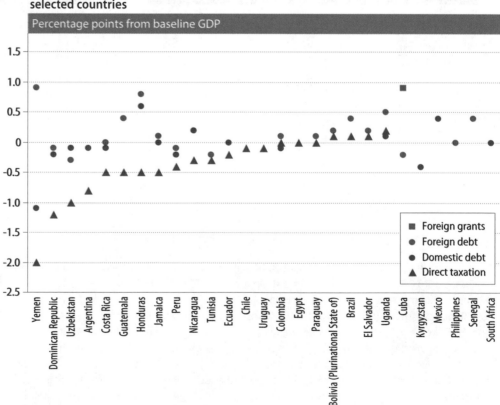

Source: Based on MAMS simulation results reported in Sanchez and others (2010) and Sanchez and Vos (2013).

---

17   We leave aside extreme cases where expenditures relative to GDP are about 0.2 per cent and 8 per cent of GDP and above.

Figure V.9
Energy and the post-2015 vision

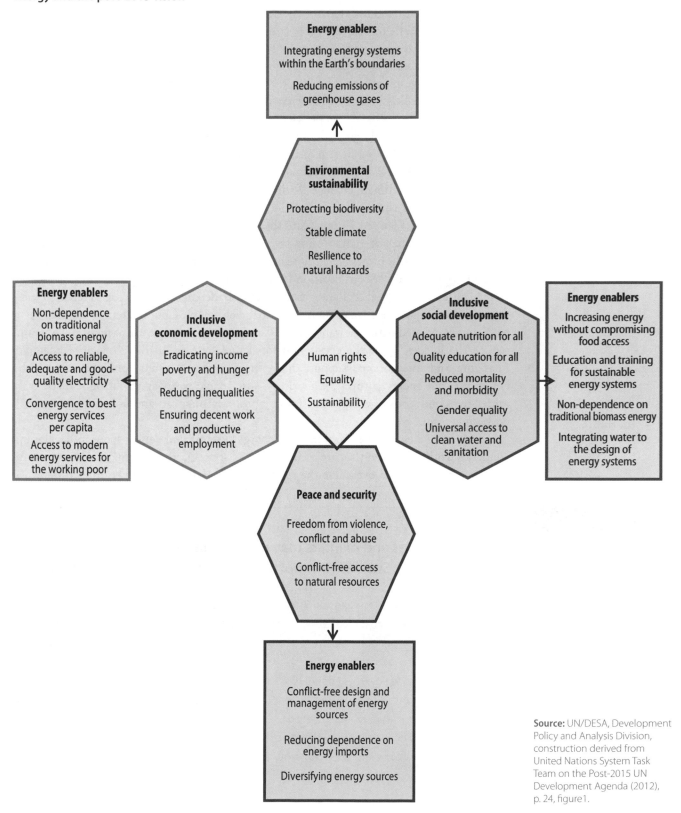

Source: UN/DESA, Development Policy and Analysis Division, construction derived from United Nations System Task Team on the Post-2015 UN Development Agenda (2012), p. 24, figure1.

contributions. Public investments are used to trigger the private investment and market forces that have so far lain dormant and hence are unable to generate the type of changes needed if world demand is to remain within the Earth's carrying capacity. However, policymaking also needs to deal with a host of market and public sector failures and to be able to elaborate well-crafted interventions, as proposed in the OECD, World Bank and UNEP green economy strategies. To illustrate the unexpected ways in which public sector interventions can spur market forces, it is useful to look at how a nationally oriented environmental policy in Sweden later developed into a market-mediated regional trash recycling activity (see box V.3 on policies and markets).

The potential relevance of the big-push approach and its emphasis on comprehensive coherent policies and strong international cooperation is illustrated by the case of Bangladesh which has rightly identified adaptation as the issue of utmost concern when dealing with climate change. Without losing sight of adaptation, the country has also been active in the area of mitigation, with such policies as the promotion of solar renewable sources (United Nations, 2011b). Furthermore, Bangladesh is considering an energy strategy aimed at guaranteeing the energy supply needed by the country to continue growing and improving energy security by reducing dependency on imports. One possible approach under consideration for achieving these goals entails basing the energy system on enhanced coal technologies. Use of enhanced coal technologies leads to a reduction in emissions relative to traditional coal technologies, but to an increase relative to pathways associated with renewable sources; and a more extensive use of renewables would reduce the locking in of the country to fossil fuel sources. In the absence of adequate financing and international support, however, Bangladesh should probably choose the enhanced coal energy pathway. Choosing a sustainable pathway might be realistic only under the conditions of a big-push strategy properly financed and assisted (see box V.4 on Bangladesh).

Policies designed to transform energy systems and deploy them in developing countries work best when they are comprehensive, strategic and systematic. Policymaking in these areas needs to overcome the tendency to oversimplify the planning framework

---

Box V.3

Policies and markets may provide unintended welcoming effects: Sweden is importing garbage to generate electricity

With a strong tradition of recycling and incinerating, Sweden now has too many waste-to-energy incinerators and not enough rubbish to meet demand. While Germany, Belgium and the Netherlands are also importing trash from other countries, with Germany importing the most, Sweden is the leading importer in terms of the share of rubbish burned.

To date, Sweden has imported mainly from Norway. However, as the European Union seeks to reduce the dumping of 150 million tons of rubbish in huge landfills each year, Sweden sees a chance to import more waste from other States of the European Union too.

According to Weine Wiqvist, head of the trade association Swedish Waste Management: "It sounds almost foul to be importing waste, but the import to Sweden is not a problem. The dumping in landfills abroad is a huge problem."

Source: Ringstrom (2012).

Box V.4

Bangladesh: between a coal-based energy system at hand and a promising but distant sustainable energy system

Bangladesh is likely to experience severe negative impacts from climate change and it is preparing for them.[a] The Government has already formulated its National Adaptation Programme of Action and has taken measures to reduce climate change hazards, including community-led coastal afforestation, construction of dual-use flood shelters and programmes to reduce salinity, among others. Bangladesh is also taking important steps towards mitigation. Notably, it has formulated an energy strategy up to 2030, the Power System Master Plan 2010. The Plan, which identifies this strategy as based on a "fuel diversification" scenario considers that it addresses the three main concerns, related to the economy, the environment, and energy security. On the economic front, the Plan aims to eliminate power shortages and to renovate the power infrastructure created during the first phase. In terms of the environment, while the use of coal is central to the Plan, Bangladesh expects to lower carbon emissions by improving the thermal efficiency of coal plants using Japan's clean coal technology. The plan seeks energy security by lowering its current reliance on imported oil.

The power strategy relies on energy generation from coal. Currently, gas is the main source of energy (60-70 per cent) and oil is second in importance (15-30 per cent). The Plan anticipates changing this composition dramatically. The share of coal in power generation will increase from less than 5 per cent in 2012 to about 50 per cent in 2030. Gas will account for 25 per cent and oil for 5 per cent. Nuclear and hydroelectric—domestic and imported, including wind and solar renewables—will account for 20 per cent. The main reason behind the choice of coal as the main source of energy is its comparatively low and stable price and the discovery of high-quality coal deposits in the northern part of the country.

Mondal, Mathur and Denich (2011) argue that a policy package of carbon taxes and regulations placing caps on emissions could have positive sustainability effects. Using a MARKAL model for energy the authors run simulations showing that a policy package of mandated reductions in CO2 emission and carbon taxes directly decreases the use of high-carbon fossil-based technologies in favour of clean renewable energy technologies. A cumulative CO_2 emissions reduction target of 10 and 20 per cent reduces cumulative net energy imports by 39-65 per cent, while a carbon tax of 2,500 taka/ton reduces imports by 37 per cent by 2035. The simulated emissions reduction targets and the carbon tax results suggest that the country can decrease its total primary energy use by 5-22 per cent, relative to the baseline, and do so while satisfying the energy needs of an economy growing at 6.8 per cent per year. Thus, the adoption of low-carbon policies could allow the country to reduce emissions, guarantee energy security, increase efficiency and expand the use of renewables, with the added well-known health benefits.

This quick review invites the following question, which might be relevant not only for Bangladesh but also for many other developing countries: Why not adopt ambitious low-carbon policies? The nature of the answer is, in large part, of course, related to the difficulties of implementing, in the real world, the assumptions made in the modelling realm. Implementation problems need to be overcome in the area of financing of investments in energy generation and infrastructure and, of technology development and adaptation; and political economy-related obstacles need to be overcome in order to implement carbon taxes and regulations on capping emissions, which is known to require complementary policies designed to neutralize or compensate for negative impacts on vulnerable population groups. The adoption of sustainable development paths by developing countries initially depends on effective internaitonal (sp) cooperation, including financial and technical assistance.

Source: UN/DESA, Development Policy and Analysis Division.
a See, for example, World Bank (2010b); and Thurlow, Dorosh and Yu (2011).

in terms of its scope, to focus on a narrow set of energy options, and to ignore trends in other economic and social sectors. Policies will have to specify goals, establish standards for performance, exploit niche markets and adopt a portfolio approach rather than pick a few winning projects or technologies. Policies should be geared towards end users, with specific goals for energy services, markets and the portfolio of technologies to be considered. Given multiple interrelations, the policy focus should be on clusters and should be based on integrated assessments. Examples of integrated approaches to energy policies are the water-energy-food nexus (NEXUS) and the climate-land-energy-water (CLEW) inter-linkage. A best-practice energy policy feeding into the national biofuel policy of Mauritius turns out to be inconsistent with respect to future water availability, the cost of extraction and the energy security goals of the country. These inconsistencies were revealed only

---

Box V.5

Mauritius: coping with climate and land-use, energy and water resources

Land, energy and water are among our most precious resources, but the manner and extent to which they are exploited contributes to climate change. Meanwhile, the systems that provide these resources are themselves highly vulnerable to changes in climate. Efficient resource management is therefore of great importance, for both mitigation and adaptation purposes.

The lack of integration in resource assessments and policymaking leads to inconsistent strategies and inefficient resource utilization, especially at the national level.

In Mauritius, a national biofuel policy that made sense from a best-practice energy, land and water planning point of view was shown to be strongly inconsistent. This was discovered only when the Government and international analysts modelled these systems in an integrated manner. An integrated modelling approach of climate, land-use, energy and water resource systems (CLEW) was particularly useful for assessing the response to climate change-induced reductions in precipitation. The change in rainfall patterns led to increases in water withdrawals, which in turn led to higher demand for the energy needed to drive pumps bringing water from its source to the fields and to power water-desalination plants. The existence of a positive feedback loop means that this will lead to increased demand for cooling of thermal power plants and thus to additional withdrawal of water (unless they are cooled by seawater). If the increase in electricity demand is met with coal-fired power generation, as planned, then the greenhouse gas benefits of the ethanol policy are eroded by increased emissions from the power sector. Higher coal imports also have a negative impact on energy security. The benefits of this policy—aimed at reducing energy import costs and emissions—are thus clearly vulnerable to the impacts of climate change; and the long-term viability of this strategy would be at risk if rainfall were to decrease further and droughts were to continue. In this case, producers would have either to scale back production or resort to expensive water desalination. Both of these options negatively impact the expected climate and energy security benefits of the policy and both would be detrimental to the sugar and ethanol industry.

The water-constrained scenario does, however, also lead to better prospects for renewable electricity generation. Wind and photovoltaic electricity generation is typically much less water-intensive than fossil fuel generation. Furthermore, if power consumption for water desalination facilities were to make up a significant share of total system load, intermittent resources such as wind could be integrated more easily. Since water is cheap and easy to store, it is not important that it be produced at a specific time. It could therefore be treated as an interruptible load and shut down in the event that wind generation was unavailable during times of high system load.

In response to these factors, the Government of Mauritius has appointed a high-level CLEW panel to ensure consistency among its climate, land, energy and water strategies.

by an integrated assessment of the biofuel policy which included the potential effects of climate-change on water precipitation (box V.5). Increasing the production of biofuels is a natural candidate for the role of addressing energy insecurity and rising greenhouse gas emissions. Burkina Faso, like many other developing countries, would do well to consider expanding the production of biofuels to address energy security concerns and cope with greenhouse gas emissions, even at the cost of accelerating the rapid deforestation that affects the country. However, an integrated assessment recommended the implementation of policies that intensify the use of land for agriculture production (see discussion in chap. III). Even if there are inevitable trade-offs, increasing the intensity of land use leads to net reductions in emissions, contained deforestation and improved energy security (box V.6).

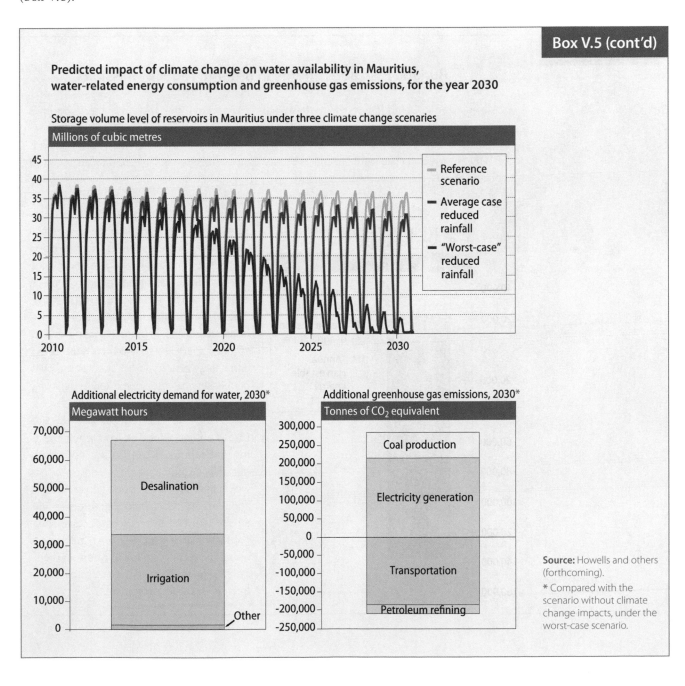

Box V.5 (cont'd)

Predicted impact of climate change on water availability in Mauritius, water-related energy consumption and greenhouse gas emissions, for the year 2030

Storage volume level of reservoirs in Mauritius under three climate change scenaries

Millions of cubic metres

Legend:
— Reference scenario
— Average case reduced rainfall
— "Worst-case" reduced rainfall

Additional electricity demand for water, 2030*

Megawatt hours

Desalination / Irrigation / Other

Additional greenhouse gas emissions, 2030*

Tonnes of CO_2 equivalent

Coal production / Electricity generation / Transportation / Petroleum refining

Source: Howells and others (forthcoming).

* Compared with the scenario without climate change impacts, under the worst-case scenario.

Integrated energy
assessment and planning
constitute a critical tool for
the design of sustainable
strategies, particularly in
developing countries

Integrated energy assessment and planning constitute a critical tool for the design of sustainable strategies, particularly in developing countries—and even more so in those countries that are likely to be affected by climate variability. However, these countries rarely have the capacities needed to undertake such analysis. Widespread access to integrated energy assessment and planning tools should be part of the international co-operation framework for sustainable development. It is important to harness the expertise on energy systems acquired by a number of research institutions throughout the world to assist developing countries in the task of building sustainable energy systems. It will thus be important to establish a network of independent centres for energy systems analysis with a mandate to assist the design and implementation of sustainable energy plans in developing and least developed countries.

Box V.6

Burkina Faso adds energy in order to reduce emissions

Policies to reduce emissions have to take into consideration the fact that the economic-environment system is complex, specific and interlinked. In Burkina Faso, a country with rapid de-forestation, growing energy insecurity and greenhouse gas emissions, an integrated approach finds that a measure with damaging direct effects on each of these factors has disproportionately positive knock-on effects. This phenomenon is uncovered by an integrated modeling of the system, allowing for appropriate national development actions.

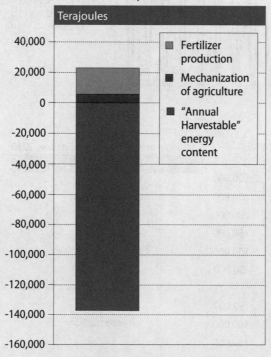

Changes in the energy balance in Burkina Faso, 2030

Source: Hermann and others, 2012.

In summary, agriculture is expanding rapidly, eating into forest, a natural "carbon sink". Forest supplies vital fuel wood used for cooking and heating. As forest is displaced, people are forced, for energy needs, to use oil, which is imported and expensive. Emissions are increasing as the carbon sink is disappearing and oil use is increasing. Energy security is reduced as more oil is imported, and energy poverty is increased as the price of the new energy source (oil) is relatively expensive.

However, agriculture in Burkina Faso is not intensive. The land requirements for similar outputs can be significantly reduced by changing practices. Those changes would include higher application of fertilizer and mechanization. To fully grasp these linkages it is useful to recall that conventional production and application are highly greenhouse gas-intensive and increased mechanization requires higher volumes of oil use in tractors and other equipment.

More broadly, significant investments will be needed in technological innovation and adaptation, supported by efficient technology transfers and cooperation at the regional and international levels (United Nations, 2011b). The design of sustainable energy systems as part of national development strategies calls for capacities and skills that are not abundant in many countries of the world. Building such capacities will enable countries to undertake transformative energy plans that would otherwise be considered completely out of reach.

It will be important to establish a network of independent centres for energy systems analysis to assist in the design and implementation of sustainable energy plans in developing and least developed countries

Sustainable energy systems in a global development agenda

The transformation of the energy system should be a core element in a post-2015 development agenda. The four dimensions integrated in the UN-System view of the post-2015 development agenda provide a useful reference for framing the transformation of the energy system (United Nations System Task Team on the Post-2015 UN Development Agenda, 2012). Each of the four dimensions can be mapped to further detail for relevant energy transformative policies. For example, the environmental sustainability dimension can be directly linked to the promotion of renewables and energy efficiency, as well as linked with integrated energy policies (figure V.9). The inclusive economic development dimension can relate to policies for reducing dependence on traditional biomass energy and policies aimed at providing universal access to electricity, among others. The inclusive social development dimension can be mapped to integrated policies for ensuring access to modern energy and food security, and to strategies for integrating access to water and provisioning energy, for example. The dimension of peace and security can be related to policies designed to lessen dependence on energy imports or policies for diversifying sources of energy. Member States currently working to define the main threads of the post-2015 development agenda might wish to take note of the importance of explicitly incorporating energy goals.

Member States currently working on defining the main threads of the post-2015 development agenda might take note of the importance of explicitly incorporating energy goals

Bibliography

Abdallah, S. S., and others (2009). *The (un)Happy PlanetIndex 2.0.: Why Good Lives don't Have to Cost the Earth*. London: new economics foundation.

Abel, Jaison, and Richard Deitz (2012). Job polarization and rising inequality in the nation and the New York-northern New Jersey region. *Current Issues in Economics and Finance*, vol. 18, No. 7, pp. 1-7.

Africare, Oxfam America and WWF-ICRISAT Project (2010). More rice for people, more water for the planet. Hyderabad, India.

Agrawala, Shardul, and Samuel Fankhauser, eds. (2008). *Economic Aspects of Adaptation to Climate Change: Costs, Benefits and Policy Instruments*. Paris: Organization for Economic Cooperation and Development.

AIV (2011). The post-2015 development agenda: the Millennium Development Goals in perspective, No. 74 (April). The Hague: Advisory Council on International Affairs.

Alire, Rod (2011). The reality behind biodegradable plastic packaging material: the science of biodegradable plastics. Fremont, California: FP International. Available from http://www.fpintl.com/resources/wp_biodegradable_plastics.htm (accessed 3 March 2013).

Altieri, Miguel A. (2008). Small farms as a planetary ecological asset: five key reasons why we should support the revitalization of small farms in the global South. Oakland, California: Food First/Institute for Food and Development Policy. 15 April. Available from http://www.foodfirst.org/en/node/2115.

Alton, Theresa, and others (2012). *The Economic Implications of Introducing Carbon Taxes in South Africa. UNU-WIDER Working Paper*, No. 2012/46. Helsinki: United Nations University-World Institute for Development Economics Research.

Anseeuw, Ward, and others (2012). *Land Rights and the Rush for Land: Findings of the Global Commercial Pressures on Land Research Project*. Rome: International Land Coalition.

Aryeetey, Ernest, and others (2012). *Getting to zero: finishing the job the MDGs started*. Paper prepared by members of the Global Agenda Council on Bench-making progress convened by the World Economic Forum.

Asheim, Geir B., and Martin L. Weitzman (2001). Does NNP growth indicate welfare improvement? *Economics Letters*, 73, No. 2 (November), pp. 233-239.

Audretsch, David B., Albert N. Link and John T. Scott (2002). Public/private technology partnerships: evaluating SBIR-supported research. *Research Policy*, vol. 31, No. 1 (January), pp. 145-158.

Ayres, Robert (2007). On the practical limits to substitution. *Ecological Economics*, vol. 61, No. 1, pp. 115-128.

Baker, Judy L., ed. (2012). *Climate Change, Disaster Risk, and the Urban Poor: Cities Building Resilience for a Changing World*. Urban Development Series. Washington, D.C.: World Bank.

Bangladesh (2010). Power system master plan 2010. Available from http://www.powerdi-vision.gov.bd/pdf/SUMMARYPSMP2010.pdf.

Barnosky, Anthony, and others (2012). Approaching a state shift in Earth's biosphere. *Nature*, vol. 486, No. 7401 (7 June), pp. 52-58.

Baumert, Kevin A., Timothy Herzog and Jonathan Pershing (2005). *Navigating the Numbers: Greenhouse Gas Data and International Climate Policy*. Washington, D.C.: World Resources Institute.

Beall, Jo, Basudeb Guha-Khasnobis and Ravi Kanbur, eds. (2012). *Urbanization and Development in Asia*. Multidimensional Perspectives. New York: Oxford University Press.

Beatley, Timothy, ed. (2012). *Green Cities of Europe: Global Lessons on Green Urbanism*. Washington, D.C.: Island Press.

Beddington, J., and others (2012). Achieving food security in the face of climate change. Final report from the Commission on Sustainable Agriculture and Climate Change. Copenhagen: CGIAR Research Program on Climate Change, Agriculture and Food Security.

Beintema, Nienke, and Howard Elliott (2009). Setting meaningful investment targets in agricultural research and development: challenges, opportunities and fiscal realities. Paper prepared for the Expert meeting on "How to Feed the World in 2050", organized by the Food and Agriculture Organization of the United Nations, Rome, 24-26 June 2009.

Bellard, Celine, and others (2012). Impacts of climate change on the future of biodiversity. *Ecology Letters*, vol. 15, No. 4 (April), pp. 365-377.

Benin, S., and others (2010). Monitoring African agricultural development processes and performance: a comparative analysis. ReSAKSS Annual Trends and Outlook Report 2010. Washington, D.C.: International Food Policy Research Institute.

Berg, Andrew, and Jonathan Ostry (2011). Inequality and unsustainable growth: two sides of the same coin? IMF Staff Discussion Note. SDN/11/08. Washington, D.C.: International Monetary Fund. 8 April.

Besley, Timothy, and Louise J. Cord, eds. (2007). *Delivering on the Promise of Pro-Poor Growth: Insights and Lessons from Country Experiences*. Washington, D.C.: World Bank; Basingstoke, United Kingdom: Palgrave Macmillan.

Bhagwati, Jagdish (2005). Development aid: getting it right. *OECD Observer*, No. 249 (May).

Biodiversity International and others (2012). Sustainable agricultural productivity growth and bridging the gap for small-family farms: interagency report to the Mexican G20 Presidency. 12 June.

Birdsal, Nancy, and Lawrence McDonald (2013). Could China and its fellow Brics nations lead the way on climate change? *Guardian*, 28 January. Available from http://go.nature.com/wqdizO.

Birkmann, Jörn, and Korinna von Teichman (2010). Integrating disaster risk reduction and climate change adaptation: key challenges - scales, knowledge, and norms. *Sustainability Science*, vol. 5, No. 2, pp. 171-184.

Boon, Ronald G.J., Anastasia Alexaki and Ernesto Herrera Becerra (2001). The Ilo Clean Air Project: a local response to industrial pollution control in Peru. *Environment and Urbanization*, vol. 13, No. 2 (October), pp. 215-232.

Bowen, Alex (2012). "Green" growth: what does it mean? Environmental Scientist, pp. 7-11. London: Grantham Research Institute on Climate Change and the Environment.

Braun, Arnoud, and Deborah Duveskog (2008). The Farmer Field School approach: history, global assessment and success stories. Background paper commissioned by the International Fund for Agricultural Development for the *IFAD Rural Poverty Report 2009* (October).

Brookes, L. (1990). The Greenhouse effect: the fallacies in the energy efficient solution. *Energy Policy*, vol. 18, No. 2 (March), pp. 199-201.

Brooks, S., and M. Loevinsohn (2011). Shaping agricultural innovation systems responsive to food insecurity and climate change. Background paper prepared for *World Economic and Social Survey 2011*.

Brown, Judy, and Michael Fraser (2006). Approaches and perspectives in social and environmental accounting: an overview of the conceptual landscape. *Business Strategy and the Environment*, vol. 15, No 2, pp. 103-117.

Brysse, Keynyn, and others (2012). Climate change predictions: erring on the side of least drama? *Global Environmental Change*, vol. 23, No. 1 (February 2013), pp. 327-337. Available from http://dx.doi.org/10.1016/j.gloenvcha.2012.10.008.

Burritt, Roger L., Tobias Hahn and Stefan Schaltegger (2002). Towards a comprehensive framework for environmental management accounting: links between business actors and environmental management accounting tools. *Australian Accounting Review*, vol. 12, No. 27 (July), pp. 39-50.

Campbell-Lendrum, D. (2009). Saving lives while saving the planet: protecting health from climate change. Background paper prepared for *World Economic and Social Survey 2009*.

Cannady, Cynthia. (2009). Access to climate change technology by developing countries: a practical strategy. *ICTSD Intellectual Property and Sustainable Development Series Issue Paper*, No. 25. Geneva: International Centre for Trade and Sustainable Development. September.

Castaldi, Carolina, and others (2009). Technological learning, policy regimes, and growth: the long-term patterns and some specificities of a "Globalized" economy. In *Industrial Policy and Development: The Political Economy of Capabilities Accumulation*, Mario Cimoli, Giovanni Dosi and Joseph Stiglitz, eds. Oxford: Oxford University Press.

Cattaneo, Olivier, Gary Gereffi and Cornelia Staritz (2010). Global value chains in a postcrisis world: resilience, consolidation, and shifting end markets. In *Global Value Chains in a Postcrisis World*, Olivier Cattaneo, Gary Gereffi and Cornelia Staritz, eds. Washington, D.C.: World Bank.

Chant, Lindsay, Scott McDonald and Arjan Verschoor (2008). Some consequences of the 1994-1995 coffee boom for growth and poverty reduction in Uganda. *Journal of Agricultural Economics*, vol. 59, No. 1 (February), pp. 93-113.

Chen, Shaohua, and Martin Ravallion (2010). The developing world is poorer than we thought, but no less successful in the fight against poverty. *Quarterly Journal of Economics*, vol. 25, No. 4, pp. 1577-1625.

Cohen, Barney (2006). Urbanization in developing countries: current trends, future projections, and key challenges for sustainability. *Technology in Society*, vol. 28, Nos. 1-2 (January-April), pp. 63-80.

Cohen, Joel (2010). Beyond population: everyone counts in development. Center for Global Development Working Paper 220. Washington, D.C.: Center for Global Development. July.

Committee on World Food Security, High-level Panel of Experts on Food Security and Nutrition (2011). Price volatility and food security. HLPE report 1. Rome. July.

Daly, Herman (1991). *Steady State Economics*, Washington, D.C.: Island Press.

_____ (1996). *Beyond Growth: The Economics of Sustainable Development*. Boston, Massachusetts: Beacon Press.

Dasgupta, Partha (1994). Optimal development and the idea of net national product. In *Sustainable Economic Development: Domestic and International Policy*, I. Goldin and A. Winter, eds. Cambridge, United Kingdom: Cambridge University Press. Pp. 111-142.

_____, B. Kristrom and K. G. Maler (1997). The environment and the net national product. In *The Environment and Emerging Development Issues*, P. Dasgupta and K. G. Maler, eds. Oxford: Clarendon Press. Pp. 129-139.

Davis, Kristin, and others (2007). Strengthening agricultural education and training in sub-Saharan Africa from an innovation systems perspective: case studies of Ethiopia and Mozambique. IFPRI discussion Paper, No. 00736 (December). Washington, D.C.: International Food Policy Research Institute.

Deininger, Klaus, and others (2010). *Rising Global Interest in Farmland: Can It Yield Sustainable and Equitable Benefits?* Washington, D.C.: World Bank.

Deloitte (2012). eTransform Africa: agriculture sector study: sector assessment and opportunities for ICT. 4 February.

Derviş, Kemal (2012). Convergence, interdependence, and divergence. *Finance and Development*, vol. 49, No. 3, pp. 10-14.

Devarajan, Shantayanan, and others (2011). Tax policy to reduce carbon emissions in a distorted economy: illustrations from a South Africa CGE model. *B.E. Journal of Economic Analysis and Policy*, vol. 11, No. 1. Available from http://www.bepress.com/bejeap/vol11/iss1/art13.

Dobbs, Richard, and others (2011a). *Resource Revolution: Meeting the World's Energy, Materials, Food, and Water needs*. McKinsey Global Institute. November.

Dobbs, Richard, and others (2011b). Urban world: mapping the economic power of cities. McKinsey Global Institute. March.

Dobbs, Richard, and others (2011c). Resource revolution: meeting the world's energy, materials, food and water needs. McKinsey Global Institute, McKinsey Sustainability and Resource Productivity Practice. November.

Dong, Fengxia and Frank H. Fuller (2007). Changing diets in china's cities: empirical fact or urban legend? Working Paper 06-WP 437. Ames, Iowa: Center for Agricultural and Rural Development, Iowa State University. September.

Dregne, H. E. (1990). Erosion and soil productivity in Africa. *Journal of Soil and Water Conservation*, vol. 45, No. 4 (July/August), pp. 431-436.

Drèze, J. and A. Sen, eds. (1991). *The Political Economy of Hunger*: vol. 1, *Entitlement and Well-being*; vol. 2, *Famine Prevention*; vol. 3, *Endemic Hunger*. *WIDER Studies in Economics*. New York: Oxford University Press.

Dubin, H. J., and John P. Brennan (2009). Fighting a "shifty enemy": the international collaboration to contain wheat rusts. In *Millions Fed: Proven Success in Agricultural Development*, David J. Spielman and Rajul Pandya-Lorch, eds. Washington, D.C.: International Food Policy Research Institute. Pp. 19-24.

Durrmeyer, Isis, Philippe Février and Xavier D'Haultfoeuille (2011). The Willingness to pay for global warming reduction: lessons from the French automobile market. Paper prepared for the Eighteenth Annual Conference of the European Association of Environmental and Resource Economists, Rome, 29 June-2 July 2011.

Earth Security Initiative (2012). The Land Security Agenda: how investor risks in farmland create opportunities for sustainability. London. March.

Echeverria, Ruben G., and Nienke M. Beintema (2009). Mobilizing financial resources for agricultural research in developing countries: trends and mechanisms. Rome: Global Forum on Agricultural Research (GFAR).

Elliot, Kimberley Ann (2010). Pulling agricultural innovation and the market together. Working paper No. 215 (June). Washington, D.C.: Centre for Global Development.

Epstein, Gerald (2005). Introduction: financialization and the world economy. In *Financialization and the World Economy*, Gerald Epstein, ed. Cheltenham, United Kingdom: Edward Elgar.

Erten, Bilge, and Jose Antonio Ocampo (2012). Super-cycles of commodity prices since the mid-nineteenth century. DESA Working Paper No. 110. ST/ESA/2012/DWP/110. February. Available from http://www.un.org/esa/desa/papers/2012/wp110_2012.pdf.

Ervin, David E., Leland L. Glenna and Raymond A. Jussaume, Jr. (2010). Are biotechnology and sustainable agriculture compatible? *Renewable Agriculture and Food Systems*, vol. 1, No. 1 (18 February), pp. 1-15.

Evans, Alex (2010). Globalization and scarcity: Multilateralism for a world with limits. New York: Center on International Cooperation, New York University. November.

_____ (2011). Resource scarcity, fair shares and development. WWF/Oxfam discussion paper. Available from http://www.oxfam.org/sites/www.oxfam.org/files/rr-resource-scarcity-fair-shares-200711-en.pdf.

Fan, Shenggen, and Mark W. Rosegrant (2008). Investing in agriculture to overcome the world food crisis and reduce poverty and hunger. IFPRI Policy Brief, No. 3. Washington, D.C.: International Food Policy Research Institute. June. Available from http://www.ifpri.org/sites/default/files/publications/bp003.pdf.

Falconer, Gordon, and Shane Mitchell (2012). Smart City Framework: a systematic process for enabling Smart+Connected Communities. Cisco Internet Business Solutions Group (IBSG). September.

Foley, Jonathan, and others (2005). Global consequences of land use. *Science*, vol. 309, No. 5734 (22 July), pp. 570-574.

Food and Agriculture Organization of the United Nations (2003). World agriculture: towards 2015/2030 prospects for food nutrition, agriculture and major commodity groups - interim report. Rome.

_____ (2004). Incorporating nutrition considerations into development policies and programmes. Brief for policy-makers and programme planners in developing countries. Rome.

_____ (2008). Crop prospects and food situation, No. 2: Benin. Rome.

_____ (2009a). *How to Feed the World in 2050: Proceedings of the Expert Meeting on How to Feed the World in 2050.* Rome. 24-26 June 2009, FAO Headquarters, Rome.

_____ (2009b). Investing in food security. Rome. November.

_____ (2009c). *The State of Food Insecurity in the World 2009: Economic Crises - Impacts and Lessons Learned.* Rome.

_____ (2009d). Expert papers from the High-Level Expert Forum on How to Feed the World, Rome, 12 and 13 October 2009. Available from http://www.fao.org/wsfs/forum2050/wsfs-background-documents/wsfs-expert-papers/en/.

_____ (2009e). *The State of Food and Agriculture 2009: Livestock in the Balance.* Rome.

_____ (2010). *The State of Food Insecurity in the World 2010: Addressing Food Insecurity in Protracted Crises.* Rome.

_____ (2011a). *The State of the World's Land and Water Resources for Food and Agriculture: Managing Systems at Risk—Summary Report.* Rome.

_____ (2011b). *The State of Food and Agriculture 2010/2011: Women in Agriculture-Closing the Gender Gap for Development.* Rome.

_____ (2011c). *The State of the World's Land and Water Resources for Food and Agriculture: Managing Systems at Risk.* Abingdon, United Kingdom: Earthscan.

_____ (2011d). *The State of Food Insecurity in the World 2011: How Does International Price Volatility Affect Domestic Economies and Food Security.* Rome.

_____ (2011e). Global food losses and food waste: extent, causes and prevention. Study conducted for the International Congress Save Food! at Interpack2011, Düsseldorf, Germany. Rome.

_____ (2012a). Towards the future we want: end hunger and make the transition to sustainable agricultural and food systems. Rome.

_____ (2012b). *The State of Food Insecurity in the World 2012.* Rome.

_____ (2012c). Food wastage footprints. Factsheet. Available from http://www.fao.org/fileadmin/templates/nr/sustainability_pathways/docs/Factsheet_FOOD-WASTAGE.pdf.

_____ (2013). *The State of Food and Agriculture 2013: Food Systems for Food Security and Better Nutrition.* Rome.

_____, International Fund for Agricultural Development and International Labour Organization (2010). *Gender Dimensions of Agricultural and Rural Employment: Differentiated Pathways out of Poverty.* Rome.

Foresight (2011). The future of food and farming: challenges and choices for global sustainability. London: Government Office for Science.

Fuglie, K. O. (2012). Productivity growth and technology capital in the global agricultural economy. In *Productivity Growth in Agriculture: An International Perspective*, K. O. Fuglie, S. L. Wang and V. E. Ball, eds. Wallingford, United Kingdom: CABI.

Galbraith, James K. (2012). *Inequality and Instability: The Study of the World Economy Just before the Great Crisis*. Oxford: Oxford University Press.

Galloway, James, and others (2003). The nitrogen cascade. *BioScience*, vol. 53, No. 4, pp. 341-356.

Georgescu-Roegen, N. (1971). *The Entropy Law and the Economic Process*. Cambridge, Massachusetts: Harvard University Press.

Gereffi, Gary (2005). The global economy: organization, governance, and development. In *The Handbook of Economic Sociology*, Neil Smelser and Richard Swedberg, eds. Princeton, New Jersey: Princeton University Press.

Gilbert, Christopher L. (2008). How to understand high food prices. Discussion paper, No. 23. Trento, Italy: Department of Economics, University of Trento. Available from http://www.unitn.it/files/23_08_gilbert.pdf.

Global Footprint Network (2010). Ecological footprint and biocapacity, 2007: results from Natural Footprint Accounts 2010 edition. Oakland, California. Available from http://www.footprintnetwork.org/en/index.php/GFN/page/footprint_for_nations.

Godfray, H. Charles J., and others (2010). Food security: the challenge of feeding 9 billion people. *Science*, vol. 327, No. 5967 (12 February), pp. 812-818.

Gollier, Christian, and Martin L. Weitzman (2010). How should the distant future be discounted when discount rates are uncertain? *Economic Letters*, vol. 107, No. 3 (June), pp. 350-353.

Gonzalez, Fidel (2012). Distributional effects of carbon taxes: the case of Mexico. *Energy Economics*, vol. 34, No. 6, pp. 2102-2115. doi: 10.1016/j.eneco.2012.03.007.

Group of Eight (2008). Leaders' statement on global food security, Hokkaido, Japan, 8 July. Available from http://www.mofa.go.jp/policy/economy/summit/2008/doc/doc080709_04_en.html.

Grübler, Arnulf, and others (2012a). Energy primer. In International Institute for Applied Systems Analysis, *Global Energy Assessment: Toward a Sustainable Future*. New York: Cambridge University Press; Laxenburg, Austria: IIASA. Chap. 1, pp. 99-150.

Grübler, Arnulf, and others (2012b). Policies for the Energy Technology Innovation System (ETIS). In International Institute for Applied Systems Analysis, *Global Energy Assessment: Toward a Sustainable Future*. New York: Cambridge University Press; Laxenburg, Austria: IIASA. Chap. 24, pp. 1665-1744.

Grübler, Arnulf, and Thomas Buettner (2013). Urbanization past and future. In *Energizing Sustainable Cities: Assessing Urban Energy*, Arnulf Grubler and David Fisk, eds. Abingdon, United Kingdom: Routledge.

Grübler, Arnulf, and David Fisk, eds. (2013). *Energizing Sustainable Cities: Assessing Urban Energy*. Abingdon, United Kingdom: Routledge.

Hall, Andy, Jeroen Dijkman and Rasheed Sulaiman V (2010). Research into use: investigating the relationship between agricultural research and innovation. UNU-MERIT Working Paper Series, No. 2010-44 (July). Maastricht, Netherlands: United Nations University–Maastricht Economic and Social Research and Training Centre on Innovation and Technology.

Hallam, David (2009). International Investment in agricultural production. Paper presented at the Expert Meeting on How to Feed the World in 2050, held at FAO Headquarters, Rome, from 24 to 26 June 2009.

Hartwick, J. (1990). National resources, national accounting, and economic depreciation. *Journal of Public Economics*, vol. 43, pp. 291-304.

Hazell, Peter B.R., and others (2010). The future of small farms: trajectories and policy priorities. *World Development*, vol. 38, No. 10 (October), pp. 1453-1526.

Headey, Derek, Sangeetha Malaiyandi and Shenggen Fan (2010). Navigating the perfect storm: reflections on the food, energy, and financial crises. *Agricultural Economics*, vol. 41, No. S1, pp. 217-228.

Henley, David (2012). The agrarian roots of industrial growth: rural development in South-East Asia and sub-Saharan Africa. *Development Policy Review*, vol. 30, Supplement s1 (February), pp. 25-47.

Hermann, S., and others (2012). Climate, land, energy and water (CLEW) interlinkages in Burkina Faso: an analysis of agricultural intensification and bioenergy production. *Natural Resources Forum*, vol. 36, No. 4 (November), pp. 245-262.

Hoekstra, Arjen, and Merfin Mekonnen (2012). The water footprint of humanity. *Proceedings of the National Academy of Sciences*, vol. 109, No. 9, pp. 3232-3237.

Hoffman, D.J., and others (2000). Why are nutritionally stunted children at increased risk of obesity? studies of metabolic rate and fat oxidation in shantytown children from São Paulo, Brazil. *American Journal of Clininical Nutrition*, vol. 72, No. 3 (September), pp. 702-707.

Holian, Matthew J., and Matthew E. Kahn (2013). The rise of the low carbon consumer city. *NBER Working Paper*, No. 18735 (January). Cambridge, Massachusetts: Natural Bureau of Economic Research.

Howells, M., and others (forthcoming). Integrated analysis of climate change, land-use, energy and water strategies. *Nature Climate Change*.

Huesemann, M. (2003). The limits of technological solutions to sustainable development. *Clean Technologies and Environmental Policy*, vol. 5, pp. 21-34.

_____ (2004). The failure of eco-efficiency to guarantee sustainability: future challenges for industrial ecology. *Environmental Progress*, vol. 3, No. 4, pp. 264-270.

Hoff, Karla, and Priyanka Pandey (2004). Belief systems and durable inequalities: an experimental investigation of Indian caste. *World Bank Policy Research Working Paper* 3351. Washington, D.C: World Bank. June.

Horton, Sue, and others (2008). The challenges of hunger and malnutrition. Washington, D.C.: Copenhagen Consensus Center. May.

Institute of Development Studies (2010). Special issue: the MDGs and beyond. *IDS Bulletin*, vol. 41, No. 1 (January). Brighton, United Kingdom.

Institution of Mechanical Engineers (2013). Global food: waste not, want not. London. January.

Intergovernmental Panel on Climate Change (2007a). *Climate Change 2007: Synthesis Report*. Geneva.

_____ (2007b). *Climate Change 2007: Mitigation*. Contribution of Working Group III to the Fourth Assessment Report of the Intergovernmental Panel on Climate Change, Bert Metz and others, eds. Cambridge, United Kingdom: Cambridge University Press.

_____ (2012a). Summary for policymakers. In *Managing the Risks of Extreme Events and Disasters to Advance Climate Change Adaptation*. A Special Report of Working Groups I and II of the Intergovernmental Panel on Climate Change, C. B. Field and others, eds. Cambridge, United Kingdom: Cambridge University Press.

_____ (2012b). *Managing the Risks of Extreme Events and Disasters to Advance Climate Change Adaptation*. Special report of the Intergovernmental Panel on Climate Change. New York: Cambridge University Press.

_____ (2012c). *Renewable Energy Sources and Climate Change Mitigation*. Special Report of the Intergovernmental Panel on Climate Change. Ottmar Edenhofer and others, eds. New York: Cambridge University Press.

International Assessment of Agricultural Knowledge, Science and Technology for Development (2009). *Agriculture at a Crossroads: Global Report*, Beverly D. McIntyre and others, eds. Washington, D.C.: Island Press.

International Energy Agency (2012). *World Energy Outlook 2012*. Paris: OECD/IEA.

International Food Policy Research Institute (2002). Green revolution, curse or blessing? Washington, D.C.

_____ (2005). The future of small farms. Proceedings of a research workshop, Wye, United Kingdom, 26-29 June 2005, jointly organized by International Food Policy Research Institute (IFPRI)/2020 Vision Initiative, Overseas Development Institute (ODI) and Imperial College, London. Washington, D.C.

International Fund for Agricultural Development (2011). *Rural Poverty Report 2011: New Realities, New Challenges — New Opportunities for Tomorrow's Generation*. Rome.

International Institute for Applied Systems Analysis (2012). *Global Energy Assessment: Toward a Sustainable Future*. New York: Cambridge University Press; Laxenburg, Austria: IIASA.

International Monetary Fund (2012). The liberalization and management of capital flows: an institutional view. Staff paper. Washington, D.C. 14 November.

_____ (2013). Energy subsidy reform: lessons and implications. Washington, D.C. 28 January.

Islam, Nazrul (2012). Towards a sustainable social model: implications for the post-2015 agenda. Background paper prepared for *World Economic and Social Survey 2013*.

IUCN-The World Conservation Union, UNEP-United Nations Environment Programme and WWF-World Wide Fund for Nature (1991). *Caring for the Earth: A Strategy for Sustainable Living*. Gland, Switzerland. October.

Jackson, Tim (2009). *Prosperity without Growth: Economics for a Finite planet.* Abingdon, United Kingdom: Earthscan.

_____ (2010). Philosophical and social transformations necessary for the green economy. Background paper prepared for *World Economic and Social Survey 2011.*

Jaafar, Abdul Hamid, Abul Al-Amin and Chamhuri Siwar (2008). A CGE analysis of the economic impact of output-specific carbon tax on the Malaysian economy. MPRA Paper, 10210. Munich Personal RePEc Archive. Available from http://mpra.ub.uni-muenchen.de/10210/.

Jovanovic, Boyan, and Peter Rousseau (2005). General purpose technologies. In *Handbook of Economic Growth*, Philippe Aghion and Steven Durlauf, eds. Amsterdam: Elsevier. Pp. 1181-1224.

Kaeb, Harald (2011). European bioplastics: introduction. Available from www.european-bioplastics.org (accessed 23 February 2011).

Kaplinsky, Raphael (2006). Revisiting the revisited terms of trade: will China make a difference? *World Development*, vol. 34, No. 6, pp. 981-995.

_____, and Masuma Farooki (2010). Global value chains, the crisis, and the shift of markets from North to South. In *Global Value Chains in a Postcrisis World*, Olivier Cattaneo, Gary Gereffi and Cornelia Staritz, eds. Washington, D.C.: World Bank.

Kapur, Devesh, and John McHale (2005). *Give Us Your Best and Brightest: The Global Hunt for Talent and Its Impact on the Developing World.* Washington, D.C.: Center for Global Development.

Kates, Robert, Thomas M. Parris and Anthony A. Leiserowitz (2005). What is sustainable development? goals, indicators, values, and practice. *Environment: Science and Policy for Sustainable Development*, vol. 47, No. 3, pp. 8-21.

Keane, Jodie-Ann (2012). The governance of global value chains and the effects of the global financial crisis transmitted to producers in Africa and Asia. *Journal of Development Studies*, vol. 48, No. 6, pp. 783-797.

Kees van Donge, Jan, David Henley and Peter Lewis (2012). Tracking development in South-East Asia and sub-Saharan Africa: the primacy of policy. *Development Policy Review*, vol. 30, Supplement s1 (February), pp. s5-s24.

Kenny, Charles, and Andy Sumner (2011). More money or more development: what have the MDGs achieved? Center for Global Development Working Paper, No. 278. Washington, D.C.: Center for Global Development. December.

Kindleberger, Charles, and Robert Aliber (2011). *Maniacs, Panics and Crashes: A History of Financial Crises*, 6th ed. Basingstoke, United Kingdom: Palgrave Macmillan.

Krausmann, Fridolin, and others (2009). The global socio-metabolic transition: past and present metabolic profiles and their future trajectories. *Journal of Industrial Ecology*, vol. 12, No. 5-6, pp. 637-656.

Laeven, Luc, and Fabian Valencia (2012). Systemic banking crises database: an update. IMF Working Paper WP/12/163. Washington, D.C.: International Monetary Fund.

Layard, R. (2005). The national income: a sorry tale. In *Growth Triumphant: The 21ˢᵗ Century in Historical Perspective*, R. Easterlin, ed. Ann Arbor, Michigan: University of Michigan Press.

Lee, Bernice, and others (2012). *Resources Futures*. Chatham House Report. London: Royal Institute of International Affairs. December.

Leeuwis, Cees, and Andy Hall (2010). Facing the challenges of climate change and food security: the role of research, extension and communication institutions - final report. Rome: Food and Agriculture Organization of the United Nations, Wageningen University and UNU-MERIT. October.

Lele, Uma, and others (2010). Transforming agricultural research for development. Paper commissioned by the Global Conference on Agricultural Research (GCARD) for the Global Conference on Agricultural Research in Development, Montpellier, France, 28-31 March 2010.

Lenton, Timothy, and Juan-Carlos Ciscar (2012). Integrating tipping points into climate impact assessments *Climate Change* (29 August), pp. 1-13. doi:10.1007/s10584-012-0572-8.

Li, Y., and C. Hewitt (2008). The effect of trade between China and the UK on national and global carbon dioxide emissions. *Energy Policy*, vol. 36, No. 6 (June), pp. 1907-1914.

Lim, William S.W. (2012). *Incomplete Urbanism: A Critical Urban Strategy for Emerging Economies*. Singapore: World Scientific Publishing Company.

Lobell, David, Wolfram Schlenker and Justin Costa-Roberts (2011). Climate trends and global crop production since 1980. *Science*, vol. 333, No. 6042 (29 July), pp. 616-620.

Lofgren, Hans, Martin Cicowiez and Carolina Díaz-Bonilla (2013). MAMS: a computable general equilibrium model for developing country strategy analysis. *In Handbook of Computable General Equilibrium Modeling*, vol. 1A, Peter B. Dixon and Dale W. Jorgenson, eds. Amsterdam: North Holland.

Lund, Susan, and others (2013). Financial globalization: retreat or reset?—global capital markets 2013. McKinsey Global Institute.

Lutz, Wolfgang, Warren Sanderson and Sergei Scherbov (2008). The coming acceleration of global population ageing. *Nature*, vol. 451, No. 7179, pp. 716-719.

Lyubormirsky, S., K. Sheldon and D. Schkade (2005). Pursuing happiness: the architecture of sustainable change. *Review of General Psychology*, vol. 9, pp. 111-131.

Lipton, Michael (2010). From policy aims and small-farm characteristics to farm science needs. *World Development*, vol. 38, No. 10 (October), pp. 1399-1412.

MacKay, David J.C. (2009). *Sustainable Energy—Without the Hot Air*. Cambridge, United Kingdom: UIT Cambridge.

Mathews, M.R. (1997). Twenty-five years of social and environmental accounting research: is there a silver jubilee to celebrate? *Accounting, Auditing & Accountability Journal*, vol. 10, No. 4, pp. 481-531.

Matovu, John Mary, and others (2013). Uganda. In *Financing Human Development in Africa, Asia and the Middle East*, Marco V. Sánchez and Rob Vos, eds. United Nations Series on Development. London: Bloomsburg Academic. McGranahan, Gordon, and David Satterthwaite (2003). Urban centers: an assessment of sustainability. *Annual Review of Environment and Resources*, vol. 28, pp. 243-274.

Meadows, Donella H., and others (1972). *The Limits to Growth*. New York: Universe Books.

Meadows, Donella H., Jorgen Randers and Dennis Meadows (2002). *Limits to Growth: The 30-Year Update*. White River Junction, Vermont: Chelsa Green Publishing Company.

Mehra, Rekha, and Mary Hill Rojas (2008). A significant shift: women, food security and agriculture in a global marketplace. Washington, D.C.: International Center for Research on Women (ICRW).

Milanovic, Branko (1999). True world income distribution, 1988 and 1993: first calculations based on household surveys alone. *World Bank Policy Research Working Paper*, No. 2244. Washington, D.C.: World Bank. November. WPS2244.

_____ (2011a). Global inequality: from class to location, from proletarians to migrants. *World Bank Policy Research Working Paper*, No. 5820. WPS5820. Washington, D.C.: World Bank. September.

_____ (2011b). *The Haves and the Have-Nots: A Brief and Idiosyncratic History of Global Inequality*. New York: Basic Books.

_____ (2012). Global income inequality by the numbers: in history and now: an overview. *World Bank Policy Research Working Paper*, No. 6259. Washington, D.C.: World Bank. November. WPS6259.

Melamud, Claire (2012). After 2015: contexts, politics and processes for a post-2015 global agreement on development. London: Overseas Development Institute. 4 January.

Milberg, William, and Deborah Winkler (2010). Trade, crisis, and recovery: restructuring global value chains. In *Global Value Chains in a Postcrisis World*, Olivier Cattaneo, Gary Gereffi and Cornelia Staritz, eds. Washington, D.C.: World Bank.

Millennium Ecosystem Assessment (2005). *Ecosystems and Human Well-Being: Synthesis Report*. Millennium Ecosystem Assessment Series. Washington, D.C.: Island Press.

Mitchell, Donald (2008). A note on rising food prices. *World Bank Policy Research Working Paper*, No. 4682. Washington, D.C.

"Mitigating circumstances: there are many barriers that must be overcome if South Africa is to control its greenhouse-gas emissions" (2013). *Nature Climate Change*, vol. 3, No. 4 (April) Editorial.

Mitlin, Diana, and David Satterthwaite (2012). *Urban Poverty in the Global South: Scale and Nature*. Abingdon, United Kingdom: Routledge.

Mondal, Alam Hossain, Jyotirmay Mathur and Manfred Denich (2011). Impacts of CO_2 emission constraints on technology selection and energy resources for power generation in Bangladesh, *Energy Policy*, vol. 39, No. 4, pp. 2043-2050.

Montgomery, R. Mark, and others, eds. (2004). *Cities Transformed: Demographic Change and its Implications in the Developing World*. London: Earthscan.

Mowlds, Sinead, William, Nicol and Ernán ó Cléirigh (2012). Aid for food and nutrition security. Paris: Organization for Economic Cooperation and Development, Development Co-operation Directorate. Available from http://www.oecd.org/dac/povertyreduction/Brochure%20on%20Food%20Security%20FINAL%2013%20July%202012.pdf.

MS Swaminathan Research Foundation and World Food Programme (2008). Report on the state of food insecurity in rural India. Rome: WFP.

Mutizwa-Mangiza, Naison (2012). Sustainable urbanization in the post-2015 UN development agenda. Power Point presentation prepared for the Experts Group Meeting on the Post-2015 UN Development Agenda, New York, 27-29 February 2012. Available from http://www.un.org/en/development/desa/policy/untaskteam_undf/pres_sustainable_habitat_mutizwa-mangiza.pdf.

Nelson, Gerald C., and others (2009). *Climate Change: Impact on Agriculture and Costs of Adaptation*. IFPRI Food Policy Report. Washington, D.C.: International Food Policy Research Institute. October.

Nordhaus, William D., and Edward C. Kokkelenberg, eds. (1999). *Nature's Numbers: Expanding the National Economic Accounts to Include the Environment*. Washington, D.C.: National Academies Press.

Nordhaus, Ted, Michael Shellenberger and Linus Blomqvist (2012). The planetary boundaries hypothesis: a review of the evidence. Oakland, California: Breakthrough Institute. June.

Nussbaum, Martha C. (2011). *Creating Capabilities: The Human Development Approach*. Cambridge, Massachusetts: Harvard University Press.

O'Connor, David (2009). Clarifying climate change financing estimates. Informal note. New York: Division for Sustainable Development, Department of Economic and Social Affairs of the United Nations Secretariat.

O'Rourke, Kevin, and Jeffrey Williamson (2004). Once more: when did globalisation begin? *European Review of Economic History*, vol. 8, No. 01 (April), pp. 109-117.

Ocampo, Jose Antonio (2009). The macroeconomics of the green economy. Paper contained in the report of a Panel of Experts entitled "The transition to a green economy: benefits, challenges and risks from a sustainable development perspective", presented at the Secondary Preparatory Committee Meeting for the United Nations Conference on Sustainable Development.

_____, Shari Spiegel and Joseph Stiglitz (2006). Capital market liberalization and development. In *Capital Market Liberalization and Development*, Jose Antonio Ocampo and Joseph Stiglitz, eds. Oxford: Oxford University Press.

Olivier, Jos, Greet Janssens-Maenhout and Jeroen Peters (2012). *Trends in Global CO_2 Emissions: 2012 Report. Background Studies*. The Hague: PBL Netherlands Environmental Assessment Agency.

Omilola, Babatunde, and others (2010). Monitoring and assessing targets of the Comprehensive Africa Agriculture Development Programme (CAADP) and the first Millennium Development Goal (MDG) in Africa. ReSAKSS Working Paper, No. 31. Washington, D.C.: International Food Policy Research Institute. July.

Organization for Economic Cooperation and Development (2010). Measuring aid to agriculture. April.

_____ (2011a). Tools for delivering on green growth. Prepared for the OECD Meeting of the Council at Ministerial Level, 25-26 May 2011, Paris.

_____ (2011b). *Towards Green Growth*. Paris.

_____ (2012a). Obesity update 2012. Available from www.oecd.org/health/49716427. pdf.

_____ (2012b). *Development Co-operation Report 2012: Lessons in Linking Sustainability and Development*. Paris. Available from http://dx.doi. org/10.1787/dcr-2012-en.

_____ (2012c). *OECD Environmental Outlook to 2050: The Consequences of Inaction*. Paris. doi: http://dx.doi.org/10.1787/9789264122246-en.

_____ and Food and Agriculture Organization of the United Nations (2010). *OECD-FAO Agricultural Outlook 2010-2019*. Paris and Rome.

Orrenius, Pia M., and Madeline Zavodny (2009). Do immigrants work in riskier jobs? *Demography*, vol. 46, No. 3 (August), pp. 535-551.

Owen, David (2008). Chronicles of wasted time: a personal reflection on the current state of, and future prospects for, social and environmental accounting research. *Accounting, Auditing & Accountability Journal*, vol. 21, No. 2, pp. 240-267.

Oxfam (2012). *"Our Land, Our Lives": Time Out on the Global Rush*. Oxfam briefing note. Oxford, United Kingdom. October.

Palley, Thomas (2007). Financialization: what it is and why it matters. Levy Economics Institute of Bard College Working Paper No. 525. Annandale-on-Hudson, New York. December.

Palma, Gabriel (2011). Homogeneous middles vs. heterogeneous tails, and the end of the "inverted-U": it's all about the share of the rich. *Development and Change*, vol. 42, No. 1, pp. 87-153.

Pardey, Philip G., and Nienke M. Beintema (2001). *Slow Magic: Agricultural R & D a Century after Mendel*. Washington, D.C.: International Food Policy Research Institute. 26 October.

Passel, Jeffrey S. (2006). The size and characteristics of the unauthorized migrant population in the U.S.: estimates based on the March 2005 Current Population Survey. Research report. Washington, D.C.: Pew Hispanic Center. 7 March.

Patel, Raj (2010). *The Value of Nothing*. New York: Picador.

Pearce, David, Anil Markandya and Edward Barbier (1989). *Blueprint for a Green Economy*. London: Earthscan.

Pearce, Fred (2012). *The Land Grabbers: The New Fight over Who Owns the Earth*. Massachusetts: Beacon Press.

Pemberton, H., and D. Ulph (2000). Measuring income and measuring sustainability. *Scandinavian Journal of Economics*, vol. 103, No. 1 (March), pp. 25-40.

Peters, Glen P., and E. Hertwich (2008). CO_2 embodied in international trade with implications for global climate policy. *Environmental Science and Technology*, vol. 42, No. 5 (1 March), pp. 1401-1407.

Peters, Glen P., and others (2012). Rapid growth in CO_2 emissions after the 2008-2009 global financial crisis. *Nature Climate Change*, vol. 2 (January), pp. 2-4.

Pickett, Kate, and others (2005). Wider income gaps, wider waistbands? an ecological study of obesity and income inequality. *Journal of Epidemiology Community Health*, vol. 59, No. 8 (August), pp. 670-674.

Pickett, Kate, and Richard Wilkinson (2009). *The Spirit Level: Why Greater Equality Makes Societies Stronger*. New York: Bloomsbury Press.

Piketty, Thomas, and Emmanuel Saez (2003). Income inequality in the United States, 1913-1998. *Quarterly Journal of Economics*, vol. 118, No. 1 (February), pp. 1-39.

Polèse, Mario (2009). *The Wealth and Poverty of Regions: Why Cities Matter*. Chicago, Illinois: University of Chicago Press.

Polyani, Karl (1944). *The Great Transformation: The Political and Economic Origins of Our Times*. Boston, Massachusetts: Beacon Press.

Potts, Deborah (2006). Urban growth and urban economies in Eastern and Southern Africa: trends and prospects. In *African Urban Economies: Viability, Vitality or Vitiation?*, Deborah Fahy Bryceson and Deborah Potts, eds. Basingstoke, United Kingdom: Palgrave Macmillan. Pp. 67-98.

Prasad, Eswar, Raghuram Rajan and Arvind Subramanian (2007). Foreign capital and economic growth. *NBER Working Paper*, No. 13619. Cambridge, Massachusetts: Natural Bureau of Economic Research. November.

Pretty, J. N., and others (2006). Resource-conserving agriculture increases yields in developing countries. *Environmental Science and Technology*, vol. 40, No. 4, pp. 1114-1119.

PricewaterhouseCoopers (2012). Cities of the future: global competition, local leadership—connected thinking.

Rahman, Anisur Md. (2011). *Social and Environmental Thinking of Rabindranath Tagore in the Light of Post-Tagorian World Development*. Dhaka: Bangla Academy.

Rahman, Fazlur Md. (2012). Sustainable banking is the way forward. Daily Star, 22 October. Available from http://www.thedailystar.net/newDesign/news-details.php?nid=254912.

Rajan, Raghuram (2010). *Fault Lines: How Hidden Fractures Still Threaten the World Economy*. Princeton, New Jersey: Princeton University Press.

Raupach, Michael R., and others (2007). Global and regional drivers of accelerating CO_2 emissions. *Proceedings of the National Academy of Sciences of the United States of America*, vol. 104, No. 24, pp. 10288-10293. Available from http://ateson.com/ws/r/www.pnas.org/content/104/24/10288.full (accessed 28 March 2013).

Ravallion, Martin (2012). Benchmarking global poverty reduction. *World Bank Policy Research Working Paper*, No. 6205. Washington, D.C.: World Bank. September. WPS6205.

Resnick, Danielle, Finn Tarp and James Thurlow (2012). *The Political Economy of Green-Growth: Illustrations from Southern Africa. UNU-WIDER Working Paper*, No. 2012/11. Helsinki: United Nations University-World Institute for Development Economics Research.

Rayner, Geof, and Timothey Lang (2012). Waste lands? In Revaluing Food, N. Doron, ed. Fabian policy report. London: Fabian Society.

Rees, William E. (1992). Ecological footprints and appropriated carrying capacity: what urban economics leaves out. *Environment and Urbanisation*, vol. 4, No. 2 (2 October), pp. 121-130. doi:10.1177/095624789200400212.

Riahi, Keywan, and others (2012). Energy pathways for sustainable development. In International Institute for Applied Systems Analysis, *Global Energy Assessment: Toward a Sustainable Future*. New York: Cambridge University Press; Laxenburg, Austria: IIASA. Chap. 17, pp. 1203-1306.

Ringstrom, Anna (2012). Sweden turns trash into cash as EU seeks to curb dumping. *Reuters*. 26 November. Available from http://www.reuters.com/article/2012/11/26/us-sweden-environment-garbage-idUSBRE8AP0MI20121126.

Rockstroem, Johan, and others (2009). A safe operating space for humanity. *Nature*, vol. 461, No. 24, pp. 472-475.

Rodrik, Dani (2011). *The Globalization Paradox. Democracy and the Future of the World Economy*. New York: W.W. Norton and Company.

_____ (2012). Unconditional convergence in manufacturing. *Quarterly Journal of Economics* (18 November). doi:10.1093/qje/qjs047.

Rogelj, Joeri, David L. McCollum and Keywan Riahi (2013). The UN's "Sustainable Energy for All" initiative is compatible with a warming limit of 2° C. *Nature*. Published online 24 February. doi: 10.1038/NCLIMATE1806.

Rothman, Dale (1998). Environmental Kuznets curves: real progress or passing the buck?—a case for consumption-based approaches. *Ecological Economics*, vol. 25, No. 2 (May), pp. 177-194.

Saez, Emmanuel (2013). Striking it richer: the evolution of top incomes in the United States (updated with 2011 estimates). 23 January. Available from http://elsa.berkeley.edu/~saez/saez-UStopincomes-2011.pdf.

Sahan, Erinch, and Monique Mikhail (2012). *Private Investment in Agriculture: Why It's Essential, and What's Needed*. Oxfam Discussion Paper. Oxford, United Kingdom: Oxfam GB. 25 September.

Sánchez, Marco V. (2011). Welfare effects of rising oil prices in oil-importing developing countries. *The Developing Economies*, vol. 49, No. 3 (September), pp. 321-346.

_____, and Martín Cicowiez (2013). Inter-temporal macroeconomic trade-offs and payoffs of human development strategies: an economy-wide modelling analysis. Background paper prepared for *World Economic and Social Survey 2013*.

Sánchez, Marco V., and Rob Vos (2010). Impact of the global crisis on the achievement of the MDGs in Latin America. DESA Working Paper, No. 74. June 2009 (revised May 2010). ST/ESA/2009/DWP/74. Available from http://www.un.org/esa/desa/papers/2009/wp74_2009.pdf.

_____, eds. (2013). *Financing Human Development in Africa, Asia and the Middle East*. United Nations Series on Development. London: Bloomsbury.

Sánchez, Marco V., and others, eds. (2010). *Public Policies for Human Development: Achieving the Millennium Development Goals in Latin America*. Basingstoke, United Kingdom: Palgrave Macmillan.

Sanchez, Pedro A. (2002). Soil fertility and hunger in Africa. *Science*, vol. 295, No. 5562 (15 March), pp. 2019-2020.

Sarris, Alexander (2009). Evolving structure of world agricultural trade and requirements for new world trade rules. Paper presented at the FAO Expert Meeting on "How to feed the world in 2050", Rome, 24-26 June 2009.

Satterthwaite, David (1992). Sustainable cities: introduction. *Environment and Urbanization*, vol. 4, No. 2 (October), pp. 3-8.

_____ (2007). *The Transition to a Predominantly Urban World and its Underpinnings*. Human Settlements Discussion Paper: theme - urban change-4. London: International Institute for Environment and Development (IIED).

_____ (2009). The implications of population growth and urbanization for climate change. In *Population Dynamics and Climate Change*, José Miguel Guzmán and others, eds. United Nations publication, Sales No. E.09.III.H4.

_____ (2010). *Urban Myths and the Mis-use of Data that Underpin Them. UNU-WIDER Working Paper*, No. 2010/28. Helsinki: World Institute for Development Economics Research. March.

_____, and Alice Sverdlik (2013). Energy access and housing for low-income groups in urban areas. In *Energizing Sustainable Cities: Assessing Urban Energy*, Arnulf Grubler and David Fisk, eds. Abingdon, United Kingdom: Routledge.

Schaltegger, S., and R. Burritt (2000). *Contemporary Environmental Accounting: Issues, Concepts and Practice*. Sheffield, United Kingdom: Greenleaf Publishing

Sen, Amartya K. (1981). Ingredients of famine analysis: availability and entitlements. *Quarterly Journal of Economics*, vol. 96, No. 3 (August), pp. 433-464.

_____ (1999). *Commodities and Capabilities*. New Delhi: Oxford University Press.

_____ (2000). *Development as Freedom*. New York: Alfred A. Knopf.

Simms, Andrew, Victoria Johnson and Peter Chowla (2010). *Growth Isn't Possible: Why We Need a New Economic Direction*. London: new economics foundation.

Spratt, Steven, and others (2010). *The Great Transition: A Tale of How It Turned Out Right*. London: new economics foundation.

Spielman, David J, and Rajul Pandya-Lorch (2009). Fifty years of progress. In *Millions Fed: Proven Successes in Agricultural Development*, David J. Spielman and Rajul Pandya-Lorch, eds. Washington, D.C.: International Food Policy Research Institute. Pp. 1-18.

Steffen, Will, and others (2011). The anthropocene: from global change to planetary stewardship. *Ambio*, vol. 40, No. 7, pp. 739-761.

Stern, Nicholas (2007). *The Economics of Climate Change: The Stern Review*. Cambridge, United Kingdom: Cambridge University Press.

Stiglitz, Joseph E. (2004). Capital-market liberalization, globalization, and the IMF. *Oxford Review of Economic Policy*, vol. 20, No. 1, pp. 57-71.

_____ (2012). *The Price of Inequality: How Today's Divided Society Endangers Our Future*. New York: W.W. Norton and Company.

_____, Amartya K. Sen and Jean-Paul Fitoussi (2010). *Mismeasuring Our Lives: Why GDP Doesn't Add Up*. Report by the Commission on the Measurement of Economic Performance and Social Progress. New York: New Press.

Sturgeon, Timothy, and Richard Florida (2000). Globalization and jobs in the automotive industry. Massachusetts Institute of Technology Working Paper. MIT-IPC-00-012. Cambridge, Massachusetts: MIT Industrial Performance Center. November. Available from http://web.mit.edu/ipc/publications/pdf/00-012.pdf.

Sumner, Jenny, Lori Bird and Hillary Smith (2009). Carbon taxes: a review of experience and policy design considerations. Technical report NREL/TP-6A2-47312. December.

te Lintelo, Dolf, and others (2013). The Hunger and Nutrition Commitment Index: measuring the political commitment to reduce hunger and undernutrition in developing countries. Brighton, United Kingdom: Institute of Development Studies. April.

The Hague Conference on Agriculture, Food Security and Climate Change (2010). Chair's summary.

Thurlow, James, Paul Dorosh and Winston Yu (2011). *A Stochastic Simulation Approach to Estimating the Economic Impacts of Climate Change in Bangladesh. UNU-WIDER Working Paper*, No. 2011/86. Helsinki: United Nations University-World Institute for Development Economics Research. December.

Toye, John (2012). Human development in an environmentally constrained world in the post-2015 era. Background paper prepared for *World Economic and Social Survey 2013*.

Turner, G. (2008). A comparison of The Limits to Growth with 30 years of reality. *Global Environmental Change*, vol. 18, pp. 397-411.

United Kingdom, Department for Environment, Food and Rural Affairs (2010). The 2007/2008 agricultural price spikes: causes and policy implications. London.

United Nations (1993). *Report of the United Nations Conference on Environment and Development, Rio de Janeiro, 3-14 June 1992*, vol. I, *Resolutions Adopted by the Conference*. Sales No. E.93.I.8 and corrigendum. Resolution I, annex I (Rio Declaration on Environment and Development). Resolution I, annex II (Agenda 21).

_____ (1997). *Report of the United Nations Conference on Human Settlements (Habitat II)*, Istanbul, 3-14 June 1996. Sales No. E.97.IV.6. Chap. I resolution 1, annex II (Habitat Agenda).

_____ (2007). *The United Nations Development Agenda: Development for All*. Sales No. E.07.I.17.

_____ (2008). Comprehensive framework for action. Prepared by the High-level Task Force on the Global Food Crisis. 15 July.

_____ (2009). *World Economic and Social Survey 2009: Promoting Development, Saving the Planet*. Sales No. E.09.II.C.1.

_____ (2010a). *World Economic and Social Survey 2010: Retooling Global Development*. Sales No. E.10.II.C.1.

_____ (2010b). Shanghai manual: a guide for sustainable urban development of the 21st century. Outcome of the World Expo 2010. Available from http://sustainabledevelopment.un.org/content/documents/shanghaimanual.pdf.

_____ (2011a). *The Millennium Development Goals Report 2011*. Sales No. E.11.I.10.

_____ (2011b). *World Economic and Social Survey 2011: The Great Green Technological Transformation.* Sales No. E.11.II.C.1.

_____ (2012a). *World Economic Situation and Prospects 2012.* Sales No. E.12.II.C.2.

_____ (2012b). *Back to Our Common Future. Sustainable Development in the 21ˢᵗ Century (SD21) Project: Summary for policymakers.* New York: Department of Economic and Social Affairs, Division for Sustainable Development.

_____ (2012c). *The Millennium Development Goals Report 2012.* Sales No. E.12.I.4.

_____ (2012d). Sustainable energy for all. New York. Available from http://www.un.org/en/events/sustainableenergyforall/background.shtml.

_____ (2013). *World Economic Situation and Prospects 2013.* Sales No. E.13.II.C.2.

_____, Department of Economic and Social Affairs (2008). Don't forget the food crisis: new policy directions needed. UN/DESA Policy Brief, No.8. October.

_____ (2012). *Back to Our Common Future: Sustainable Development in the 21ˢᵗ century (SD21) Project: Summary for Policymakers.* May.

_____, Population Division (2011). World Population Prospects: The 2010 Revision, vol. I, Comprehensive Tables, and vol. II, Demographic Profiles. ST/ESA/SER.A/313 and ST/ESA/SER.A/317.

_____ (2012). World Urbanization Prospects: The 2011 Revision - Methodology. April.

United Nations, Economic Commission for Latin America and the Caribbean (2012). Population, territory and sustainable development. LC/L.3474(CEP.2/3). June.

United Nations Conference on Trade and Development (2010). *Technology and Innovation Report 2010: Enhancing Food Security in Africa through Science, Technology and Innovation.* Sales No. E.09.II.D.22.

_____ (2012a). *Trade and Development Report 2012: Policies for Inclusive and Balanced Growth.* Sales No. E.12.II.D.6.

_____ (2012b). *World Investment Report 2012.* Sales No. E.12.II.D.3.

United Nations Convention to Combat Desertification (2012). Worsening factors. Bonn: UNCCD Secretariat. Available from http://www.unccd.int/en/programmes/Thematic-Priorities/Food-Sec/Pages/Wors-Fact.aspx.

United Nations Development Programme (2010). *Human Development Report, 2010: The Real Wealth of Nations - Pathways to Human Development*, 20ᵗʰ anniversary ed. Basingstoke, United Kingdom: Palgrave Macmillan.

_____ (2013). *Human Development Report 2013: The Rise of the South: Human Progress in a Diverse World.* New York.

United Nations Environment Programme (2010a). Green economy report: a preview. Châtelaine, Switzerland.

_____ (2010b). Driving a green economy through public finance and fiscal policy reform. Working paper v. 1.0. Geneva.

_____ (2011). *Towards a Green Economy: Pathways to Sustainable Development and Poverty Eradication.* Nairobi. Available from www.unep.org/greeneconomy.

_____ (2012a). *GEO5: Global Environment Outlook - Environment for the Future We Want.* Nairobi. Available from http://www.unep.org/geo/pdfs/geo5/GEO5_report_full_en.pdf.

_____ (2012b). The Emissions Gap Report 2012: A UNEP Synthesis Report. Nairobi. November.

United Nations Human Settlements Programme (UN-Habitat) (2002). *Sustainable Urbanisation: Achieving Agenda 21*. Nairobi: UN-Habitat; London: Department for International Development.

_____ (2010). *State of the World's Cities 2010/2011: Bridging the Urban Divide*. Abingdon, United Kingdom: Earthscan.

_____ (2012). Sustainable cities and human settlements in the post-2015 UN development agenda. Concept note. Available from http://www/worldwewant2015.org/node/302328. Accessed 8 April 2012.

United Nations Office for Disaster Risk Reduction (2012). *Making Cities Resilient Report 2012: My City is Getting Ready! — A Global Snapshot of How Local Governments Reduce Disaster Risk*. Available from http://www.unisdr.org/files/28240_rcreport.pdf. Geneva.

_____ (2013). Resilient cities. Unpublished notes prepared as substantive input for *World Economic and Social Survey 2013*.

United Nations Population Fund (2011). *Population Dynamics in the Least Developed Countries: Challenges and Opportunities for Development and Poverty Reduction*. New York.

United Nations Standing Committee on Nutrition (2010). Progress in nutrition. *Sixth report on the world nutrition situation*. Geneva: UNSCN Secretariat.

United Nations System Task Team on the Post-2015 UN Development Agenda (2012). Realizing the future we want for all: report to the Secretary-General. Available from http://www.un.org/millenniumgoals/pdf/Post_2015_UNTTreport.pdf.

United States of America, Congress of the United States, Congressional Budget Office (2011). Trends in the distribution of household income between 1979 and 2007. Publication No. 4031. Washington, D. C. October.

van der Ploeg, Frederick, and Cees Withagen (2011). Optimal carbon tax with a dirty backstop: oil, coal, or renewables? CESifo Working Paper, No. 3334. 12 January. Munich, Germany: CESifo Group.

Vandemoortele, Jan (2010). Taking the MDGs beyond 2015: hasten slowly. *IDS Bulletin*, vol. 41, No. 1, pp. 60-69.

_____ (2011). If not the Millenium Development Goals, then what? *Third World Quarterly*, vol. 31, No. 1, pp. 9-25.

_____ (2012). Advancing the UN development agenda post-2015: some practical suggestions. Report submitted to the UN Task Force regarding the post-2015 framework for development. Bruges, Belgium. January.

Vieira, Sergio (2012). Inequalities on the rise. Background paper prepared for the *World Economic and Social Survey 2012*.

von Braun, Joachim (2009). Overcoming the world food and agriculture crisis through policy change and science. Prepared for the Trust for Advancement of Agricultural Sciences (TAAS), Fourth Foundation Day Lecture, organized by International Food Policy Research Institute, New Delhi, 6 March 2009. Available from http://www.ifpri.org/publication/overcoming-world-food-and-agriculture-crisis-through-policy-change-and-science.

Vuuren, Detlef P., and others (2013). The role of negative CO2 emissions for reaching 2° C—insights from integrated assessment modeling. *Climate Change*. 6 February. doi: 10.1007/slos84-012-0680-5.

Wackernagel, M. (1994). Ecological footprint and appropriated carrying capacity: a tool for planning toward sustainability. PhD thesis. School of Community and Regional Planning of the University of British Columbia. OCLC 41839429. Available from https://circle.ubc.ca/bitstream/handle/2429/7132/ubc_1994-954027.pdf?sequence=1.

Waggoner, Paul, and Jesse Ausubel (2002). A framework for sustainability science: renovated IPAT identity. *Proceedings of the National Academy of Sciences*, vol. 99, No. 12, pp. 7860-7865.

Weitzman, Martin L. (1976). On the welfare significance of national product in a dynamic economy. *Quarter Journal of Economics*, vol. 90, No. 1 (February), pp. 55-68.

_____ (1984). *The Share Economy: Conquering Stagflation*. Cambridge, Massachusetts: Harvard University Press.

_____ (1985). Profit sharing as macroeconomic policy. *American Economic Review*, vol. 75, No. 2 (May), pp. 41-45.

_____ (1997). Sustainability and technical progress. *Scandinavian Journal of Economics*, vol. 99, No. 1, pp. 1-13.

_____ (2000). The linearized Hamiltonian as comprehensive NDP. *Environment and Development Economics*, vol. 5, No. 1 (February) pp. 55-68.

_____ (2003). *Income, Wealth, and the Maximum Principle*. Cambridge, Massachusetts: Harvard University Press.

Wilkinson, R. (2005). *Impact of Inequality: How to Make Sick Societies Healthier*. London: Routledge.

_____, and K. Pickett (2008). *The Spirit Level: Why Equal Societies Almost Always Do Better*. London: Allen Lane.

Woodward, David (2013). Global growth, inequality and the prospects for poverty eradication in a carbon-constrained world. Background paper prepared for *World Economic and Social Survey 2013*.

_____, and Andrew Simms (2006). *Growth Isn't Working: The Unbalanced Distribution of Benefits and Costs from Growth*. London: new economics foundation.

World Bank (2005). *World Development Report: Equity and Development*. Washington, D.C.

World Bank (2006). *Repositioning Nutrition as Central to Development: A Strategy for Large-Scale Action*.

World Bank (2008a). *World Development Report 2008: Agriculture for Development*. Washington, D.C.

_____ (2008b). Food price crisis imperils 100 million in poor countries. News and Broadcast. Available from http://web.worldbank.org/WBSITE/EXTERNAL/NEWS/0,,contentMDK:21729143~pagePK:64257043~piPK:437376~theSitePK:4607,00.html.

_____ (2009). *World Development Report 2009: Reshaping Economic Geography*. Washington, D.C.

_____ (2010a). *World Development Report 2010: Development and Climate Change.* Washington, D.C.

_____ (2010b). Economics of adaptation to climate change: Bangladesh. Washington, D. C. Available from http://climatechange.worldbank.org/sites/default/files/documents/EACC_Bangladesh.pdf.

_____ (2011). *Rising Global Interest in Farmland.* Washington, D.C.

_____ (2012a). Turn down the heat: why a 4ºC warmer world must be avoided. Report for the World Bank by the Potsdam Institute for Climate Impact Research and Climate Analytics. Washington, D.C. November.

_____ (2012b) *Inclusive Green Growth: The Pathway to Sustainable Development.* Washington, D.C.

_____ (2012c). Toward a green, clean, and resilient world for all: A World Bank Group environment strategy 2012-2022.

_____ (2013). *Planning, Connecting and Financing Cities–Now: Priorities for City Leaders.* Washington, D.C.

World Commission on Environment and Development (1987). *Our Common Future.* Oxford: Oxford University Press.

World Economic Forum (2013). *The Green Investment Report: The Ways and Means to Unlock Private Finance for Green Growth—A Report of the Green Growth Action Alliance.* Geneva.

World Health Organization (2008). *2008-2013 Action Plan for the Global Strategy for the Prevention and Control of Noncommunicable Diseases.* Geneva.

_____ (2012a). Millenium Development Goals (MDGs). Fact sheet No. 290. November. Available from http://www.who.int/mediacentre/factsheets/fs290/en/index.html.

_____ (2012b). *World Health Statistics 2012.* Geneva.

_____ (2013). Fact Sheet No. 311. March. Available from http://www.who.int/mediacentre/factsheets/fs311/en/.

World Vision (2011). *Reaching the MDGs 2.0: Rethinking the Politics.* World Vision International policy briefing. Uxbridge, United Kingdom: World Vision International. September.

Wright, Brian, and Tiffany Shih (2010). Agricultural innovation. *NBER Working Paper,* No. 15793 (March). Cambridge, Massachusetts: National Bureau of Economic Research.

Wu, Jing, and others (2013). Incentives and outcomes: China's environmental policy. *NBER Working Paper,* No. 18754. Cambridge, Massachusetts: National Bureau of Economic Research. February.

WWF (2012). *Living Planet Report 2012: Biodiversity,Biocapacity and Better Choices.* Gland, Switzerland: WWF International.

Yunus, Muhammad (2007). *Creating a World without Poverty: Social Business and the Future of Capitalism.* New York: PublicAffairs.

_____ (2010). *Building Social Business: The Kind of New Capitalism That Serves Humanity's Most Pressing Needs.* New York: PublicAffairs.

Yusuf, Arief Anshory, and Arief Ramayandi (2008). Reducing fuel subsidy or taxing carbon: comparing the two instruments from the economy, environment, and equity perspective for Indonesia. Working Paper in Economics and Development Studies, Padjadjaran University, Bandung, Indonesia.

Xiao, Y. L., and F. Y. Nie (2009). *A Report on the Status of China's Food Security.* Beijing: China Agricultural Science and Technology Press.

WITHDRAWN

United Nations publication
Sales No. E.13.II.C.1
ISBN 978-92-1-109167-0
eISBN 978-92-1-056082-5

Copyright © United Nations, 2013
All rights reserved

13-29677